"Sit back and enjoy as Dr. Simmons leads you on an exhilarating romp through your own anatomy. Journey past your taste buds. (Did you know they're in your throat, too?) Explore the complexity of reproduction. Celebrate the miracle of your birthday. Examine the differences between man and ape. And in the end, be prepared to confront the overwhelming evidence against Darwin's explanation for your existence."

— Dr. Jed Macosko,
professor, University of New Mexico,
and molecular biologist

"In *What Darwin Didn't Know*, Dr. Simmons gives a marvelous, entertaining, physician's-eye view of the intricate functioning of the human body. The relentless detailing of biological elegance and complexity overwhelms facile Darwinian stories as a tidal wave overwhelms a beach."

— Michael J. Behe, Ph.D.,
professor of biochemistry, Lehigh University,
and author of the bestselling book
Darwin's Black Box: The Biochemical Challenge to Evolution

"Several years ago the prestigious peer-reviewed journal *Science* carried a research article titled 'Did Darwin Get It All Right?' The subtitle answered the question with a 'No.' There is a tide of data mounting against the Darwinian (though not necessarily Darwin's) concept that randomness can explain the wonder of life. In *What Darwin Didn't Know*, Geoffrey Simmons converts that tide into a tidal wave of evidence.

"In his book, Simmons treats us to the respect for the complexity of life he has gained as a doctor with 35 years of experience. His frontline experience with the challenges of maintaining life has given him insights that armchair and laboratory biologists never have."

— Gerald Schroeder, Ph.D.,
MIT-trained nuclear physicist
and earth and planetary scientist;
author of *The Science of God*

WHAT
DARWIN
DIDN'T
KNOW

GEOFFREY SIMMONS, M.D.

HARVEST HOUSE PUBLISHERS

EUGENE, OREGON

Cover by Terry Dugan Design, Minneapolis, Minnesota

Cover image courtesy of Galleria dell' Accademia, Venice, Italy/Bridgeman Art Library

Author photo on back cover by Mikala A. Wood

WHAT DARWIN DIDN'T KNOW
Copyright © 2004 by Geoffrey Simmons, M.D.
Published by Harvest House Publishers
Eugene, Oregon 97402
www.harvesthousepublishers.com

Library of Congress Cataloging-in-Publication Data

Simmons, Geoffrey S.
    What Darwin didn't know / Geoffrey Simmons.
        p. cm.
    Includes bibliographical references.
    ISBN 0-7369-1313-0 (pbk.)
    1. Creationism. 2. Evolution—Religious aspects—Christianity. 3. Evolution (Biology)—
    Religious aspects—Christianity. 4. Darwin, Charles, 1809-1882. I. Title.
    BS652.S56 2004
    231.7'652—dc22   2003015099

Printed in the United States of America

04 05 06 07 08 09 10 11 / VP-MS / 10 9 8 7 6 5 4 3 2 1

To my wife, Sherry,
and my children, Erik, Tara, Brad, and Anaïs

and

To the memory of Barry Hull, Damon Knight,
my father, Col. Theodore R. Simmons,
and my mother, Jane Lavander

Acknowledgments

I would like to express my appreciation to Lance Sparks, Doctor of Arts, and my wife, Sherry, for their extraordinary proofreading, as well as Chuck Freedenberg for his technical assistance.

I would like to thank Terry Glaspey, acquisition editor for Harvest House Publishers, who happened into my life, by coincidence or design, the same week I finished writing this book. His immediate enthusiasm and subsequent suggestions were invaluable.

I would also like to thank Paul Gossard, project editor for Harvest House Publishers, for doing such a nice job of editing my manuscript and for so adeptly carving my material into smaller, more comprehensible packets.

I have enormous admiration for the authors within the bibliography. I owe much of my work to theirs.

Lastly, I would like to acknowledge Ross Sandler, professor at NYU Law School (and my cousin) for coming up with the right title, and thank Harvest House Publishers for their interest and support.

Previous Publications
by Geoffrey Simmons

The Z Papers (Arbor House, Bantam)
The Adam Experiment (Arbor House, Berkley)
Pandemic (Arbor House, Berkley)
MURDOCK (Arbor House)
The Glue Factory (Beckett)
To Glue or Not To Glue (Beckett)

Contents

List of Illustrations

The Gig
Is Up

Foreword by William A. Dembski, Ph.D.

Arthur Miller's play *The Crucible* is about the Salem witch trials. Even at the start of the play, the evidence for Salem being a hotbed of witchcraft is not good. But as the play unfolds, it becomes clear to the judges overseeing the witch trials that the evidence was utterly fabricated and bogus. Unfortunately, by this time several people have already been executed for witchcraft. What are the judges to do? At a key point in the play, the judges decide that they had better keep the executions going since otherwise their credibility will be shot.

A similar inertia drives Darwinism. The evidence for Darwinism was never any good—even in Darwin's day. But with advances in contemporary science, Darwinism becomes utterly insupportable. What are Darwinists to do? Rather than admit that their theory is at fault (and thus lose credibility), they keep the propaganda mills running overtime, inflating Darwinism's paltry successes and charging critics like Geoffrey Simmons with being "unscientific" and "religiously motivated" and with committing the "intellectual sin" of merely picking holes in evolutionary theory.

David Berlinski, a prominent critic of Darwinism, once remarked to me that "a shift in prevailing scientific orthodoxies will come only when the objections to Darwinism accumulate so forcefully that they can no longer be ignored." In this book, Geoffrey Simmons reviews the many discoveries and advances in science since Darwin that point to intelligent design in human biology. By providing numerous clear evidences of the intelligent design of human biological systems, this book is bringing about the shift in scientific orthodoxies to which Berlinski refers. *What Darwin Didn't Know* leaves none of Darwinism's grandiose claims standing. Its critique is cumulative, relentless, and overwhelming.

Why Darwinism?

Why does Geoffrey Simmons focus on Darwinism? It is no accident that in debates over biological evolution, Darwin's name keeps coming up. Nor are repeated references to Darwin and Darwinism simply out of respect for the history of the subject, as though evolutionary biology needed constantly to be reminded of its founder. Darwin looms larger than life in the study of biological origins because his theory constitutes the very bedrock of evolutionary biology. Indeed, nothing in evolutionary biology makes sense apart from Darwinism.

To see this, we need to understand how Darwinism makes evolutionary biology tick. Darwinism is really two claims. The less crucial claim is that *all organisms trace their lineage back to a universal common ancestor.* Thus you, the fly buzzing around your head, and the bacteria sitting on the fly all share the same great-great-great grandparent. This claim is referred to as "common descent." Although evolutionary biology is committed to common descent, that is not its central claim.

The Mechanism for Change That Darwinism Proposes

The central claim of evolutionary biology, rather is that *an unguided physical process can account for the emergence of all biological complexity and diversity.* Filling in the details of that process remains a matter for debate among evolutionary biologists. Yet it is an in-house debate, and one essentially about details. In broad strokes, however, any unguided physical process capable of producing biological complexity must have three components: 1) *hereditary transmission,* 2) *incidental change,* and 3) *natural selection.*

Think of it this way: We start with some organism. It incurs some change. The change is *incidental* in the sense that it doesn't anticipate future changes that subsequent generations of organisms may experience (neo-Darwinism, for instance, treats such changes as random mutations or errors in genetic material). What's more, incidental change is *heritable* and therefore can be transmitted to the next generation. Whether it actually is transmitted to the next generation, however, depends on whether the change is in some sense beneficial to the organism. If so, then natural selection will be likely to preserve organisms exhibiting that change.

Evolutionary biologists debate the precise role and extent of hereditary transmission and incidental change. The debate can even be quite sharp at times. But no evolutionary biologist challenges Darwinism's holy of holies—*natural selection.* Darwin himself was unclear about the mechanisms of hereditary transmission and incidental change. But whatever form they took, Darwin was convinced that natural selection was the key to harnessing them. The same is true for contemporary evolutionary biologists. That's why to this day we hear repeated references to Darwin's theory of natural selection...but not to Darwin's theory of variation or Darwin's theory of inheritance.

An Intellectual Swindle

Apart from intelligent design, what can coordinate the incidental changes that hereditary transmission passes from one generation to the next? To perform such coordination, evolution requires a designer substitute. *Darwin's claim to fame was to propose natural selection as a designer substitute.* In making that proposal, Darwin perpetrated the greatest intellectual swindle in the history of ideas.

Natural selection is no substitute for intelligence. All natural selection does is narrow the variability of incidental change by weeding out the less fit. What's more, it acts on the spur of the moment, based solely on what the environment at present deems fit, and thus without any foresight of future possibilities. And yet this blind process, when coupled with another blind process (incidental change), is supposed to produce designs that exceed the capacities of any designers in our experience.

Where is the evidence that natural selection can accomplish the intricacies of bioengineering that are manifest throughout the living world? Where is the evidence that the sorts of incidental changes required for large-scale evolution ever occur? The evidence simply isn't there. To appreciate what's at stake, imagine what would happen to the germ theory of disease if scientists never found any microorganisms or viruses that produced diseases. That's the problem with Darwinism. In place of detailed, testable accounts of how a complex biological system could realistically have emerged, Darwinism offers handwaving just-so stories for how such systems might have emerged...in some idealized conceptual space far removed from biological reality.

It's All Smoke and Mirrors

Why, then, does Darwinism continue to garner such a huge following, especially among the intellectual elites? Two reasons:

1) It provides *a materialistic creation story that dispenses with any need for design or God* (this is very convenient for those who want to escape the demands of religion, morality, and conscience). 2) *The promise of getting design without a designer* is incredibly seductive—it's the ultimate free lunch. No wonder Daniel Dennett, in *Darwin's Dangerous Idea,* credits Darwin with "the single best idea anyone has ever had." Getting design without a designer is a good trick indeed.

Darwinism is a magic trick performed far enough away from the audience to dazzle them…until someone starts handing out binoculars. With the advances in the life sciences that he recounts in this book, Geoffrey Simmons is handing out a great pair of binoculars and making Darwinism's sleight of hand plain to see. Darwinism, though always a trick, has in the past been a remarkably successful trick. *What Darwin Didn't Know* shows why the Darwinian magic gig is now up.

—William A. Dembski, Ph.D., Baylor University
   Author of *The Design Revolution*

The Ever-Increasing Problems of Darwin's Theories

If Charles Darwin were to submit *On the Origin of Species* to a university press today, would his work be published? What if a savvy editor were to replace the outdated English with contemporary phrasing and delete all the politically incorrect comments—would that help? Any answer, of course, would be purely conjecture, but there are reasons to believe that Darwin's most famous manuscript would face repeated rejections. Some of these might arise out of modern medicine, a profession I have practiced for more than 35 years. Others might arise from contemporary modifications of the theory of evolution, a kind of science that has remained a passionate interest of mine for nearly 45 years.

Given what was known about the life sciences during the 1800s, most of Darwin's theories made sense. Horses could be bred into faster horses, and dogs could be bred into better hunters. Biographical writings indicate Darwin was a thoughtful, honest, thorough, and sincere scientist, well-skilled in biology and geology, who was hesitant to publish out of respect for his wife's religious beliefs.

So, why would there be a problem?

One rejection letter might cite conflicts with cellular biochemistry, human physiology, electron microscopy, and immunology.

Darwin knew very little about genetics or endocrinology, such as why a child resembled his or her parents, that harmful bacteria existed, or how the thyroid gland worked. Another rejection letter might cite his superficiality, pointing to the incredible complexities, coordination, and feedback loops of all biological systems. Other than his study of the microscopic male barnacle, there is little evidence Darwin knew anything about cellular functions. Cellular theory was still in its infancy when he published *Origins*.

What We Know Today

The interior of the human body is a much busier place than New York City, London, Mexico City, Tokyo, and Bombay combined. Ten to seventy-five trillion cells participate in more than a quadrillion purposeful chemical interactions each day that help us walk, breathe, think, sleep, procreate, see, hear, smell, feel, digest food, eliminate waste, write, read, talk, make red cells, remove dead cells, fight infections, behave, misbehave, absorb nutrients, transport oxygen, eliminate carbon dioxide, maintain balance, carry on dialogue, understand instructions, argue, and make complex decisions, just to name a few common activities. In addition, each of these processes has dozens—and sometimes hundreds—of smaller, interacting steps, checks, counterchecks, balances, and regulatory mechanisms. And further, all of these steps have smaller chemical substeps. In many ways the human body functions like an extremely well-organized blizzard of invisible chemical responses and rapidly-changing electrical impulses. The human brain is a convoluted continent swept by microscopic electrical hurricanes and chemical tidal waves that somehow make sense out of reality on a microsecond-by-microsecond basis. Darwin didn't have a clue how these mechanisms truly worked. For the most part, he didn't know they even existed.

During the 1800s some people believed bats navigated at night by touch, the moon was populated by furry, winged humans, decaying meat spontaneously turned into maggots, grain changed into rodents, and mud became frogs. Human conception was mysterious, and menopause was almost unheard of (women rarely lived beyond 50). Diseases were treated—but rarely cured—with fresh air, open windows, closed windows, open wounds, covered wounds, homes by the sea, homes away from the sea, hot water baths, cold water baths, salt water baths, alternating hot and cold baths, laxatives, bag balms, dubious tonics from charlatans, short walks, long walks, and bloodletting. Broken legs were treated with amputation, people were transfused with dog and cow blood (and died), and the use of chloroform as an anesthetic was deemed antireligion.

> The human brain is a convoluted continent swept by microscopic electrical hurricanes and chemical tidal waves that somehow make sense out of reality on a microsecond-by-microsecond basis.

It Seemed to Make Sense

My interest and belief in the theory of evolution began in high school. I was fascinated by it then, and I have remained fascinated ever since. And why not? Nature has numerous examples of unicellular organisms banding together to accomplish very complex goals. For example, millions of slime mold cells can come together to form a single, much taller organism to hoist new spores to wind currents. Or take coral reefs. Or the killing red tides. We know that lungfish can breathe air—so why couldn't fish have come ashore and evolved into amphibians? Fossil evidence indicates that a select group of dinosaurs had feathers—so why couldn't they, given enough time, have evolved into birds? Monkeys certainly resemble humans. Every mammal has a heart, lungs, kidneys, and a gastrointestinal tract—we all eat, sleep, drink, and mate in mostly similar ways. Why not have had a common ancestor?

My teachers taught evolution at every grade level; biology textbooks still display the parade of fish to amphibian to reptile to mammal to monkey to man. Their theories are backed up by radioactive dating, relative dating, and mitochondrial mutation counts. Although no true transition fossils have been found, the theory of evolution continues to make sense to many people. And without question, natural selection is real. It can easily be viewed all around. Just look out any window and see how the healthier trees crowd out weaker ones—or observe how the runt of the litter often dies. Is it the earliest worm that gets eaten, or the earliest bird that gets breakfast? Does it matter? Both systems are proof of natural selection. In my mind, Darwin's theories had to be correct—or if they weren't correct, they certainly were close enough.

It's not as if I were alone in these thoughts. My company included the likes of Sagan, Gould, Eldredge, Tattersall, Margulis, Diamond, and Leakey. Many professors expounded the details of evolution as if they were foregone conclusions; school boards insisted that evolution was the only explanation. My conclusions were locked in early—or so I thought. Yes, perhaps there was a God. Certainly, there were many things I couldn't explain, and there were millions who relied on faith. For me, however, evolution seemed factual. The faster rabbits outlived the slower rabbits; the chameleon probably outlived the more-conspicuous lizards.

I majored in "pre-vet" for two years at the University of Illinois and was readily accepted into their veterinary school. One week before the start of classes, however, I changed my major to "pre-med." Medicine had suddenly become my aspiration. I loved animals, but I wanted to help people. Cats, hamsters, birds, and dogs might be fun and interesting, but people were more fun and more interesting. I also thought I could make a difference. Idealism of youth, I suppose—but I have held onto those feelings.

Throughout undergraduate studies, graduate school, and during my days of private practice, I continued a zealous hobby of reading books and articles on the life sciences. Although I loved an occasional Vonnegut, Crichton, Hesse, Arthur C. Clarke, Heinlein, Grisham, or C.S. Lewis, nearly every one of my nonfiction selections involved the biological sciences, with a bias toward evolution.

I also had a deep respect for people who follow any religious doctrine—I just didn't understand certain items. How could God create and watch over the billions of microorganisms found in a handful of soil, let alone the infinite-seeming number of organisms of all sizes and shapes everywhere on Earth? It didn't seem possible. And why would a God allow famine, disease, war, and birth defects? It didn't seem godly. How could God know what was happening to everyone at all moments? Quite incomprehensible. Natural laws, slow evolution, and survival of the fittest seemed to make better sense. Good things happen and bad things happen—it's all random, the so-called luck of the draw. My teachers had said evolution was a fact; my textbooks portrayed evolution as a fact; and my colleagues said it was a fact. It must be a fact...or was it? That the world was flat was once a fact. That malaria came from heavy air in the swamps was once a fact. And, that man could talk long-distance or fly to the moon was a fantasy.

Questioning My Views

My ideas started to slowly change when I married my wife, Sherry, in 1985. She is a Christian and an ardent believer in the infallibility of the Bible. Out of respect and love, I listened to what she had to say. We had a few polite debates, but for the most part, I was a scientist and not truly persuaded. She never budged.

Another impetus to question my views on evolution came in the late 1980s from the book *The Neck of the Giraffe* by Francis Hitching. I don't recall how I came upon it (perhaps by rummaging through a used bookstore, a hobby of mine), but I know that I've read it several times. This is an easy-to-understand, nonreligious book that cites many flaws in Darwin's theories. Hitching's facts and arguments are on the opposition's playing field. He notes that, among the missing fossils or predecessors are shorter-necked "pre-giraffes." Stephen Gould confirmed this in his column in *Natural History:* "Giraffes provide no established evidence whatsoever for the mode of evolution of their undeniably useful necks."

Hitching also writes about reptile fossils having multiple bones in their lower jaw and mammals having only one lower jawbone—with no transitional forms found. He points to the unusual tail of the whale and the dolphin, which swings up and down, rather than side to side like those of all other mammals and fish. He discusses the Cambrian Period, 540 million years ago, when thousands of organisms exploded onto the scene, without any evidence of predecessors. Even Stephen Gould has been quoted as saying that this period is "the enigma of paleontological enigmas."

After reading and savoring nearly every word of Hitching's book, I tracked down extra copies and shared them with my friends. Hitching had raised the question for me: Now, by close to the twenty-first century, was not the fossil record complete enough to draw logical conclusions? I began to seek out authors who discussed this. There weren't many. Along the way I procured William Paley's *Natural Theology*, an antique book from the year 1800, and enjoyed his attempt to connect natural systems to an Intelligent Designer. I also found Patrick Glynn's *God, the Evidence: The Reconciliation of Faith and Reason in a Postsecular World* very insightful. Glynn has traveled down a path not unlike my own.

But I was not seeking religious arguments. I wanted to hear from the experts on natural selection, fossil dating, and genetic changes, the professionals who felt Darwin's proponents might be mistaken. I wanted to hear the scientific arguments. I wanted to know how random changes could cause the tail to merely drop off, how cold-blooded animals changed into warm-blooded animals, and how the laying of eggs changed to internal fertilization. These are massive, purposeful genetic changes that lack the evidence of transitional species. Where is the animal with lukewarm blood or partial live births?

> In my mind, Darwin's theories had to be correct—or if they weren't correct, they certainly were close enough.

The Challenges of Complex Systems and Built-In Information

The next book that truly affected my views was Michael Behe's *Darwin's Black Box*. His bottom line is that chemical reactions in the human body require multiple, useless (when isolated) steps. One example is the clotting of blood, which involves multiple "interlocking" chemical steps. He asks, how could the first and second steps, or even the tenth step, have come about without a plan? Just having step one and two in the right order is complicated, yet it's useless for clotting. An analogy might be that of a dog's tail somehow adding a useless leg, reproducing as a leg–tail for a million years, then adding another leg, reproducing as a two-legged tail for another million years, then adding a kidney, a liver, a heart, and two more legs at million-year intervals—until finally getting a head with ears that flop. None of these steps would be capable of functioning alone. And so it is with the multiple steps needed to cause a wound to clot or to manufacture the incredible myriad of molecules in the human body.

Two other books that played a significant role were William Dembski's *No Free Lunch* and *Intelligent Design: The Bridge Between Science & Technology*. Professor Dembski, who holds a Ph.D. in mathematics and a Ph.D. in philosophy, argues from a statistical perspective that random occurrences could not lead to life as we know it. He also introduces the terms *specified complexity* and *complex specified information* to help scientists define and identify design in nature. For example, if one were to find on a table Scrabble letters spelling out a Shakespeare sonnet, one would readily assume intelligent design was at work. And so it must be with the human body, where trillions of chemical sonnets are written daily. To many people his argument is compelling.

And then, of course, there is the fact that Darwin's own writings piqued my curiosity and doubts. He intermittently expressed concerns about his work and seemed to worry about the incomplete fossil record and the enormous complexity of things. These are exactly the same difficulties that plague his work now.

More Than a Wondrous Accident

As a physician, I have had increasing problems fitting most of Darwin's theories and many of the newer modifications into the field of medicine. Some of his ideas might work in a smaller sphere, but many are appearing increasingly tenuous when applied to human anatomy, physiology, cellular functions, hematology, biochemistry, endocrinology, cardiology, immunology, and electron microscopy. In fact, they sometimes look downright impossible. Our body is way too complicated to be merely a wondrous accident.

I once asked Carl Sagan why he thought humans could have developed into such complex beings through mere evolution. His answer, simply stated, was "six billion years." I thought he was wrong then, and I know he's wrong now. Modern technology has muddied the waters in regard to the theory of evolution. I hope to show you why. For some, this book may further muddy the waters; for others, it may make them clearer.

—Geoffrey Simmons, M.D.
October 2003

PART I
Basic Issues

False facts are highly injurious to the progress of science, for they often endure long….

—Charles Darwin, *The Descent of Man*

1

The Scope of
the Challenges

In many regards the theory of evolution seems to make sense. Approximately three billion years ago, lightning may have struck a primordial soup, creating a few reactive amino acids, the building blocks of life…or perhaps an asteroid loaded with organic compounds from another planet crashed into the Earth's surface and began sprouting life-forms like sown seeds. As millions of years passed, these compounds might have combined and recombined to form complex organisms that began competing, reproducing, mutating, and steadily improving, until eventually humans arrived about a hundred thousand years ago. Everyone has heard the story. The progression from unicellular organisms to primates can be found in every biology book, on T-shirts and bumper stickers, on posters, and in movies.

The Problem of Change

Ironically, one of the major problems is change itself. Scientific evidence suggests that the human brain has tripled in size from 400 to 1350 cubic centimeters. Human beings have gone from walking on all fours to bipedal locomotion, lost most of their fur (hair), silenced ovulation (eggs are released without a female going into "heat"), gained millions of sweat glands, developed breasts (when not lactating), nearly doubled in height, lengthened their arms or shortened their legs, and learned to communicate in extremely complex ways. Yet there are many animal and plant species in our environment that have not changed appreciably during the same period. The modern dolphin is a prime example. This mammal looks, and probably acts, the same as it did long before humans arrived—about five million years ago. A similar pattern exists for crocodiles, turtles, jellyfish, sharks, clams, certain fish, and numerous insects. In fact, the crocodile and cockroach have remained virtually unchanged for 200 million years, and there is evidence that certain jellyfish have not changed in 550 million years. The coelacanth fish and the ginkgo tree are considered living fossils.

Why would man steadily improve in size, skills, and intelligence—given the exposure to the same air, radiation, climate, and foods—while other species have remained unimproved? Did human changes come about by accident, or were they the result of intelligent design? Or could they be both? These have been, and continue to be, major questions—and there are many very strongly held beliefs. Curiously, in 1860, Darwin declared, "I had no intent to write atheistically." Yet that is exactly how he has been interpreted.

Although the theories of natural selection, survival of the fittest, and random mutations have retained their appeal for nearly a hundred-and-fifty years, these processes have had little to no impact on many species. One might therefore ask if the "minimum-changers" are innately resistant to mutagens (factors causing mutations), such as variations in global temperature, radiation, ultraviolet light, pathogenic viruses, and toxic chemicals. This is unlikely since all living cells are exquisitely sensitive. Have these steady-state species reached the pinnacle of evolutionary perfection? This is also doubtful, but pinnacles are hard to define. Are they the toughest, smartest, most prolific, fastest, best-camouflaged, or meanest members of their group around? If one looks closely, this is often not the case. Do animals go through short evolutionary bursts or pauses (millions of years)…and the exceptions of today are merely in a pause? No one can answer this, but it defies contemporary scientific principles. Did an asteroid strike near the Yucatán Peninsula 65 million years ago, causing tidal waves and nuclear winters that selectively drove dinosaurs to extinction and yet spared many prehuman mammals? If so, one might wonder why the entire evolutionary clock wasn't set back. Then again, is surviving a matter of survival of the *fittest*—or of the *luckiest?* Questions such as these cloud evolutionary thought. Even the most ardent supporters of the theory of evolution still call it a theory—with very good reason: no knowledgeable scientist has ever called it the "facts of evolution."

> Why would man steadily improve in size, skills, and intelligence—given the exposure to the same air, radiation, climate, and foods—while other species have remained unimproved?

The Problem of Complexity

Complexity is another major problem for Darwin's theories. In *On the Origin of Species,* he wrote, "The eye to this day gives me a cold shudder." Imagine walking past the fanciest Ferrari ever made and assuming that only evolution was responsible for its existence. There is a parallel logic. First came the wheel, then the cart, the wagon, the unicycle, the bicycle, the Model-T Ford, a sedan, a convertible, and then a Ferrari. It should be obvious to any passerby that this car was man-made, not derived from a series of mutations (accidents)…and yet many people believe that the human body, a considerably more complex machine, came about, in part, through a series of lucky genetic accidents. (Accidents, in my mind, are burns and broken bones.) Nearly all accidents (mutations) in nature are either silent and useless, extremely challenging, outright deforming, or simply incompatible with life. They are not capable of creating complex individuals who can paint beautiful pictures, write wonderful stories, repair cleft palates, debate political issues, or build racing cars.

The Genes

Everything that transpires within the body is controlled by the three billion base pairs that make up the 100,000 genes that form the 23 paired chromosomes within the nucleus of nearly every cell. The amount of information stored within a single nucleus is equal to a library of 1000 encyclopedias, each with 1000 pages. Multiply that by the 35 billion cells in a brain, not to mention the ten or more trillion cells in a single body, and the amount of information moving about the body in each second becomes astronomical. Yet if one could put all of the DNA coordinating the growth, development, and functioning of every human on Earth into a single pile, it would weigh barely 50 grams. How could a particle smaller than dust have enough knowledge to, as it were, multiply into a trillion-room skyscraper—and also know the color, shape, and size of every room, every worker who would ever be employed in it, and every speck of furniture, wiring, and plumbing? (This speck might even know the past, the present, and the future.)

Did these all-knowing genes come about through a series of accidents? If so, that would mean that an average of two bases were added to our chromosomes per year throughout the presumed three billion years of life. They were also placed in the right order at the right time on the correct chromosomes, and were fully capable of coordinating with the other genes. For example, the genes that control human eye color and shape must either reside close by each

Human Chromosomes

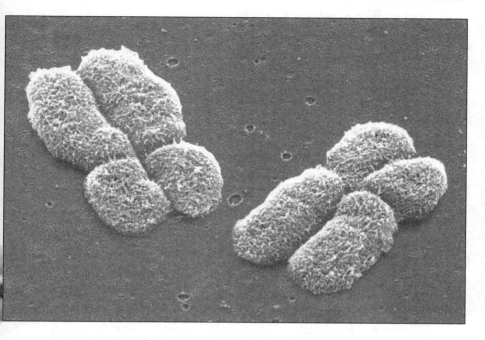

Scanning electron micrograph (SEM) of pairs of human chromosomes. One chromosome of each pair has replicated during cell division to form an identical copy, or *chromatid*. Chromatids are joined together at the *centromere*, the region of a chromatid that also divides it into two asymmetrical "arms." Magnification: x9450 at 5x7 cm size.

other or have a way of communicating. The gene specifying the texture of a person's hair would not function well if it were placed with the genes for the ear or for bladder function. A major challenge to evolution has been whether repeated mutations could truly have created changes in the correct order.

Interactivity

Every aspect of human physiology has multiple facets, steps, purposes, managers, feedback loops, and anticipated outcomes. The idea that ten or more trillion cells can even coordinate with each other is mind-boggling. How can the sight of a tennis ball's shape, size, color, and speed be sent to dozens of spots in the brain at the same time, be recombined into a functional image, and then result in an action—all in less than a second? The fact that a mother and her baby simultaneously know when it's time to be delivered, and the baby knows when to take its first breath, seems like a miracle. A breath taken too early would result in drowning or suffocation; one too late would cause permanent brain damage. The process that causes a baby to suckle and a mother's breasts to start releasing milk simultaneously cannot have come about with a few random changes. And why is it that lactation is a natural contraceptive? To lessen sibling competition for mother's milk? Why does a nursing baby lack teeth the first seven to nine months? To lessen breast injuries? The chances of multiple, purposeful, interacting mutations happening to two individuals and then being passed down the generations is beyond calculation. If one were to try to argue to the contrary, one would need to find examples of newborns that progressed through tiny, incremental steps: from those that didn't breast-feed, to species that partially breast-feed, to present-day mammals.

No such data exists.

How does the liver know to grow in synchrony with the other organs? Why do all lungs always look like lungs? How do the calves and thighs know to grow at the same rate as the knees and toes? Leonardo da Vinci's famous Vitruvian Man (at right) demonstrates this symmetry. With outstretched arms and legs, this man's 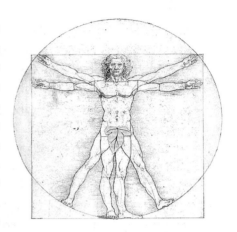 fingers and toes touch the circumference of a circle, and his navel lies exactly in the center. If his extremities remain perpendicular, their further points touch all sides of a square.

The body automatically maintains its design integrity. There are no fossils found with lopsided extremities. Somehow the top half coordinates with the bottom half, the left side with the right side, the front with the back. Just the complexity of managing simultaneous, coordinated growth alone is overwhelming. Can it possibly be coincidence?

Look at how we transfer sugar, minerals, proteins, fats, carbohydrates, and vitamins from our dinner plates to our mouths, down to the gastrointestinal tract, through the walls of the small bowel, into the bloodstream, through the liver, and ultimately to every cell in the body. Millions of macroscopic and microscopic processes are utilized. How does the body even know which sugar (and there are many types) to absorb, or which protein (and there are hundreds) goes where, when, and in what quantity? How does it know which substances are safe to absorb, and which should be ignored, quickly eliminated, or destroyed? How does the small bowel know how to cooperate with the 500 different kinds of bacteria that live in it?

These are incredibly complex functions that work together—and only together—to maintain the health of an individual.

How does the body know when there's too much or too little sugar in the bloodstream and whether more or less insulin should be secreted? How does it mobilize the sugar stored in the liver and change it into energy, using as many as 1000 mitochondria per cell? Questions such as these are endless, yet they address important bodily functions that were unknown at Darwin's time. Evolution says we easily changed from prehistoric fish digesting algae to primates who savor meat. But not only do humans have many more and different digestive processes than our presumed forebears, but experts overlook the relatively sudden appearance of a tongue and a full set of teeth—with a total lack of precedents. There are few, if any, examples of mouths with partial tongues, a single, odd tooth, or both.

The Problem of the Whole-Package Phenomenon

A third problem for Darwin is Michael Behe's concept of *irreducible complexity*—or what might also be called "all-or-none," or the *whole-package phenomenon* (WPP). He cites the process of blood clotting (mentioned in the introduction of this book), but there

Simple Feedback System for Wounds

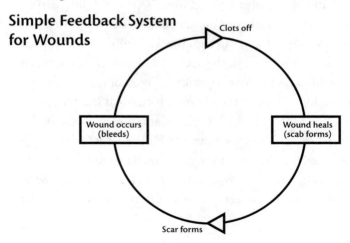

Wounds: What Really Happens

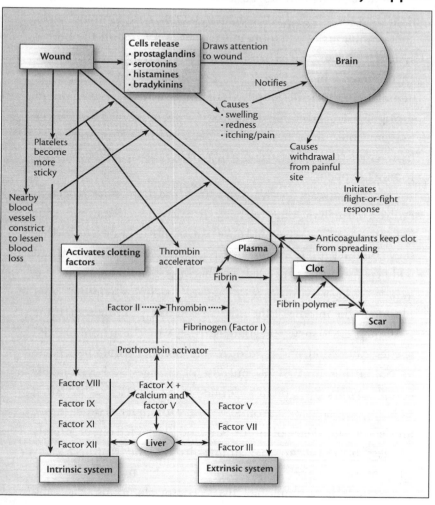

are hundreds of examples, all made up of "useless" intermediate steps. Take the body's ability to fight infections. A dirty wound might contain billions of microorganisms, yet every step in the body's system for protecting us from intruders—even those never before encountered—has to have been in place beforehand. Or take the hemoglobin molecule. Hundreds of amino acids have to be put in the right order and configuration, or else the molecule cannot carry oxygen. Could there have been a species with only intermediate, useless molecules of hemoglobin floating around in its bloodstream? It didn't happen.

Six billion years doesn't even come close to the time needed to evolve a ten-trillion-plus-cell body. To start, the active amino acids in the primordial soup would have had to link up in such a way that they could reproduce, protect themselves, find nourishment, and add new functions as needed. The likelihood of that happening is akin to having a swimmer from England meeting a swimmer from Florida in the middle of the Atlantic without a GPS system. If the swimmers are to survive beyond that, they would also need to build shelter, catch food, and reproduce—or else they would perish.

To further understand purposeful changes and irreducible complexity, imagine a prehistoric blind man called Gene who started building a wooden bridge off Key West. Although he could not see and lacked knowledge of any distant lands, he added one seemingly "useless" plank after another, aiming directly for Portugal. One day when he was extremely old, he completed the ten-million-plus plank connection. He accomplished this task despite lightning strikes and hurricanes, without making any significant errors. And so it goes with human evolution. There are thousands of such lengthy bridges, and millions of well-aimed, individually useless steps (planks)… and yet, according to evolutionists, we came about without a plan.

An incredible number of steps (planks) are needed to manufacture and use insulin. We all secrete this twisted, multifaceted hormone after each meal to control sugar. A shortage results in uncontrolled sugar levels in the bloodstream, or diabetes; an excess may cause hypoglycemia or fainting. In the process of insulin manufacture, none of the several "pre-insulin" molecules are useful (envision a car being made along an assembly line). Not only is this an all-or-none process, but so are the mechanisms that tell the body when to secrete insulin, how much insulin to produce or secrete, for how long, where to send it, how to link it to nutrients in the blood, how to transport it, and how to turn it off when the job is done.

> The idea that ten or more trillion cells can even coordinate with each other is mind-boggling.

The Problem of Intermediates

A fourth problem with Darwin's theories is the lack of intermediate species. Thousands of animal species suddenly exploded on the scene in the Cambrian period, and many more "sudden-species" have shown up since. Some experts have argued that there was an atmospheric problem, like low oxygen tension, that prevented fossil formation in certain areas—yet there are much older, unrelated fossils in the same areas. Note that the whale, the largest animal on the planet, lacks significant fossil evidence. (Darwin said whales came from bears, but there are no part-bear, part-whale fossilized bones.)

If humans truly had monkeys as prehistoric intermediates, shouldn't there still be, somewhere in the world, a remote family of humans that still walk on all fours, or a few folks with very long arms, or people who hang from and procreate in trees, or groups who still eat ticks found on their spouses? Shouldn't some humans have retained a hairy coat? Desmond Morris wrote that there are 193 living species of monkeys and apes and that 192 are covered with hair. It seems odd that only one line requires parkas, gloves, and electric heating for chilly nights. Survival of the fittest should have enhanced those who had natural protection from the cold. And where did that tail go? The entire appendage just dropped off.

Listen to Mr. Darwin's worries on the subject:

> The number of intermediate varieties which have formerly existed on the Earth must be enormous. Why then is not every geological formation and every stratum full of such intermediate links? Geology assuredly does not reveal any such finely graduated organic chain: and this, perhaps, is the most obvious and gravest objection which can be urged against my theory.

Ape babies pass through the birth canal with their faces looking up, whereas most human babies face downward. How did the birth of a child swing around 180 degrees without any intermediate stages? It seems as though the entire human race would have perished if that change had evolved slowly—a baby would die quickly if its head passed through the pelvis sideways and got stuck; it would probably kill the mother as well. If this flip-over had happened suddenly, the change would have required an immeasurable number of simultaneous, purposeful, genetic mutations in both mother and baby. It couldn't have just happened. So if it could not have happened slowly and it could not have come about quickly, where's the answer? That depends on one's belief system, not known facts. It's also odd that the gorilla, which is double human-size, delivers an infant that is 50-percent smaller than the average human baby. Maybe we humans should have smaller babies, which favors survival—not ones whose heads are so large they can damage and sometimes kill their mothers. Perhaps the original primates delivered their babies face down, and apes (not us) are the changed ones. If so, one would then have to explain how the intermediate monkeys survived childbirth.

The Problem of Purposeful Function

A fifth problem involves the issue of purposeful function, or intelligent design. Why are we born with the thickest skin on the bottom of our feet (where it needs to be), the most sensitive skin on our fingertips and lips (where it should be), the thinnest and most transparent skin in our eyelids (so we wake when the sun rises), chemically different tears for crying, happiness, and lubrication, adrenaline for sudden energy bursts, a nose situated above the mouth to assess food before it enters the system, taste buds to catch a poison before it goes down (or vomiting, aided by gagging, if the bad stuff slips through), a thumb that opposes the other fingers (where are the hands with trial thumbs elsewhere?), endorphins to lessen pain, killer sperms, a rectum and bladder strategically located to aid elimination, genitals that naturally fit together, eyelids that close snugly, a rectum that seals shut, a heart with a backup electrical system, body language skills, ear wax that kills mites, stomach acid that kills bacteria, white cells that destroy viruses, nipples that face outward to aid a nursing babe in arms, waterproof skin, and a conscience that usually helps us make our lives reasonable and rational? Why are eating, drinking, sleeping, and having sex so pleasurable? Could the enjoyment be a result of a design to promote these activities and thereby promote the species? Or is enjoyment merely a mutation or a result of natural selection?

I believe that the latter arguments stretch logic. Too many complex, internal systems are involved.

The Problem of "Gifts"

A sixth problem with Darwin's theories has to be *gifts*. These are attributes like laughing, singing, dancing, reading, playing, understanding, complex thinking, offering sympathy, and simply smiling. Experts on evolution rarely tackle these qualities because they can't explain them. Is Albert Einstein a product of natural selection, or is he merely a product of many genetic mutations? Or Mark Twain? Or Gandhi? Or Shakespeare? Or Mother Teresa? What about "idiot savants" who can play thousands of songs on the piano without a lesson? Evolutionary theories do not explain these special skills.

What Darwin Didn't Know

Despite having been given enormous credit for insight into biological processes, Darwin knew very little about human cells when he wrote *On the Origin of Species*. His knowledge of human physiology was sparse and mostly mistaken. In that book he wrote,

> The laws governing inheritance are quite unknown;
> no one can say why the same peculiarity in different
> individuals of the same species, and in individuals of
> different species, is sometimes inherited and sometimes
> not so.

If a pig could be made into a fatter pig, Darwin felt that gills could change into lungs, fins into legs, and a monkey into a man. Although an artist makes it look simple, the genetic change from one species to another is more complicated than transforming Paris into Hong Kong. Although man and monkey are 95 to 98 percent genetically similar, the difference at the chemical base level is still in the millions. (Note that the DNA of the zebra fish is 92 percent similar to humans. Why don't zebra fish and monkeys hang out together?)

Despite huge gaps in the fossil evidence, and though he lacked even the simplest of genetic information, Darwin's guesses have dominated modern scientific thought like no other. Even his strongest proponents have admitted there have been significant problems with his theories and have merely offered Band-Aid guesses of their own. What Bertrand Russell once said may readily apply:

> The fact that an opinion is widely held is no evidence whatsoever that it is not utterly absurd.

Bottom-Line Points

- *Given the exposure to the same air, radiation, climate, and foods, why would man steadily improve in size, skills, and intelligence while other species like the dolphin, cockroach, and crocodile have remained unimproved for millions of years?*

- *Natural selection may be a very legitimate law of nature, much like gravity or water freezing, but it falls way short of explaining evolution. Fast rabbits still remain rabbits; they do not become jaguars.*

- *Science has been wrong many times in the past; why are we so certain evolutionary science is correct now?*

- *Every aspect of human physiology has multiple facets, steps, purposes, managers, feedback loops, anticipated outcomes, and double checks. Every function is too complex to have been formed by slow, accidental changes that luckily fit together.*

- *Darwin knew very little about genetics, cell theory, or human physiology.*

To postulate that the development and survival of the fittest is entirely a consquence of chance mutations seems to me a hypothesis based on no evidence and irreconcilable with the facts. These classical evolutionary theories are a gross oversimplification of an immensely complex and intricate mass of facts, and it amazes me that they are swallowed as uncritically and readily, and for such a long time, by so many scientists without a murmur of protest.

—Professor Sir Ernst Chain, 1945 Nobel Prize Laureate for Medicine or Physiology

2

The Cell

To understand the real complexity of a human being and to further appreciate why some scientists believe that intelligent design is responsible, it's best to start with the cells, whose numbers are staggering. Every human body contains between 10 and 75 trillion, depending on a person's age and size, and there are 200 known variations, ranging from microscopic red blood cells to long, skinny nerve cells that stretch from the base of the spine to the foot, from cells that prevent infection to those that fight infection, and from cells that help us remember to cells that help us forget. The female *ovum,* or egg, is a fraction smaller than the period at the end of this sentence, while the sperm is a hundred times smaller.

Compounds and Chromosomes

Every cell contains an estimated one billion compounds. That's as many as 75,000,000,000,000,000,000,000 (75 sextillion) compounds per person—give or take a billion—and among these compounds are approximately five million different kinds of proteins. These proteins are highly varied in shape and size, but in the simplest of terms, most look like partially unraveled, tangled balls of yarn; they can have more than one function or electrical charge, they all know where to go and how to get there, when to act, how fast to react, and when to stop. Nearly every chemical reaction is helped along by one or more of the 3000-plus different enzymes. Some of these chemical reactions take only a millionth of a second.

The nucleus of each cell contains 23 pairs of very complex chromosomes (DNA), with 100,000 genes that can be further broken down into six billion chemical bases. There are only four kinds of these bases, abbreviated A, G, C, and T; yet these four bases, which are relatively simple compounds, appear in such varying combinations that they tell the cell, and ultimately the body, everything that it needs to know about growing up, surviving, fighting, fleeing, digesting food, breathing, thinking, pumping blood, eliminating wastes, and perpetuating the species. The first few cells in an embryo already know what a person's height will be, his or her propensity to be obese, the color of his or her eyes, the number of curls in his or her hair, whether he or she will have musical skills, if his or her teeth will grow in crooked, and whether he or she is vulnerable to certain diseases such as breast cancer or Huntington's chorea. Some scientists call the DNA-coded instructions the Book of Life; it's a book like no other.

Knowledge Today vs. Knowledge in Darwin's Day

Each cell has an assigned location, a seemingly lifetime role, a lifestyle, hundreds to thousands of complex tasks to accomplish, and a distinct longevity. Each cell is also programmed to take care of its own needs—as well as the entire being. Proof of this became evident with cloning. If the nucleus from a skin cell is placed inside a female egg after its nucleus has been removed, the skin's (hidden?) DNA Book of Knowledge can duplicate an entire individual.

During the 1800s, cells were thought to be nothing more than tiny building blocks, like bricks in a building, or passageways for special juices. Improved microscopy, however, has shown them to be highly variable. Muscle cells are long and spindly, and most nerve cells look like deranged octopi. Cells can be flat and rectangular in the skin, rounded in the bloodstream, torpedolike in the testes, or amoeba-like when fighting infections. Many are extremely flexible; some can stretch to double their size, and others shrink to half. They can be stationary or mobile or both. Billions ride the currents of the bloodstream every day, tumbling, surfing, floating, and swimming. Some can suddenly latch onto a cell wall as if it were lined with Velcro; others can slip in between cells to fight intruders. Some bring manufactured products; others take them away. Certain cells are heavily armed and patrol the blood vessels for signs of intruders, ready to engage in combat at a moment's notice; still others can engulf invaders. Some make antibodies and carry biological walkie-talkies to coordinate their attack. Many secrete pyrogens to raise body temperature.

Nowadays, scientists can tease out a few cells from a biopsy specimen, such as prostate or skin, and watch them grow and reproduce in the culture. Many crawl about and ingest nourishment as if they were free-living unicellular organisms. Skin cells will link up and try to form skin; muscle cells will try to form muscle bundles. Nerve cells send out tentacles in an attempt to connect to their neighbors. Are we just a huge collection of cells that have learned to work together?

> Some scientists call the DNA-coded instructions the Book of Life; it's a book like no other.

Functions and Messages

Cell surfaces can be highly variable, too. Some have thousands of cilia—tiny waving projections—such as those that move irritants out of the lungs or nutrients along the bowel. Others, like those in the inner ear, have microscopic wheat fields that sway with sounds.

Specialized cells monitor the environment for worrisome chemicals, toxins, allergens, sights, sounds, smells, sensations, and tastes. They send warnings to the brain, which in turn recruits other cells for appropriate responses or inaction. Other cells have regulatory responsibilities, such as monitoring blood pressure and heart rate, sensing changes in body temperature, or adjusting concentrations of salts, nutrients, and water.

Cells have variable life spans. Certain bone cells cease to grow when a person is fully grown. Millions of skin cells slough every day. Red blood cells live 120 days, while certain brain cells linger for years, maybe for life. Some cells dwindle with advancing age, like cells responsible for female hormone production and fat cells in the skin (that's why elderly skin is so fragile). Others proliferate, giving elderly folks larger ears and noses, bulkier eyebrows, and bone spurs. A female newborn arrives with half a million potential eggs, and yet she will only ovulate 500 of them during her lifetime. Which ova are selected, or how selection comes about, is a mystery. Is the egg picked to match the suitor? No one knows.

All cells use chemical and electrical messages. Certain nerve cells telegraph pain and heat or cold to the brain, and other nerve cells carry the response back to muscles, joints, and ligaments at lightning speed. Heart cells use electricity to make heart muscle cells contract in unison, and chemical messages from a variety of sources control the heart's speed. Chemical messages also tell the thyroid, adrenals, and ovaries to speed up or slow down hormone production.

Cell Components

Like an industrial complex, a cell has numerous factories, called *organelles*. The most commonly studied are the *endoplasmic reticulum, Golgi complexes, mitochondria, ribosomes,* and *centro-meres.* They all contribute to the making or use of proteins, carbohydrates, lipids (fats), hormones, vitamins, salt, and water. If it's hormones they are manufacturing, the finished products may be stored or moved to the cell's surface for transport.

The mitochondria (singular, *mitochondrion)* are the cell's power generators, and there can be as many as a thousand per cell in the heart. Like alkaline batteries, they store energy in the form of ATP for future use. The "TP" stands for three phosphates—and for energy needs, this battery gives up one phosphate, going from ATP to ADP, much like solar panels convert light energy into electrical energy. If a person were to become chilled, a signal would go out, and every cell would start using these batteries to warm up. One can sense that warmth by sitting on a chair that was recently occupied by someone else. More commonly, however, the energy is used for day-to-day cellular needs.

For unknown reasons, the DNA found in the mitochondria comes only from the mother and is passed through the generations with very few changes. In fact, their mutation rate is estimated to be one change every 10,000 years. This makes them a very stable item to study. This came into play when Dr. Bryan Sykes, who wrote *The Seven Daughters of Eve,* studied the mitochondria taken from the "Iceman" found in the Italian Alps in 1991. Carbon dating indicated this individual had been frozen for 5000 years—and yet Dr. Sykes was able to find modern-day relatives. Using similar mitochondrial DNA analyses, he was also able to prove Europeans are not descendants of Neanderthal man. This same technology has been used by forensic specialists in Guatemala to return the remains of victims of political homicides to their mothers and grandmothers. It only requires a speck of tissue, which is sometimes extracted from the pulp of a dead tooth.

Evolutionists cannot explain how these mitochondria came about or why they are exclusively maternal. (The fertilizing sperm sheds its mitochondria as it enters the egg.) Lynn Margulis and Dorion Sagan, in *Origins of Sex*, suggests that mitochondria were independent microorganisms, like bacteria, that joined the prehuman cell eons ago in some symbiotic relationship, shed their outer membranes, and reproduced along with our cells from then on. It's like having your mother accidentally ingest a button—and then every generation thereafter is born with buttons in their stomachs. No one can prove whether this stowaway theory is correct, but since these power units are found in all living cells, their beginning must date back to the beginning of all cell life. Somehow, they know to become more active or to multiply whenever there is a need.

The Work of a Cell

Work within each cell progresses each day as if the cell contained a book of instructions. Messenger RNA carries the instructions from a gene or genes to the workplace, where workers called ribosomes read the instructions, collect the appropriate amino acids, and begin manufacturing a specific protein or proteins. Somehow these messengers know which genes have the instructions, how to transport them, and where to deliver them. In like manner, the workers are able to read the message and carry out the instructions. When their product is complete, it folds itself spontaneously and is loaded onto or into a complex tubular system that delivers it to the proper destination, either within the cell or to the cell's shipping port. Sometimes the product is a precursor that must travel to another cell far away and be cleaved (split) or combined. If the original cell had evolved first, why did it make a compound that was useless for itself?

Most textbooks make the cell seem like some gelatin-containing plastic box with a few pieces of fruit floating about inside, but it is vastly more complicated. Using semirigid scaffolding, the cell wall maintains its shape and keeps intruders out. This wall membrane is solid enough to keep water in and yet semipermeable to certain nutrients and wastes. It is self-sealing. One can puncture the wall with a microscopic needle, and it will immediately close up. The side facing the capillary—the smallest blood vessel in the body—is covered with loading docks that have various structures to receive a long list of products. Triangle-tipped items fit into triangle-holes, and proteins that twist right may connect with docks that twist left. Opposites attract, and similarly charged particles repel each other. Passageways to the cell interior can resemble long hallways, conveyor belts, or sieves. They can be guarded or unguarded. The remaining sides of the cell tightly adhere to neighbors by a special glue that is made at the border membrane. In many instances, these membranes can bend, stretch, flex, stiffen, bulge, and retract with ease. A few can bend in half. Under certain circumstances, some can separate and move elsewhere.

How Does It Know?

Similar to a skyscraper with crisscrossing steel girders, the cell is supported by a skeleton of crisscrossing microfilaments and microtubules. Unlike a skyscraper, however, some of these structures are like movable scaffolding. They are also used for structural support and as channels to move organelles and proteins within the cell. Envision a building with changing stairwells and elevators to accommodate the changing business needs of the day. If the boss needs to check out the third floor, a stairwell will suddenly appear. If he needs to go to the basement, a chute will open up. Changes

Illustration of the Ultrastructure of a Typical Cell

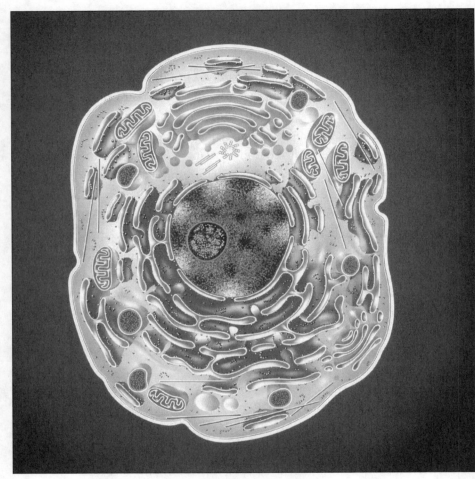

At center, the nucleus has a *nucleolus* containing the DNA genetic material. Closely associated with the *nucleus* is *endoplasmic reticulum (ER)*, a membrane system in the cytoplasm studded with *ribosomes* (sites of protein synthesis). *Golgi bodies* package products from the ER into spherical *lysosomes*. Above the nucleus, two *centrioles* made of microtubules play a role in cell division. *Mitochondria* store energy for the cell. The *cytoplasm* is bordered by a white cell membrane.

like these happen rather frequently within the cell, and the evidence indicates all the activity is purposeful.

There are numerous monitoring systems within each cell as well. The concentrations of all salts are closely watched and frequently adjusted. The same is true for water. If the body is chilling, metabolism increases to increase warmth; if the body is overheating, metabolism slows to effect cooling. The kidney cells are constantly changing their hormone production to adjust for salt and water needs. If a cell is injured, a distress call is sent out.

Every cell has tiny packets of enzymes called *lysosomes,* which can be likened to vicious pit bulls living in cages inside your house. Because they can destroy most organic compounds, they can, if set loose, be very dangerous. At the cellular level, their cages are *vesicles,* and they are handled very carefully. Lysosomes have many uses; one purpose is defense. After a white cell has engulfed a bacterium, the germ is locked in a vesicle and taken to one of these pit bull cages, where it is torn apart limb by limb. The pieces are then placed in another vesicle and carried to the cell's periphery to be dumped into the bloodstream. When a cell dies, the cages break open, and the same mechanism destroys the cell. Purposeful or accidental?

> Most textbooks make the cell seem like some gelatin-containing plastic box with a few pieces of fruit floating about inside, but it is vastly more complicated.

There are many other types of enzymes. Forty or more can be found inside a particular set of chambers called *peroxisomes.* Each peroxisome has very specific responsibilities—to snip this, attach that, glue those, or hurry up some chemical reaction. Some are secreted at specific times, such as those found in the pancreas, which are released when food needs digesting. These enzymes know their target, work in a fraction of a second, and then self-destruct.

Materials pass in and out of cells in a variety of ways. In some locations they travel in one direction only; in others there's an exchange. Sometimes it's merely a matter of concentration, meaning the item flows from the more concentrated solution to the less. Specialized cells remove nutrients from the gut, using a particular mechanism for each type of material. Other specialized cells actively remove waste items from the blood and excrete it into the stool or urine.

Phagocytosis (cell eating) is the mechanism by which white cells, using pseudopods, engulf intruders or worrisome debris. *Pinocytosis* (cell drinking) is the method by which cells collect fluid. The cell wall caves inward, surrounding the material, and then closes it off into a vacuole. *Exocytosis* is the opposite process, used to eliminate waste. This is how breast milk is moved from the cell's interior into the ducts and how a sperm releases enzymes to penetrate the egg.

Each cell is also a combination metallurgist, pharmacist, and chemist. It handles and stores a number of vitamins, chemicals, and toxic metals and is able to release whichever one(s) it needs. Knowing how to store, retrieve and transport these items had to have come about as a WPP—whole-package phenomenon, as discussed in chapter 1. Knowing how and where to store calcium without knowing how to absorb, transport, and use it just couldn't happen. It just couldn't be the result of separate systems that luckily came together. How would the body know how to store iron if it didn't know how to absorb it, transport it, and use it?

What remains overwhelmingly impressive is that a single cell can do more than our most powerful computers, that it can be completely different from, yet totally compatible with, its neighbor cells, and that every function is predetermined on a submicroscopic level. Often the billions of results are a domino effect; one development leads to another, to another, and to another.

Bottom-Line Points

- *The formation of each cell and every function thereof follows a blueprint that is drawn up at the union of the egg and sperm. What has been called a "blank slate" actually has millions of instructions that unfold like a three-dimensional game of dominoes.*

- *Every human body contains between 10 and 75 trillion cells, depending on the person's size; there are 200 known kinds of cells and thousands of different functions.*

- *Every cell contains dozens of tiny factories that make billions of compounds.*

- *These compounds are highly variable in shape, size, electrical charge, and configuration; many can complete a function in a millionth of a second.*

- *Anatomy, physiology, and genetics—from a single freckle on the cheek to a bend in the colon—are predetermined. Personalities, preferences, and susceptibilities may also be. The "blank slate" is a very crowded board.*

Faced with the enormous sum of lucky
draws behind the success of the evolutionary
game, one can legitimately wonder to what
extent this success is actually written into
the fabric of the universe.

—Christian de Duve, 1974 Nobel Laureate
for Medicine or Physiology

3

Reproduction: Macroscopic

All aspects of human reproduction either had to have evolved in unbelievably specific, compatible, and parallel ways—or else all these aspects arrived simultaneously (WPP). Every significant change in the male's reproductive system had to have been met with a reciprocal change in the female's (or vice versa). There could not have been sexual drive or attraction without matching desire, anatomy for thrusting without anatomy for receiving, a fully functional penis without complementary female vagina, male hormones without female hormones, mobile sperm without a mature egg, 23 male chromosomes without 23 compatible female chromosomes, an opening into the cervix for the sperm to enter without an opening in a fallopian tube for the egg, or a maturation plan for the embryo without a uterus to receive and nurture it. Having all these steps plus a live birth is close to unique in nature. Other than microorganisms, which reproduce in a totally different way, we share this distinction with cockroaches, fleas, some sharks, certain snakes, and all other mammals except the platypus and the spiny anteater.

Compatibility

Human genitals are designed to fit snugly together. A man's erection, if it were to be sustained 24/7, would make life very uncomfortable and urination quite difficult. Instead, the penis is designed to remain limp and yet maintain a hydraulic-like system that knows when and how to fill up with blood when an erection is needed. The erectile tissue in the penis is designed to respond to visual, auditory, imaginary, and tactile stimuli; nocturnal erections in prepubescent males might well be practice drills. Post-ejaculation, the hydraulic system knows to release the blood. On the other hand, the female has a clitoris that acts in similar ways, swelling with sexual excitement and aiding the climax. She also secretes mucus, and her uterus changes shape, to aid the sperm's journey inward.

The testicles are designed to respond to hormones secreted by the pituitary, and during puberty this becomes readily apparent. Testosterone levels skyrocket, changing a boy into a man with a beard and a deeper voice, who can make sperm. A single male will produce about 100 million new sperm each day, essentially a thousand with each heartbeat, and over a trillion in a lifetime. These torpedolike cells with flagellating tails have a head that is loaded with explosive enzymes. They must also have a homing device, since sperm that are injected into the abdominal cavity of experimental animals will still find their way to the fallopian tubes.

The human female's bony pelvis protects her ovaries, uterus, and any pregnancies. The vaginal vault is shaped to receive and stimulate an erect penis, and it can increase lubrication to aid penetration. It is also protected by a hymen during the formative years. Although the egg is only .004 inches across, it knows where to go and how to get there. The uterus will adjust as the embryo grows; it will nourish the developing embryo through the growth of a placenta, stretch as much as is needed, and then, at a precise moment, push the baby down the birth canal. Redundancy is built into the system. One ovary would probably be sufficient, but humans have two. The reason may be for backup.

Like the chicken-and-egg riddle, there could not have been an egg or a sperm without a male and female—and there could not have been two compatible adults without compatible eggs and sperm. If evolution were the explanation, millions of intermediate species as well as numerous genetic mistakes should have been found in the fossil record. As yet, there are virtually none. And citing fish, salamanders, lizards, birds, mammals, and primates as connected, intermediate steps is like having a giant take a walk from New York to Los Angeles, stepping only in Cleveland, Chicago, Omaha, Denver, and Las Vegas—and then declaring that the entire country is one big city.

> Every significant change in the male's reproductive system had to have been met with a reciprocal change in the female's (or vice versa).

Arguments in favor of evolution must explain how so many genes made so many huge, simultaneous alterations, substitutions, and additions to set up functions such as reproduction, digestion, immunity, motor skills, breathing, circulation, the five senses, and thinking. A congenital "freak" (a presumed improvement) that was capable of producing sperm with a new characteristic would have needed a perfectly timed congenital "freak" of the opposite sex. Human males also need a means to manufacture sperm, store them, mobilize them on a moment's notice, mix them in a fluid that will cut through vaginal mucus, and deliver them in the correct manner. In a similar fashion, the egg needs to know when it's time to ovulate, how to pop out, how to travel through the fallopian tubes, how to receive a single sperm and close out the other sperm, and how to eventually implant in the uterus. That's a lot to achieve by accident.

Billions of interactions are needed to make the entire fertilization process a success. If conception does not occur, millions of additional interactions are needed to undo the monthly effort—involving the recognition of a failure, menstruation, and preparation for the next cycle. The body is designed to keep trying until it decides we're too old. Conception does not easily fit into development through random mutation. An egg is either fertilized and nourished in the proper way or it isn't; a person is either born or not born. Where are the intermediate steps?

Chromosomes and Changes

Every living species has its own unique, matching number of chromosomes. An animal with 13 chromosomes cannot mate with a species with 12 or 14 chromosomes. Whenever that rare mismatch does happen, such as a horse mating with a donkey to produce a mule, the offspring are usually sterile or monster-like. Cats cannot mate with dogs, mosquitoes with flies, lizards with amphibians, or humans with monkeys. Nor do they care to.

It is difficult to find an explanation of how chromosomes were added or subtracted from each cell as species evolved. Did the sudden appearance of a fin (hand precursor) cause the hand chromosomes to appear? Or did genes for hands appear spontaneously? In either case, it had to have happened in both the male and the female at the same time, or else their chromosomes might not have matched up. (There are no prehistoric hands with three fingers.) Fossil evidence seems to indicate there were fins and then there were hands. Quite a giant step.

A toad has 11 pairs of chromosomes, an alligator 16, a cat 19, a rhesus monkey 21, a human 23, a potato 24, a dog 39, and a chicken 39. If we are descendants of amphibians, which have 13 pairs of chromosomes, not only did the original 13 chromosomes change, but

10 pairs of chromosomes, with approximately 130 million chemical bases on each, were added. That would be like replacing half the books in the Library of Congress and then adding ten new wings full of books, one text at a time, in correct numerical order... all without a plan. All, perhaps, done by a blind librarian.

Evolutionary theory suggests that the progression from species to species could have easily happened if given enough time. As an argument, some have said that, given infinite time and an infinite number of monkeys with typewriters, one of them would eventually type the Bible. Others say, given infinite monkeys and infinite time we would use up all of our forests and be lucky to get a single useful sentence. The latter more closely approaches reality.

According to evolution, before mammals appeared on earth, eggs were fertilized outside the female's body (as with fish) or were laid already fertilized (as with birds). The questions that follow are how and why fertilization and maturation shifted inside. Natural selection could be one explanation—an embryo residing inside its mother's womb would be less vulnerable to predators, warmer, more easily transported, and better nourished—but the genetic jump would be huge, and there is no fossil evidence that some embryos lived an intermediate life (partially inside and partially outside). Just consider how many changes would be necessary.

Why and How?

As noted, every female child is born with an estimated half million immature eggs split between two ovaries, yet less than 500 will mature during her reproductive years. Which egg will leave the ovary (or how it is selected) remains a mystery. Can the partner's pheromones have an influence? And why is there usually just one egg released?

A similar mystery surrounds the selection of the single sperm that will ultimately fertilize an egg. We know that many will race inside and struggle to penetrate the egg's outer lining, but only one will be admitted. The winner is not always the first one to arrive, however. Does the egg somehow recognize which sperm will create the best offspring, or do they merely have a matching lock and key? The trip up through the uterus may involve survival of the fittest, but there is a gamelike strategy. Blocker and killer sperm will stay behind and stop any competitor's sperm, while the female genital tract is loaded with traps and chemical barriers.

Scientific facts regarding reproduction are truly scarce. We do know that a woman who is not sexually active and is not expecting to engage in sex in the near future (for example, a nun), may menstruate without ovulating. It's as if the body is saying, *Don't waste an egg.* Intelligent design or accident? Women who may be temporarily celibate, but are expecting to engage in intercourse in the near future, will ovulate. Women who are suffering from enormous emotional stress, are living in areas of famine, or are seriously ill will skip ovulation, sometimes for months. The lack of a period or periods seems to be a natural phenomenon, as if the body knows it is physically or emotionally unable to care for a newborn at such times. Women who do extreme exercising such as cross-country running will commonly miss periods. Best guess, the body views the extreme metabolic changes as a possible famine time and puts a hold on ovulation.

Incredible Journeys

Once the egg is selected, it grows for 14 days, drastically changing its interior to support the potential embryo. At a specific moment, it pops out of the ovary and is picked up by tiny fingerlike structures called *fimbriae*, located at the outer end of the fallopian tube, where it is gently and quickly moved toward the uterus. This is a potentially treacherous journey. Picture a golf ball popping out of a randomly selected window of a huge skyscraper with 250,000 windows, and then falling into someone's outstretched hands in a window at the other end of town. The egg is the size of a period, and yet it must make a five-inch journey in 24 hours. Our golf ball, as it were, will roll down 30 miles of highway and land inside a hole on the eighteenth fairway of a golf course it has never seen. This journey is usually accomplished without a hitch. Fertilization must occur within a narrow range of time and space, or else the embryo will become an ectopic (tubal) pregnancy, which can lead to a fatal event for mother and fetus.

Sperm are considerably smaller than the egg, yet they travel five times farther. They begin at the testes in biological holding pens, travel past the prostate where they mix with seminal fluid, launch up the urethra into the vagina, and swim through the cervical opening and upstream through the uterus to reach the egg. This would be the equivalent of a guppy swimming across Lake Ontario. Somehow the sperm knows exactly where to go.

> Given an infinite number of monkeys with typewriters and infinite time we would use up all of our forests and be lucky to get a single useful sentence.

The average man ejaculates 200 to 500 million sperm during intercourse, depending on his degree of arousal, his age, and the frequency of intercourse. A man's anatomy is designed to deposit his sperm very strategically at the opening of the uterus. The oldest and least viable sperm are ejaculated first, establishing a pool with the younger, more vigorous sperm on top so they can enter the cervix first. At the same time, the cervix changes from its usual bottle-top shape to an "elephant trunk," or funnel, and it literally sucks the seminal fluid into the uterus. The sexier the woman is thought to be—a hard definition—the more intercourse…and the more likely she will conceive.

Approximately 10 percent of the ejaculate (20 to 50 million sperm) is truly capable of fertilizing the egg, but only 200 sperm actually complete the journey. After entering the cervix, they travel at an average speed of three millimeters per hour, covering a distance that is equal to a person's pinky finger in 24 hours. According to Dr. Robin Baker in his book *Sperm Wars,* they can be classed as *blockers, killers,* and *egg-getters* (fertilizers). The blockers follow the egg-getters through the cervix and plug up the holes in the woman's mucus so another man's sperm cannot make it inside. Still others, called killers, linger behind to attack any other man's sperm in case they make it past the first wall of defense. To help increase the chances of fertilization, the ejaculate contains sperm of varying ages so that some can linger and mature in crevices along the way. Presumably this allows for a second and third wave of egg-getters to fertilize the egg up to five days after contact. Design or accident?

Reciprocity and Combination

Everything about the act of fertilization is reciprocal. Not only is the female's anatomy designed to arouse the male and increase his ejaculate, but around the time of ovulation she emits hormones that entice him and make her vaginal mucus more permeable to sperm. At this time, female-initiated intercourse is most likely to occur. Orgasms tend to empty the crypts (vaginal cavities) of mucus and stretch them out, which, combined with the mucus-busting enzymes from seminal fluid, aids sperm penetration.

Each sperm is built like a torpedo, with enzymes on its tip that can break through the exterior surface of the egg. Once inside, the head detaches, and a chemical reaction follows that makes the egg's outer wall impermeable to other sperm. The 23 chromosomes, or six billion chemical bases, in the sperm readily combine with the 23 chromosomes in the egg. This is a very quick and very exacting event. Millions of characteristics are decided at the moment of conception. One gene will become dominant over another, two genes will decide to meld, or many genes will start to cooperate. The genes know whether this will be a little blond girl or a little dark-haired boy. They know which diseases this person may be prone to and, despite being only seconds old, these genes may also know what genes will be passed on to the next generation. They might even know how long a person is likely to live.

Intimacy: Designed?

Humans are among very few animals that indulge in recreational sex. Most animals show little interest in sex between estrus cycles. Some telegraph when it's time. The labia of female monkeys will swell and redden, their buttocks may change color, they will issue distinctive aromas or pheromones, and some will assume the coital position in front of the male. Every possible clue, visible and invisible, is given to the male. Bulls go crazy when a cow in a different field is ready, yet a farmer cannot detect any of those chemical changes.

Humans, in contrast, are clueless when it comes to ovulation. Some women may monitor their daily temperatures or increase the frequency of intercourse at midcycle, but the time of ovulation has remained mostly a guess. Ironically, while most animals indulge in sex to reproduce, many humans go out of their way to avoid reproducing.

What is it that drives all of us to be intimate, to long for someone else, to get aroused, and to need love? According to Richard

Dawkins in *The Selfish Gene,* it's only our genes, which want to reproduce more genes. Are we just an intermediate host to microscopic DNA entities? Ridiculous? There are precedents. Birds carry berry seeds miles from their origin and drop them in nutrient-filled globs of feces, squirrels bury acorns (and forget where they left them), and tapeworms make use of our gastrointestinal tract to perpetuate their species. The DNA or RNA in a virus can be quite similar to human DNA, only smaller. The only reason for their entering our bodies is to produce more viral particles. The disease they cause might merely be a side effect. Yet, there is a chance that some viruses are part of a species' natural defenses, benign within that species and used to keep other species away. Perhaps the green monkey virus (or ebola, or AIDS) is present to protect a certain species.

There is some evidence suggesting that human genes carry viral particles, perhaps trapped and passed on for millennia. Whether this is good or bad for us is not known. If we are to believe Dawkins' theory, we are like a chicken driven by its egg to make another egg. I don't accept his theory, but there's no question that much of our sexual behavior is written in the chromosomes.

The Attraction Is Mutual

One person's attraction to another may begin with how they are treated or with a smile, eye color, a wink, the sound of a voice, the shape of a torso, the size of her breasts, the symmetry of a face, the shape of his buttocks, personality, IQ or common sense, and even the thickness of a wallet. Although any of these may apply, attraction might also be due to pheromones. The body may use facial, armpit, and pubic hairs as wicks to waft pheromones out to the waiting *vomeronasal* (VMR) organs of others. These VMR organs are tiny collections of cells located in each nostril. Until recently, little was known about them, but newer evidence suggests they pick up sexual scents that cannot be consciously detected. Their presence might be why nasal passages swell during intercourse. Kissing may, in part, be enjoyable because we exchange pheromones close-up.

> Millions of characteristics are decided at the moment of conception. This is a very quick and very exacting event.

Obviously, sexual attraction is not entirely determined by proximity or pheromones. Many individuals find revealing photos in magazines, on TV, or in the movies enormously attractive. Some of what we take for granted, however, may not be true. Is breast size desirable because larger breasts are more attractive in lovemaking or, subconsciously, because they may be better for breast-feeding? Are wider hips on a woman more attractive in some cultures because she might be more enjoyable to be intimate with or because they might, subconsciously again, be better for birthing? When a man tries to seduce a woman, are his deeper, unrealized drives based on an inner desire to make a baby? Much of what we feel, why we react, and how we go about completing our sexual wants or needs is driven by mechanisms we don't understand. In a sense, using birth control pills or a condom is like adding artificial sugar in coffee. It fools the normal body mechanisms, but doesn't change the underlying physiology.

It's certain a man cannot consciously know that his sperm count has passed 200 million or that the seminal fluid tank is full, but these internal changes will pique a man's interest and make arousal easier. Subtle signals tell him whether he is ready or not. Even though the equipment lingers, a man cannot get a second erection until the prostate and testes say so.

In a similar sense, a woman is not aware that the pH in her vagina is conducive to keeping sperm alive, that she ovulated a certain number of hours ago, or that her cervical mucus is permeable, yet these changes increase her interest in sex. All of the male–female interactions coordinate completely. Even if a condom is interposed, the body handles intercourse as if it were being done to reproduce. The egg moves into position, and sperm charge forward. During the act of sex, respiratory rates increase and leg muscles tense up. A woman's nipples become erect, her clitoris enlarges (for increased pleasure), her labia swell (to allow easier entry), the vaginal orifice opens slightly, and secretions increase to aid penetration. Until stimulated a man's penis remains relatively small, presumably for better storage. It enlarges as dedicated arteries fill with blood while veins collapse to prevent the same blood from leaving. Seminal fluid collects near the base of the penis, where it mixes with sperm, and then the entire mixture is propelled out. The forward movement has to be coordinated, and the seminal fluid must have the correct amounts of nutrients and enzymes.

Manufacturing 200 to 500 million sperm for each encounter is no small task. The assembly plants are located in the testes, which are purposefully located outside the body, where the lower temperature prolongs survival of sperm. Each *spermatocyte* (cell that gives rise to sperm cells) divides into four *spermatozoa*, which grow long tails and trim down by extruding most of their inner cell contents. They are moved to the *vas deferens*—the sperm ducts— where they are mixed with seminal fluid. Their life expectancy would only be minutes if not bathed in this nutritive liquid. Once they have entered the uterus, other factors play a role—and some sperm may live as long as five days. Success, in part, has to do with sheer numbers. Of the hundreds of millions that are propelled with each ejaculation and the several thousand that make it into the uterus, only a few hundred make it to the egg, and only one penetrates it.

All of these well-coordinated and complex functions speak to purposeful design. It's WPP all over again. To dismiss intercourse as a simple act would be like defining an amusement park as a place to buy cotton candy. And here again, the fossil record is essentially void of transitional forms.

Bottom-Line Points

- *All aspects of human reproduction either had to have evolved in unbelievably specific, compatible, and parallel ways—or else all these aspects arrived simultaneously.*

- *Every significant change in the male's reproductive system had to have been met with a reciprocal change in the female's (or vice versa).*

- *Human males have the means to manufacture sperm, store them, mobilize them on a moment's notice, mix them in a fluid that will cut through vaginal mucus, and deliver them in the correct manner.*

- *The egg knows when it's time to ovulate, how to pop out, how to travel through the fallopian tubes, how to receive a single sperm and close out other sperm, and how to eventually implant in the uterus.*

- *Much of what we feel, why we react, and how we go about completing our sexual wants or needs is driven by mechanisms we don't understand.*

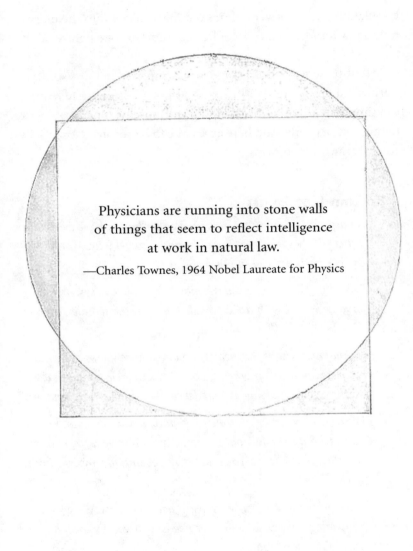

Physicians are running into stone walls
of things that seem to reflect intelligence
at work in natural law.

—Charles Townes, 1964 Nobel Laureate for Physics

4

Reproduction:
Microscopic

The union of the egg and the sperm combines two halves of the DNA Book of Knowledge. This is a peculiar book, however—full of codes, stops and starts, specific recipes, mysterious blank areas, and obscure instructions. It is not merely a thousand pages added to another thousand pages—a top half added to the bottom half, or the shuffling of pages. The halves are more like near mirror images, addressing similar issues, such as hair color or head size, from different perspectives. A person's blueprint is not only recorded in the DNA, but it is also linked to a timer. Barring something cataclysmic, growth and development will occur at predetermined times and predetermined speeds.

As the cells in the embryo divide and redivide, the subsequent generations know when (and how) to differentiate into specific cell types such as pancreas, brain, or muscle, where to position themselves, how to get there, how to interact with neighbor cells, when to start work, and how much work to do. Every stage of development is extremely well orchestrated and planned. Not only do bone cells line up in the right order, but they never end up in the spleen; ovarian cells are never found among prostate cells; and blood cells know to travel in the circulatory system, not in the common bile duct. Heart cells start beating the moment they arrive; and like a bongo player joining a street ensemble, they know innately how to beat in unison. Kidney and lung cells remain relatively quiet until called upon after birth.

Every cell has extremely specific instructions. Some bone marrow cells become white blood cells, and others become red blood cells. Some nerve cells form the brain and others the spinal column. Oftentimes there are several steps until the final cell is formed—and sometimes these cells go backward.

Reproducing a Factory

In many ways, a cell resembles an industrial complex. Throughout the day and night, it receives supplies, makes specialized products for its own needs or for distribution, and then sends different proteins or hormones to specific targets throughout the body. There's a central command post called the nucleus, where the instructions, warnings, and missions are kept. Surrounding this sphere is a gelatinous chunk of material called cytoplasm, which contains the biological equivalents of assembly lines, messenger services, snail mail and e-mail, administrative offices, copy machines, pumps and sumps, renewable energy sources, receiving departments, shipping docks, various storage areas, holding tanks, gas chambers for intruders, garbage chutes, recycle bins, containment centers, security devices, large and small highway systems, a parts department, repair crews, filing systems, pickup and delivery systems, monitoring devices, maintenance teams, and cleanup crews.

Unlike an industrial complex, however, a human cell can reproduce itself by a process called *mitosis*. Picture the same manufacturing plant—with millions of workers—shutting down to duplicate itself. The doors lock; the CEO quickly divides into two exact copies; each one migrates to an opposite end of the building and sends out fishing lines. At the same time everything else starts moving toward the absolute center of the plant: books, telephones, desks, paper clips, machinery, water fountains, lights, fax machines, fire extinguishers, chairs, file cabinets, computers, manu-factured goods, as well as every employee and every employee's belongings. A moment later, the order goes out for everything to be duplicated. Once that's done, the CEOs' fishing lines pull half of each set toward the opposite ends. The process of mitosis usually comes off without a hitch, but under unclear circumstances an employee might make a last-minute trade: a digital camera for a laptop, a stapler for an address book. And so it can happen with certain genes.

> Heart cells start beating the moment they arrive; and like a bongo player joining a street ensemble, they know innately how to beat in unison.

Once the factory has split into two equal halves, the exteriors quickly seal, and it's back to business as usual. Our chromosomes can duplicate the six billion chemical bases in a matter of six to eight hours. That means that more than 30 million copies can be made in the time it takes to read this sentence. Thousands of enzymes help this duplication—at a rate of one billion copies per hour.

The egg and the sperm come about in a slightly different way, called *meiosis*. Instead of becoming duplicates, these *gametes* (sex cells) become halves—23 chromosomes needing a complementary set of 23 chromosomes. A thousand sperm are made between every heartbeat, with an error rate of less than one in a million. Here too, the "employees" make last-minute exchanges, but they do so for very good reasons. Without this kind of shuffling, different-aged children in the same family would look and act exactly alike. Exchanges help diversity, which is vital for our species' survival. Without variety everyone would look alike. Generation after gener-ation would run at the same speed, listen to the same music, and probably think the same thoughts. Since everyone's immunity might be the same, an epidemic might kill the entire species. How these kinds of significant exchanges happen has remained a mystery, but all experts agree that this is an indispensable process.

A Package of Life's Instructions

Nearly every cell in the human body carries the DNA Book of Life around like a schoolchild might carry a backpack with all of life's instructions. Different cells select different pages or paragraphs to use for their own purposes. Instead of words, the cellular information is written in a biological code—the chemical bases abbreviated A,C,G, and T.

As a newly formed embryo divides, the Book of Life tells individual cells what shape to assume, what hormones to make, which minerals to absorb, how to communicate, which vitamins are needed, when to divide again, and much, much more. Parathyroid cells are told to monitor calcium concentrations—not sugar—and how to respond to high and low levels. Genes tell nerve cells how to sense pain, white cells how to fight infections, and gonad cells when to make testosterone or estrogen. Experts argue over how much of an individual's personality is genetically determined, but most agree that a very large percentage is already in place at birth. A kind person arrives predisposed to being kind, and a mean-spirited person arrives with a tendency to be mean. Criminals may not be born criminals, but that tendency, given the right circumstances, will show its ugly head. Circumstances can only magnify or lessen the expression of these characteristics—never eliminate them. Many diseases are also genetically predetermined. Dyslexia is found on chromosome 6, breast cancer on 13, and deafness on 17.

A child's sex is determined by the twenty-third chromosome, which is designated XY for male and XX for female. Each parent contributes one set of 23 chromosomes to their baby, but it is the sperm that determines the sex of the child. If a sperm carrying an X unites with the egg, which is

> A change in one or two DNA bases will not produce an individual with a tail any more than two monkeys with a few mutations will produce a baby without one.

always X, the baby (XX) will be a girl—but if a Y-sperm fertilizes the egg, the baby (XY) will be a boy. As mentioned in the previous chapter, many factors determine which sperm will make it to the egg, including vaginal pH, white cells, antibodies, mucus, and the presence of another man's sperm.

Sexually inherited traits such as baldness, color blindness, and hemophilia travel only on the X chromosome. For unclear reasons, the "good" X in the female embryo will dominate the XX combination and shut out baldness or hemophilia. If the male gets a "bad" X, it cannot suppress it with its Y; he will be bald at an age similar to his grandfather, not be able to distinguish red and green, or have a bleeding disorder. Since all genes come as matching pairs, a cellular system determines whether one trait will dominate or both will blend. If you look closely at a child's face, and then at its parents', you can easily recognize many blended characteristics. Although the process is very complex, it seems to happen rather easily.

Mutations: A Part of the Package?

Mutations caused by toxins, radiation, and viruses can happen during mitosis or meiosis, but they are usually inconsequential (the equivalent of a new paper clip in our factory). A change in one or two bases will not produce an individual with a tail any more than two monkeys with a few mutations will produce a baby without one. Changes of these magnitudes require huge numbers of simultaneous and well-coordinated mutations. When injuries to genetic material are major, they are usually detrimental and incompatible with life. (Imagine our industrial plant missing the ceiling between the first and second floors.)

In his book *Not by Chance!* Dr. Lee Spetner has written that unless an entire population incurs the same mutation, any change will dilute out and quickly disappear. If, for example, an animal is born that can jump four feet high, while his siblings (and other herd members) can only jump three feet, and if this is an improvement, he will mate with a three-foot jumper. Some of their blended offspring may jump three-and-a-half feet. During the next mating season, most of the better jumpers will mate with the older versions, and so on—until everyone is jumping three feet again.

So why did our ancestors have longer arms, which would be better for grabbing prey or picking fruit? Why not continue to run on all fours if that's faster? Why have larger heads when increased size is more dangerous during delivery? Could these anatomical characteristics have come about for reasons other than survival of the fittest?

Bottom-Line Points

- *The union of the egg and the sperm combines two halves of the DNA Book of Knowledge; this is an incredible text full of assembly plans, codes, stops and starts, recipes, mysterious blank areas, and yet-to-be-decoded instructions.*

- *A person's blueprint is not only recorded in the DNA, but it is also linked to a timer. Barring something cataclysmic, growth and development will occur at predetermined times and predetermined rates.*

- *As the cells in the embryo divide and redivide, the subsequent generations know when (and how) to differentiate into specific cell types. Each new generation may be a very different cell type.*

- *A cell resembles a miniature industrial complex that is much more complicated than a General Motors or Boeing plant.*

- *When injuries (mutations) to genetic material are major, they are usually detrimental and incompatible with life (not an improvement). When they are minor, they typically dilute out and disappear.*

The only possible answers are religious....I find anew for God in the Universe and in my life.

—Arthur L. Schawlow, 1981 Nobel Laureate for Physics

5

The Beginning

It takes about four days for the fertilized egg to move to the uterus. As it travels, it divides into two cells, then four, then eight, frequently changing configurations and adding functions. There's a children's game in which one imagines how rich one might become if given a penny that could double every day for a month. A child's worth would be more than five million dollars on the thirtieth day. And so it goes with the fetus. By a month's time the fetus will have nearly 500 million cells. Yet, unlike new pennies, each successive generation of cells may look different, make different proteins, and divide into further newer groups. A very detailed blueprint is followed for each step.

One of the first decisions is which cells will grow to become the embryo and which will form the placenta. By the sixth day, the egg is barely the size of a pinprick, and yet it knows how to find the uterine wall, implant itself, fulfill its needs, and diversify into the 200 different kinds of 10 to 75 trillion cells that will eventually make a viable human being.

The moment that ovulation occurred, a chemical signal was sent to the mother's pituitary gland, which in turn sent hormones to the uterus to make its wall softer, thicker, and more receptive. If conception had not occurred, another signal would have been sent to the pituitary, which in turn would have caused the uterine lining to slough, initiating menstrual bleeding. The entire cycle would then repeat.

Every part of the process is complex and interdependent. Ovulation cannot occur without feedback loops between the ovaries and the pituitary; sperm formation cannot happen without the feedback loops between the testes and the pituitary; fertilization cannot happen without the interaction of the male and female reproductive anatomy; implantation cannot happen without the interaction between the uterus, the pituitary, and the embryo; and the embryo cannot grow and thrive without the DNA blueprint. Hundreds of different steps are needed at every level. To propose that a process of random mutations and accidental selections was responsible for this would be like declaring that a human could travel from Antarctica to Miami by taking a single giant step.

Transfer Mechanisms

During the first three weeks of gestation, nutrients reach the embryo by simple diffusion. Water passes through the uterine wall as if it were a sponge. Once the placenta is locked in place, supplies are transferred more directly from the cells lining the maternal blood vessels to the cells lining the placental blood vessels. Whatever may be lacking, the placenta can often make.

In Latin, *placenta* means cakelike, and indeed that's what the placenta looks like. It grows into a thick, pinkish pancake with tens of thousands of microscopic fingers that hold it to the uterine wall. Each foothold is composed of many small, tortuous blood vessels that are bathed in the mother's blood—so that oxygen easily moves toward the baby and carbon dioxide leaves; glucose, minerals, salts, and water go in and waste products like uric acid, urea, and bilirubin go out; hormones like thyroid and steroids can enter; and antibodies to many bacterial diseases like tetanus and diphtheria are passed through. Millions of chemical compounds pass both ways each day.

The placenta also secretes hormones that stop menstruation—otherwise the child would be aborted—and situated along the placenta's border are guard cells with enzymes to protect the developing baby from any dangerous maternal cells. In some senses, the mother and child are like neighboring countries with a friendly but cautious border. Some materials are denied access; other materials are accepted in limited quantities. Ultimately, the placenta reaches a diameter of nine inches and can weigh more than a pound. It knows how to connect with the uterus, how to serve and protect the fetus, and when to disconnect.

Growth and Specialization

One of the first signs a woman is pregnant may be morning sickness or vomiting. The reason for this is unknown, but one theory suggests that during its early days the fetus is most vulnerable to toxins and a mother's diet needs to be very bland. Anything that might be the slightest bit worrisome is brought back up. Another early change is in breast tissue. A combination of hormones secreted by the placenta, the maternal pituitary, and the mother's ovaries interact to change the mammary duct system so that it can make, store, and secrete milk. These cells already carry the recipes for how much water, salt, fat, sugar, minerals, vitamins, calcium, and antibodies will be needed.

> To propose that a process of random mutations and accidental selections was responsible for the DNA blueprint would be like declaring that a human could travel from Antarctica to Miami by taking a single giant step.

Highly differentiated changes in the embryo come quickly. By the third week cells responsible for the ovaries or testes begin migrating to their preassigned locations. Cells separate into three major groups: one for the skeletal system, another for skin and the neurological system, and the third for the gastrointestinal and respiratory systems. A spinal cord and brain begin to form; tubelike structures connect to make up the early heart and blood vessels. Blood vessels begin to carry nutrients and oxygen from the mother to all areas of the embryo.

By the sixth week, further specialization occurs—forming teeth, skull, all of the muscles of the body, dermis, sexual organs, connective tissue everywhere, spleen, parts of the adrenal glands, eyes, ears, mammary glands, hair, nails, liver, pancreas, the lining of the gastrointestinal tract, thyroid, major parts of the lungs, and urinary bladder. Up to now, all embryos are female, but around the seventh week the blueprint calls for appropriate changes. If the child received an X chromosome from both parents, it will remain female. If the father passed on a Y instead of an X and the child has an XY chromosome, male features begin to appear. (We do not progress through a fish and amphibian stage. There are no gills or fins.)

By the eighth week, the fetus is one-and-a-half inches long and looks human. It has two eyes with eyelids, external ears, a mouth, a jaw, a nose, and the full body shape with four extremities. All ten toes and all ten fingers are evident.

A logical progression of cell division occurs throughout the body. Certain cells will change into parent cells for the esophagus, stomach, small bowel, colon, liver, gallbladder, and pancreas. Stomach cells will then change into cells that secrete either acid, mucus, or enzymes. While the gastrointestinal cells are differentiating, they are also coordinating with nearby cells—so that the

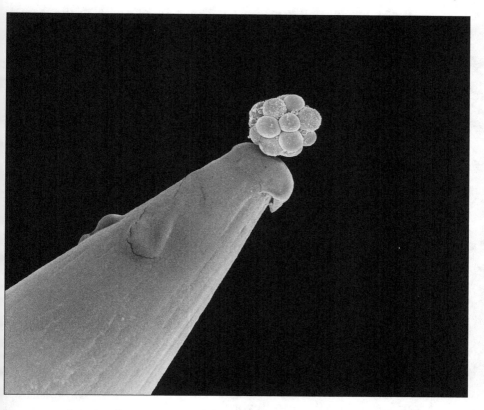

Scanning electron micrograph (SEM) of a human embryo at the 10-cell stage on the tip of a pin. The ball of cells of the embryo is known as a *morula*, a cluster of almost identical, rounded cells, each containing a central nucleus. This 10-cell embryo is about three days old. It is at the early stage of transformation from a single cell to a human composed of millions of cells. The cells multiply by repeated cleavage divisions (mitosis) and will form a hollow ball of cells (the *blastocyst*). Development of the blastocyst occurs before the embryo implants into the wall of the uterus (womb). Magnification: x130 at 6x7 cm size.

stomach connects with the duodenum, and blood vessels in the limbs are connecting with larger blood vessels in the abdomen. They all work in unison, following a master plan. Acid-secreting cells in the stomach do not precede cells secreting protective mucus. Nerve cells connect with thousands of other nerve cells.

By the tenth week, one can see fingernails and many of the finer features. By the twelfth week, the embryo is three inches long, and its sex is evident on an ultrasound. At 16 weeks, the baby is seven inches long and is perfectly formed. Cell differentiation slows while growth and maturation accelerate. By 18 weeks, the mother should feel the signs of life within her body.

Throughout the nine months of fetal growth, the umbilical cord steadily lengthens, and the placenta grows to accommodate the baby's increasing needs; the uterus expands to an incredible 16 times its normal size. Uterine rupture is exceedingly rare. Imagine how your skin might change if kept under water for a few hours—yet the baby's skin remains unaffected after nine months. It is protected by a white, cheesy substance called *vernix caseosa*, which is easily washed off with the first hospital bath.

From Speck to Baby and Beyond

For most of us, the birth of a baby seems like a miracle. It gives some people pause to wonder who we truly are and why we are here. How could two nearly invisible specks become a viable human being? To hold the tiny fingers, to view a perfectly shaped face, and to hear the first cries are among life's most moving events.

The evidence suggests that the baby's pituitary recognizes when it's time to initiate labor. It secretes a messenger hormone that crosses the placental barrier and goes to the maternal pituitary, which in turn secretes another hormone that causes the uterus to

The Head of an Eight-Week-Old Human Fetus

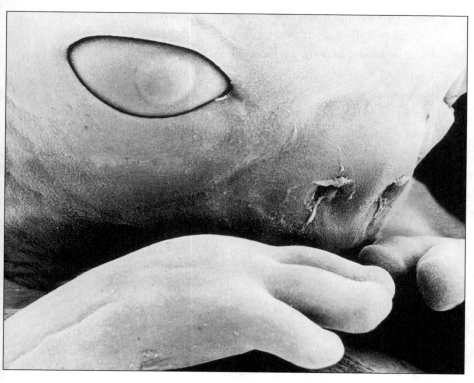

Scanning electron micrograph (SEM) of the head of an eight-week-old human fetus. The fetus's eyes, nose, and hands are visible. The eighth week of pregnancy represents the end of the formative developmental stage, and the embryo becomes a fetus. It is humanlike in appearance, with the head large in proportion to the body. The genital organs develop into male or female at seven weeks. All major organ systems are formed by the eighth week, but require much growth. By eight weeks the fetus is about 3 to 4 cm long (crown-to-rump length) and weighs under 10 grams.

start contracting. These contractions begin mildly and are widely spaced, as if the muscles are tuning up. As they intensify, the baby's head is moved into the birth canal, facing downward. The cervix begins to thin out and pull back, eventually leaving a five-inch passageway; the bag of waters ruptures, giving the uterine muscles less mass to push against. Soon, another hormone called *relaxin* causes the pelvic ligaments to relax and spread apart. The baby flexes into a tight ball and then, as if leaping through a hoop in slow motion, it extends itself forward and heads out the canal.

In most instances, the canal can accommodate the baby's head, but it can be a very tight fit. By design, the skull is still soft and can be molded to make it through. The remainder of the body slips out quite easily. How a baby can tell when it's time to take its first breath remains unknown. One theory speculates that internal oxygen levels drop, forcing the child to breathe—but breathing often starts before the umbilical cord, with its supply of highly oxygenated blood, is severed. The initiation of breathing never happens prematurely in the birth canal, even if the delivery requires days; it never happens underwater during water deliveries; and it is also not caused by the pat on the rump. Most babies take their first breath before the obstetrician can get a hand up. In fact, no mammal needs a slap on the behind. And in striking contrast to monkeys, the human child is born hairless, tailless, and plump.

Nursing begets nursing. A preplanned program kicks in the moment a baby starts suckling, and it changes with the baby's needs. The mother–child interaction sets off a reflex that causes the nipples to become erect and milk production to start. Tiny glands around the areola—the colored ring around the nipple—secrete lubricants to aid nursing, and the entire areola darkens, possibly to make the nipple easier to find. The baby is born with a natural sucking reflex.

What about the ingredients in mother's milk? Is it accidental that the vitamins A, C, D, thiamin, riboflavin, and niacin are present, as well as the proper concentrations of salts, sugars, fats, water, and antibodies? The benefits of breast-feeding appear to go way beyond mere nutritional. Children who are fed formula have two times the incidence of SIDS (Sudden Infant Death Syndrome), four times the chance of contracting RSV pneumonia, nearly three times the chance of getting ear infections, and two to seven times the chance of contracting lymphoma.

If one assumes evolution is at the root of human existence, one needs to explain how animals changed from nonlactating to lactating without any intermediate steps. Also, did nursing appear spontaneously after the advent of live births...or did it arrive simultaneously with conception, the placenta, implantation, embryo development, and delivery (WPP)? They are all intertwined. It's an all-or-none world.

Bottom-Line Points

- *During the four days the egg travels through the fallopian tube, it divides into two cells, then four, then eight, frequently changing configurations and adding complex functions.*

- *By the sixth day, the egg is barely the size of a pinprick, and yet it knows how to find the uterine wall, implant itself, fulfill its needs, and diversify into the 200 different kinds of cells that will eventually become a viable human being.*

- *Every part of the process is complex and interdependent. Ovulation cannot occur without feedback loops between the ovaries and the pituitary; sperm formation cannot happen without the feedback loops between the testes and the pituitary; fertilization cannot happen without the interaction of the male and female reproductive anatomy; implantation cannot happen without the interaction between the uterus, the pituitary, and the embryo; and the embryo cannot grow and thrive without the DNA blueprint.*

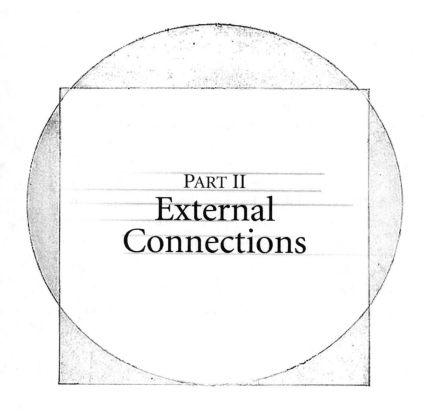

PART II
External
Connections

Men ought to know that from the brain, and
from the brain only, arise our pleasures,
joy, laughter, and jests, as well as our sorrows,
pains, griefs, and tears. Through it, in particular,
we think, see, hear, and distinguish the ugly from
the beautiful, the bad from the good, the pleasant
from the unpleasant.

—Hippocrates

The brain is a good stagehand. It gets on with its
work while we're busy acting out our scenes.

—Diane Ackerman, *A Natural History of the Senses*

6

The Neurological System

The human brain is an extraordinary multitasking, multipurpose biological computer, with capabilities that far exceed anything man may ever be able to produce. It can store between 100 trillion and 280 quintillion bits of information in three pounds of matter. It is protected by bony armor, cushioned by fluid, and serviced by a complex network of blood vessels. Everything about it exemplifies purpose and design. Life cannot begin without a brain, and life ends in four minutes without it.

Although this organ makes up less than 3 percent of the total human body weight, it consumes one-sixth of the body's oxygen and one-fifth of the body's calories. The heart, lungs, stomach, and kidneys are geared to keep it functioning. If calorie needs increase, the brain makes the person feel hungry; if oxygen levels fall, the lungs are told to breathe faster; if the blood pressure drops, the heart is told to pump harder; and if thyroid hormone is low, the thyroid gland is told to increase production.

Coordination

Every bodily action is coordinated by conference calls between millions of neurons in the brain. Imagine a multinational corporation with 35 billion employees who stay in constant touch with

The Nervous System[1]

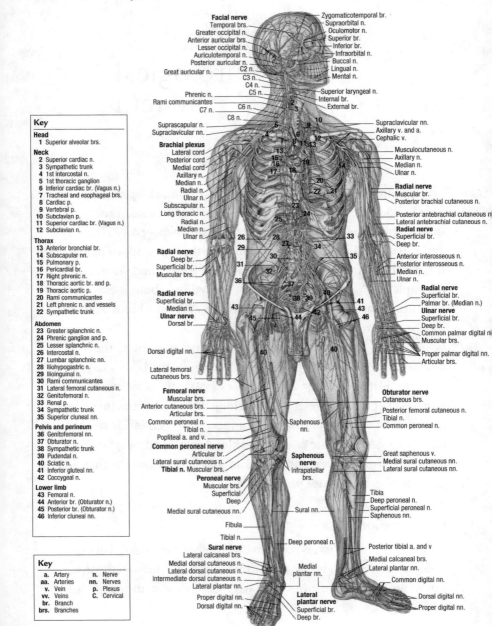

Key

Head
1 Superior alveolar brs.

Neck
2 Superior cardiac n.
3 Sympathetic trunk
4 1st intercostal n.
5 1st thoracic ganglion
6 Inferior cardiac br. (Vagus n.)
7 Tracheal and esophageal brs.
8 Cardiac p.
9 Vertebral p.
10 Subclavian p.
11 Superior cardiac br. (Vagus n.)
12 Subclavian n.

Thorax
13 Anterior bronchial br.
14 Subscapular nn.
15 Pulmonary p.
16 Pericardial br.
17 Right phrenic n.
18 Thoracic aortic br. and p.
19 Thoracic aortic p.
20 Rami communicantes
21 Left phrenic n. and vessels
22 Sympathetic trunk

Abdomen
23 Greater splanchnic n.
24 Phrenic ganglion and p.
25 Lesser splanchnic n.
26 Intercostal n.
27 Lumbar splanchnic n.
28 Iliohypogastric n.
29 Ilioinguinal n.
30 Rami communicantes
31 Lateral femoral cutaneous n.
32 Genitofemoral n.
33 Renal p.
34 Sympathetic trunk
35 Superior cluneal nn.

Pelvis and perineum
36 Genitofemoral nn.
37 Obturator n.
38 Sympathetic trunk
39 Pudendal n.
40 Sciatic n.
41 Inferior gluteal nn.
42 Coccygeal n.

Lower limb
43 Femoral n.
44 Anterior br. (Obturator n.)
45 Posterior br. (Obturator n.)
46 Inferior cluneal nn.

Key

a.	Artery	**n.**	Nerve
aa.	Arteries	**nn.**	Nerves
v.	Vein	**p.**	Plexus
vv.	Veins	**C.**	Cervical
br.	Branch		
brs.	Branches		

Facial nerve
Temporal brs.
Greater occipital n.
Anterior auricular brs.
Lesser occipital n.
Auriculotemporal n.
Posterior auricular n.
Great auricular n.
C2 n.
C3 n.
C4 n.
C5 n.
Phrenic n.
Rami communicantes
C7 n.
C6 n.
C8 n.

Zygomaticotemporal br.
Supraorbital n.
Oculomotor n.
Superior br.
Inferior br.
Infraorbital n.
Buccal n.
Lingual n.
Mental n.
Superior laryngeal n.
Internal br.
External br.
Supraclavicular nn.
Axillary v. and a.
Cephalic v.

Suprascapular n.
Supraclavicular nn.

Brachial plexus
Lateral cord
Posterior cord
Medial cord
Axillary n.
Median n.
Radial n.
Ulnar n.
Subscapular n.
Long thoracic n.
Radial n.
Median n.
Ulnar n.

Musculocutaneous n.
Axillary n.
Median n.
Ulnar n.

Radial nerve
Muscular br.
Posterior brachial cutaneous n.
Posterior antebrachial cutaneous n.
Lateral antebrachial cutaneous n.
Radial nerve
Superficial br.
Deep br.
Anterior interosseous n.
Posterior interosseous n.
Median n.
Ulnar n.

Radial nerve
Deep br.
Superficial br.
Muscular brs.

Radial nerve
Superficial br.
Median n.
Ulnar nerve
Dorsal br.

Radial nerve
Superficial br.
Palmar br. (Median n.)
Ulnar nerve
Superficial br.
Deep br.
Common palmar digital nn.
Muscular brs.
Proper palmar digital nn.
Articular brs.

Dorsal digital nn.

Lateral femoral cutaneous brs.

Femoral nerve
Muscular brs.
Anterior cutaneous brs.
Articular brs.
Common peroneal n.
Tibial n.
Popliteal a. and v.
Common peroneal nerve
Articular br.
Lateral sural cutaneous n.
Tibial n. Muscular brs.
Peroneal nerve
Muscular brs.
Superficial
Deep
Medial sural cutaneous n.

Fibula

Tibial n.
Sural nerve
Lateral calcaneal brs.
Medial dorsal cutaneous n.
Lateral dorsal cutaneous n.
Intermediate dorsal cutaneous n.
Lateral plantar nn.
Proper digital nn.
Dorsal digital nn.

Saphenous
nn.

**Saphenous
nerve**
Infrapatellar
brs.

Sural nn.

Medial
plantar nn.

Deep peroneal n.

Obturator nerve
Cutaneous brs.
Posterior femoral cutaneous n.
Tibial n.
Common peroneal n.

Great saphenous v.
Medial sural cutaneous nn.
Lateral sural cutaneous nn.

Tibia
Deep peroneal n.
Superficial peroneal n.
Saphenous nn.

Posterior tibial a. and v.
Medial calcaneal brs.
Lateral plantar nn.
Common digital nn.

**Lateral
plantar nerve**
Superficial br.
Deep br.

Dorsal digital nn.
Proper digital nn.

each other and are capable of making trillions of decisions every millisecond. They can also make millions of adjustments as needs vary. Committee members, administrators, and executives constantly change at lightning speed, and every action, or lack of action, is always well-organized.

To get a personal glimpse into the brain's complexity, take an imaginary stroll in your favorite park. The simple act of walking a dog or stopping to smell a rose requires the work of billions of neurons. Although your brain can simultaneously listen and smell, you will remain attentive to one stimulus at a time. Further, the brain acts like a billion security guards seated in front of a billion TV screens. Any sudden change or danger will draw your attention.

As you walk, your brain coordinates every muscle, bone, joint, ligament, and tendon; it maintains your balance; it monitors the ambient temperature; and it watches your breathing, pulse, and blood pressure. Millions of neurons work in tandem, in parallel, or in opposition. The brain also shifts blood from the resting muscles to active muscles and alters hormones based on moment-to-moment stresses. Add in a simultaneous conversation with a friend—and the complexity of cellular, hormonal, and metabolic interactions is beyond calculation.

Although modern science has made significant strides in understanding the neurological system, with PET scans, MRI imaging, CAT scans, nuclear medicine studies, and electron microscopy, many questions remain. For example, we know that if your eyes were to spot something falling toward you, a signal would instantly be sent through the emotion center to the visual center. The millions of cells in the emotion center decide whether you should dodge the object or knock it away. The decision may seem to be made consciously, but the brain decides whenever an instantaneous reaction is needed. Take the occurrence of an explosion or a gunshot. People commonly report having run ten to fifteen paces before they "get ahold of" themselves.

If life on Earth has existed for three billion years and our 100-billion-cell neurological system began with a single cell, it would have required an average of 33 new and different neurons to be added every year. Each neuron would also have to have been a perfect fit for many hundreds of connections. Three billion years, however, is probably not the correct length of time. Six hundred million years may be closer—and if so, that would have required the addition of a thousand perfectly functioning nerve cells per year to reach man's present brain size.

Chemical Complexity

The complexity of merely a single nerve cell challenges evolutionary theory. Each neuron is more complicated than any present-day computer. Many resemble a distorted octopus—with wiry limbs, called *dendrites,* and a long tail, called an *axon.* If the central body of a nerve cell were the size of a tennis ball, the dendrites would fill up an average living room with twisting wires, and the axon would stretch a full mile down the street. These cells communicate by electrical impulses and chemical signals. More than a hundred chemicals carry information or messages. Dopamine is one of the more commonly known neurotransmitters. A change in its secretion results in Parkinson's disease. Serotonin is another. Interference in its activity results in depression. It's not just the individual chemicals, however—it's the quantity, frequency, and speed of delivery as well as the numerous combinations that determine the message or messages.

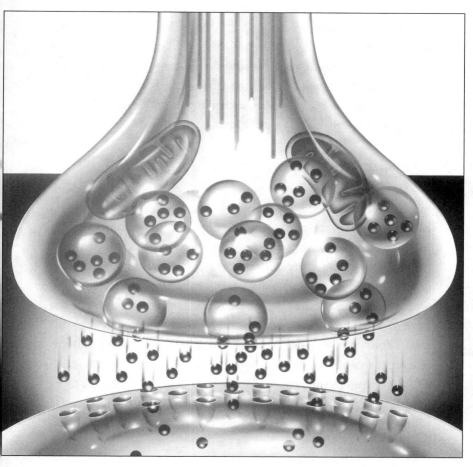

Artwork of a nerve impulse being passed across the junction, or synapse, between two nerve cells (neurons). The electrical signal has reached the end of the first neuron (upper frame), causing its vesicles (spheres) to release their neurotransmitters at the *presynaptic membrane*. These chemicals travel across the synapse and bind to the protein receptors (holes) on the *postsynaptic membrane*. This initiates a signal in the second neuron, relaying the message.

© John Bavosi/Photo Researchers, Inc.

Neurotransmitters are manufactured in the center of the nerve cell and then pass to the periphery through microscopic railways, called *microtubules,* where they are stored in small sacs called *vesicles.* The cell has a very tidy and organized way of storing and releasing them at the right moment. Then the receptor nerve cell has the means to pass the message or messages along. All of this happens at the speed of an eyeblink.

The "Spark" and Its Development

The spark of life clearly resides in the brain. Some think that's where the soul resides. Although scientists liken the brain to a modern-day computer, there are vast differences. A computer might identify the presence of chocolate, but it cannot enjoy the taste. A program might identify a laugh, but it cannot enjoy a joke. A computer can do fast calculations, but it has no consciousness of what their impact might be. A machine might be able to recite the Lord's Prayer, but when will it pray? Many assume or believe this soul is connected to God. Whatever this intangible entity might be, one needs to ask how a feeling, soul-like phenomenon—or an actual soul—evolved in the progression from fish to humans. Was there a partial soul, then half a soul, and finally a full soul? If this soul didn't evolve, then how did it come about as a whole phenomenon?

Brain development begins early. By the embryo's fourth week, there is evidence of nervous tissue, and 250,000 cells per minute (per minute!) start migrating outward. They ultimately form six layers. Each neuron knows exactly where to go, what to do, and how to link up with as many as 10,000 connections. Any exposure to toxins during this stage may alter the migration and result in congenital problems. By the fourteenth week, an actual brain is evident. A special fluid with a precise concentration of nutrients and salts bathes the brain and spinal cord, buffering them from trauma and maintaining their health. (A transitional spinal fluid would not work.)

We all have a similar internal calendar. Maternal recognition is nearly immediate. By the second day after birth, a baby should be able to detect its mother by smell, hearing, and taste. By one month, a baby will have a preference for looking at its mother. By three months, babies' eyes will follow movement, and they can smile in response to a smile. By six months, they begin to imitate sounds, grasp objects, and can roll over. At nine months, babies can sit up and understand the word "no." And by twelve months, most babies are beginning to walk and can at least say "dada" and "mama." These language skills will steadily improve, and they do so at the same rate for all children, no matter what culture, using as many as 200 distinct sounds and speaking one of 6000 possible languages. Waves of growth and pruning (refining skills) occur as the child grows. Between the ages of three and six years, there is enormous growth in the frontal lobes, allowing for very fast rates of learning. Between ages seven and fifteen there is growth in the temporal and the parietal (upper rear) lobes, partly improving motor skills. Between sixteen and twenty, there is some pruning as skills are refined.

How we establish "self" remains elusive, but clues come from the work of Dr. Elizabeth Gould and Dr. Charles Gross of Princeton. Their studies showed that thousands of newly formed neurons arrive at the frontal cortex each day, recording the day's events and interconnecting with the older neurons. Several new networks are established; they vary depending on whether the input was visual or auditory, whether it had immediate meaning or not, and whether it may be useful for the future. These collective memories help us know who we are.

Our present-day brain's size and capacity are much greater than that of our ancestors, and they seem to be slowly increasing. Perhaps this is partly due to increased memory input, but no one truly knows. We may not run faster than a cheetah, but we already know how to protect ourselves with shelters, use weapons, and avoid danger. So why do we need an enlarging brain?

> Every bodily action is co-ordinated by conference calls between millions of neurons in the brain. Imagine a multinational corporation with 35 billion employees who stay in constant touch with each other and are capable of making trillions of decisions every millisecond.

Functions and How They're Supported

The motor area and sensory area in each hemisphere are responsible for most of the movements and sensations on the opposite side of the body. Evidence suggests that huge numbers of "lost memories" are not truly lost, but are stored away in the cellular nooks and crannies. If a neurosurgeon were to stimulate the correct spot in the brain, his patient might "see" a childhood pet or smell freshly baked bread. If you were asked to sing an old song, you might stumble over a few words but readily hum the melody. Or take the example of running into an old friend. Suddenly, you can recall his or her parents or the neighborhood. Is this storage-and-retrieval mechanism a design feature or an accident?

Most cognitive functions are located toward the front of the brain. The dominant side handles analytical issues—essentially, how we think. The nondominant side looks at the world in a more subjective way, with intuition, emotions, and compassion. In many ways we are two fused people: the mathematician and the artist. Together these two decide how we should react to events (there's a "meeting of the minds"). This is more easily seen in the rare patient with a split brain, one whose right and left hemispheres were cut away from each other—usually done to control difficult seizures. These patients may find their right hand reacting to the world differently than their left. They can add up numbers on a chalkboard with one hand and not the other. And victims of certain brain injuries may exhibit behaviors that would otherwise have been curtailed.

A quart of blood is pumped through the brain every minute. Using PET scans and MRI studies, scientists have shown that blood will automatically shift to areas that are being used. For example, if one were to give a speech, the areas needed for reading or remembering the words would light up, as would the areas that control the lungs, throat, mouth, and lips—while areas that control walking or digesting food might quiet down. This is why swimmers sometimes get muscle cramps if they exercise too soon after a meal. Blood flow has left the muscles to help the stomach.

Much Is Left to Discover

Although the fields of neurology, neurophysiology, and neurobiology are expanding quickly, we truly know very little about the brain. The moment a new textbook is published, several sections are obsolete. Yet we still know a lot. There are thick books on specific functions like vision or hearing; someday the information on a single neuron will be a whole book.

The ways we treat disorders of the brain have also changed dramatically. Many of the tests from a mere ten years ago, sometimes even two years, are obsolete; many of the medications have changed; and we monitor therapeutic interventions differently. Yet our present knowledge of the brain is akin to the knowledge that the Pilgrims had about North America when they first landed.

Much of the brain's work is silent. You may think your eyes are seeing my words in front of your face, but that would be like saying a telescope sees the moon. A telescope doesn't see anything, and so it is with eyes. The back of the brain does the seeing, but it compensates to let you view your surroundings as they are. The same "ventriloquist phenomenon" applies to hearing, smelling, touching, and tasting.

Carla Shatz of the Neurobiology Department at Harvard Medical School uses an incredibly complex switchboard as an example of a neuron that sends signals on to an appropriate site or sites. The direction in which axons (telephone lines) carry messages is very specific. Nerves involved with vision must connect the eye to the visual cortex, hearing to the auditory, smell to the olfactory, fingers to the motor areas, and touch to the sensory areas. This might be compared to connecting millions of trunk lines from Boston to every household in the world. Further, each household has built-in instructions depending on the signal.

Sorting Stimuli

Although the human body is covered with sensory receptors that are constantly sending billions of messages to the brain, our nervous system is designed to select out what we truly need. If this were not so, we would be inundated with a continual tidal wave of unnecessary information. To get a rough idea how much information this might be in a day's time, multiply a few billion pieces of information by the number of milliseconds in 24 hours: 3,000,000,000 x 1000 x 60 x 60 x 24. One might liken this to the president of the United States simultaneously and constantly listening to the six billion people who inhabit Earth, selecting the many who need immediate attention, and deciding appropriate actions—all in less than a second.

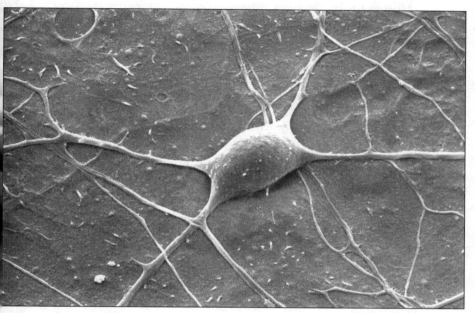

Scanning electron micrograph (SEM) of a *Purkinje nerve cell* from the *cerebellum* of the brain. The cell comprises a flask-shaped cell body, from which branch numerous threadlike dendrites. Purkinje cells form the junction between the granular and molecular layers of the gray matter of the cerebellum. Nerve impulses are relayed to a Purkinje cell through its dendrites. The cerebellum controls balance, posture, and muscle coordination. Magnification: x1700 at 6x7 cm size.

Most of the brain's work is beneath conscious awareness. If an individual were to think about every heartbeat, every breath, every peristaltic wave, every muscle contraction, every squeeze of the gallbladder, every eyeblink, every swallow, every light impulse, every sound wave, every moving joint, and every growing hair (if that were even possible), there would be no time to do anything else. We would be paralyzed by sensory overload.

Imagine trying to go about your business and yet being aware of every sensation from your skin, or hearing every sound, or seeing individual specks of color. All of this information, plus millions of bits of additional information from internal sources, is continually being fed into your brain, organized, and handled in a prompt fashion.

Your brain compiles the details, and you are given whole pictures. A distant lightning storm may catch your attention, whereas particular clouds may not. The smell of a steak sizzling on an outdoor grill may stand out among many treats. You can listen to one person in a crowd of people talking, switch to another, or ignore the entire group. You can listen to an orchestra or select out the lead violinist. Your mind will automatically notice a spark from the barbecue in the grass, and yet it ignores burning briquettes in the pit. While you are engrossed in conversation at a restaurant, your brain keeps track of every morsel of food and will automatically alert you if something's too hot, too cold, or tastes strange. In fact, you can eat an entire meal and be so engrossed in conversation that you never even taste it. No matter where you are or what you are doing, your brain constantly monitors your internal and external environment. It will also alert you to unexpected pleasures, such as an unusual flavor, your date's laugh, someone's perfume, a celebrity entering the restaurant, or an unexpected caress.

The brain treats the vast majority of incoming information as if it were background noise. This is called adaptation—it resembles a busy radar screen that alerts a traffic controller only when two planes are too close. Recall the relief you feel when refrigerator noise stops. The same process applies to the sounds of traffic. A driver may not pay any attention to car engine noise, but the squeal of brakes may readily catch his attention. Noise in a restaurant may remain in the background until a waiter drops a load of dishes.

We all have built-in gating mechanisms that block out selective stimuli. Putting an ice pack on a sprained ankle is a good example. The relief may be due partly to less inflammation, but some of it comes from a competitive stimulus; the ankle can feel only one sensation, cold or pain. In many places the nervous system has intersections with four-way stops. Only one stimulus can pass at a time—and if the cold sensation gets there first, it may hog the intersection. This is partly why acupuncture and earphones in the dentist chair work.

Growth and Adaptation

During growth and development, some neurons are strengthened and others are pruned. There are windows of opportunity to learn skills and even to practice drills. If not used, the windows disappear. For example, if a patch is placed over a newborn cat's eye, it will grow up blind in that eye. If you don't learn how to pronounce "R" at a certain age, it may always be "L."

The brain can change with the internal needs of the body or the external demands of the environment (a phenomenon called *plasticity*). It can also adapt to and recover from many physical and chemical assaults. The actor Christopher Reeve is an example of injured neurons slowly recovering. Unlike other cells in the body, however, most neurons remain for life. As we age, old cells merely learn new tricks.

Bottom-Line Points

- *The brain can store between 100 trillion and 280 quintillion bits of information in a mere three pounds of matter.*

- *Life cannot begin without a brain, and life ends in four minutes without it.*

- *If life on Earth has existed for three billion years and our 100-billion-cell neurological system began with a single cell, it would have required an average of 33 new and different neurons to be added every year. Each neuron would also have to have been a perfect fit for many hundreds of connections and would have had to bring new functions to the being.*

- *More than 100 chemicals carry information or messages between nerve cells.*

- *By the fourth week of an embryo's life, 250,000 nerve cells per minute start migrating outward. Each one knows where to locate itself and how to connect with its neighbors. Some neurons may have as many as 10,000 connections (which makes them each a small city on their own).*

- *Although the human body is covered with sensory receptors that are constantly sending billions of messages to the brain, our nervous system is designed to select out what we truly need, delete background noise, and help us make reasonable choices.*

Autonomic Nervous System[2]

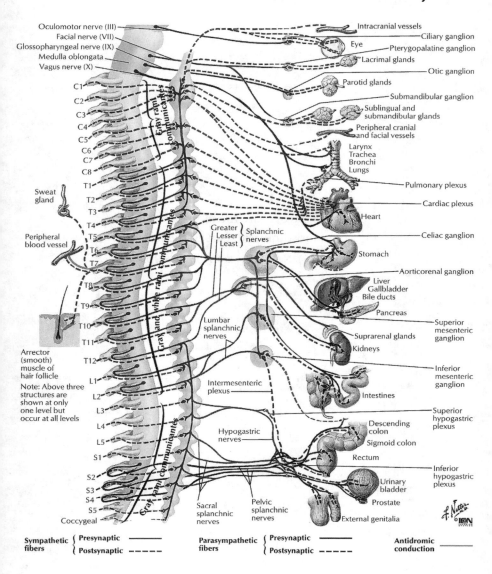

Oculomotor nerve (III)
Facial nerve (VII)
Glossopharyngeal nerve (IX)
Medulla oblongata
Vagus nerve (X)

Intracranial vessels
Ciliary ganglion
Eye
Pterygopalatine ganglion
Lacrimal glands
Otic ganglion
Parotid glands
Submandibular ganglion
Sublingual and submandibular glands
Peripheral cranial and facial vessels
Larynx
Trachea
Bronchi
Lungs
Pulmonary plexus
Cardiac plexus
Heart
Celiac ganglion
Stomach
Aorticorenal ganglion
Liver
Gallbladder
Bile ducts
Pancreas
Superior mesenteric ganglion
Suprarenal glands
Kidneys
Inferior mesenteric ganglion
Intestines
Superior hypogastric plexus
Descending colon
Sigmoid colon
Rectum
Inferior hypogastric plexus
Urinary bladder
Prostate
External genitalia

C1
C2
C3
C4
C5
C6
C7
C8
T1
T2
T3
T4
T5
T6
T7
T8
T9
T10
T11
T12
L1
L2
L3
L4
L5
S1
S2
S3
S4
S5
Coccygeal

Gray rami communicantes

Gray and white rami communicantes

Gray rami communicantes

Greater
Lesser } Splanchnic
Least } nerves

Lumbar splanchnic nerves

Intermesenteric plexus

Hypogastric nerves

Sacral splanchnic nerves

Pelvic splanchnic nerves

Sweat gland

Peripheral blood vessel

Arrector (smooth) muscle of hair follicle

Note: Above three structures are shown at only one level but occur at all levels

Sympathetic fibers	{ Presynaptic ———	Parasympathetic fibers	{ Presynaptic ———	Antidromic conduction ———
	{ Postsynaptic --------		{ Postsynaptic --------	

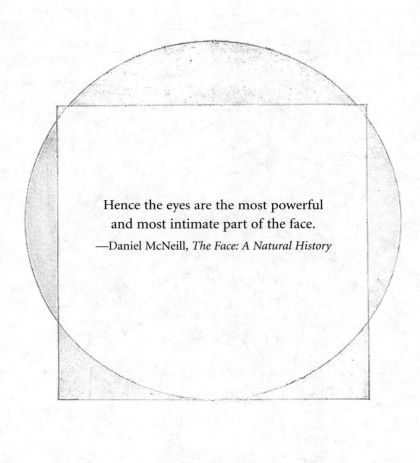

Hence the eyes are the most powerful
and most intimate part of the face.

—Daniel McNeill, *The Face: A Natural History*

7

Vision

It is readily apparent that the human race would not have survived without the ability to see—we probably would not have even come about. We depend on our eyes to warn us of impending danger, to communicate with each other, to show emotion, to find food and water, to attract partners, to help prepare shelters, to defend ourselves, to identify enemies, and to select friends. Vision is also where 70 percent of the body's sensory receptors reside. Visual cues are critical for nearly every action we take—or don't take. In olden days they helped us escape a predator, find ripe fruit, avoid a precipice, or make our way home. For the present day, one could list thousands of visual needs. Without glasses, magnifying lenses, cataract surgery, and seeing-eye dogs, however, some of us would spend a large part of our lives sitting around the house with very limited activities.

We take vision for granted. Darwin, though, found the complexity of the eye to be so daunting he feared that it challenged his most basic theories. Many of those who agree with him today continue to share that same feeling. To have changed from a unicellular animal that could sense some changes in light to a multitrillion-cell organism that can recognize hundreds of colors, sort through scores of shades and intensities, identify a multiplicity of shapes, recognize a relative not seen for 50 years, and spot the proverbial shiny needle in a haystack is an enormous, multifaceted evolutionary step that defies the theory of natural selection. Even the first steps in the development of rudimentary useful neurons to sense light would have involved a large number of purposeful mutations. For them to have progressed to the complexity of the present human eye would have required an incalculable number of continuing, purposeful mutations.

Every Aspect Suggests Design

Millions of cells lining the interior of each eye function as photochemical receivers that convert light waves into a myriad of electrical impulses, which are forwarded, at a speed of about 200 miles per hour, to the brain—and then sorted, organized, and analyzed. This is accomplished in milliseconds. Eyes are like antennae for the brain. For practical purposes, images are made to appear before us and outside our body, as well as right side up, even though the brain sees them upside down. How else might one catch a ball, throw a spear, climb stairs, or avoid an obstacle?

Every anatomical, chemical, and physiological aspect of our eyes suggests design. Notice how both eyes are set back inside bony sockets where they are well-protected from blunt trauma, yet protrude just enough to maintain a wide horizontal view. They are also set apart for depth perception. Eyeballs are spheres so that they can easily roll from side to side or up and down. Only one sixth of the eyeball is visible, however, while the remainder is constantly protected. Note that both eyes, unless damaged, move in perfect unison. Imagine how limited our vision might be if our eyeballs were triangular, square, or irregular in shape, or if their images moved in different directions or at different speeds.

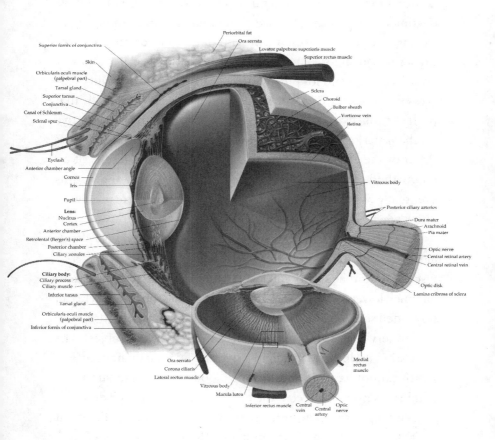

Superior fornix of conjunctiva
Periorbital fat
Ora serrata
Levator palpebrae superioris muscle
Superior rectus muscle

Skin
Orbicularis oculi muscle (palpebral part)
Tarsal gland
Superior tarsus
Conjunctiva
Canal of Schlemm
Scleral spur

Sclera
Choroid
Bulbar sheath
Vorticose vein
Retina

Eyelash
Anterior chamber angle
Cornea
Iris
Pupil

Vitreous body

Posterior ciliary arteries

Lens:
Nucleus
Cortex
Anterior chamber
Retrolental (Berger's) space
Posterior chamber
Ciliary zonules

Dura mater
Arachnoid
Pia mater
Optic nerve
Central retinal artery
Central retinal vein

Optic disk
Lamina cribrosa of sclera

Ciliary body:
Ciliary process
Ciliary muscle
Inferior tarsus
Tarsal gland
Orbicularis oculi muscle (palpebral part)
Inferior fornix of conjunctiva

Ora serrata
Corona ciliaris
Lateral rectus muscle
Vitreous body
Macula lutea
Inferior rectus muscle
Central vein
Central artery
Optic nerve

Medial rectus muscle

Eyebrows are there to protect us from glare, and they also keep perspiration from running down into the eyes. Eyelashes may make us more attractive, emphasizing the eyes with a starburst look. Along with the blink reflex they protect us from small flying debris. Pupils dilate to allow more light in for better vision at dim times and constrict to protect our retinas from excessive glare and to improve daytime vision. We are afforded further protection by squinting or closing our eyes, covering them with our hands, or merely turning away. During sleep our eyelids automatically close, and our eyeballs roll upward for protection beneath a bony ridge. Did predecessor species have eyelids that partially closed, or eyeballs that partially rolled upward during sleep—or were these protective mechanisms just a lucky confluence of multiple genetic mutations? Proof of the eyelids' protection is evident from the results of an old method of torture. When eyelids were snipped off, the victims eventually went blind. Eyelids are also translucent, perhaps so we'll know when the sun comes up.

Our eyes are kept moist and nearly sterile by tiny lacrimal glands along the outer edge of each upper eyelid. These glands secrete a viscous fluid that slowly moves downward and across the eye to an inner, lower tear duct and drains into the nasal passages. (Recall how often someone has to blow their nose after crying.) Also, note how watery an eye becomes when irritated by a foreign object. The eye washes itself. This same fluid also brings oxygen to the cornea—which cannot have vision-blocking blood vessels on its surface—and brings proteins to coat the eye. Is that accidental or design?

Blinking is another protective function that we each do about 14,000 to 20,000 times a day, or about 15 times a minute. We lose about 23 minutes of wake time by blinking, yet the brain never sees an involuntary blink, never loses the ongoing picture. Each blink lasts about a third of a second, yet for unclear reasons we can see a light flicker at one three-hundredth of a second. Deliberate eyeblinks take longer, and nobody knows why. There are three kinds of eyeblinks: protective (involuntary, in response to a loud sound or flash of light); voluntary (rock seen coming at the eye); and cyclical (also involuntary), to clean the eye like a squeegee and move tears with debris toward the lacrimal ducts.

A Tool for Communication

Our communication skills are enhanced by our eyes. They flare with anger and sparkle with love. We can tell if someone is tired or alert by looking at their eyes. The whites, or *sclerae*, primarily found in human beings, make it clear to others where we are looking. Eyes rolling up during conversation have a different meaning than eyes merely looking up. Multiple blinks may mean something different than a prolonged blink. Dilated pupils may tell us to beware. Uneven dilation of pupils may suggest there's a brain tumor. We expect eye attention when we're speaking, and we worry about someone who can't or won't make eye contact. We wonder if "someone's in there" when their eyes are closed.

The reason babies are so adorable could be because of their giant, beautiful eyes. Penny Moser wrote in *Discover* in 1999, "We are wired to adore and protect any face with what the Germans call *Kinderschema*—the flat faces, snub noses, and big eyes of the human baby." A baby's eyes take up one-third of its face—in contrast to the adult, in which the eyes make up only one-fifth. Large eyes may also lend themselves to faster, easier learning. *Kinderschema* is the source of the same appeal that we feel toward puppies and kittens.

Many people feel that the eyes see and say it all. According to Daniel McNeill, author of *The Face*, we exist just behind our eyes.

Lacrimal Apparatus[4]

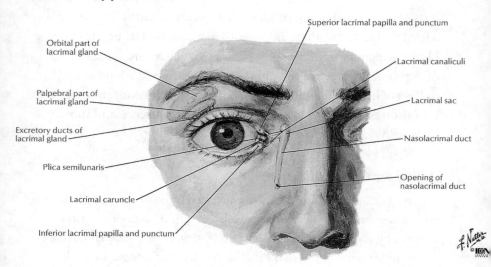

Orbital part of lacrimal gland

Palpebral part of lacrimal gland

Excretory ducts of lacrimal gland

Plica semilunaris

Lacrimal caruncle

Inferior lacrimal papilla and punctum

Superior lacrimal papilla and punctum

Lacrimal canaliculi

Lacrimal sac

Nasolacrimal duct

Opening of nasolacrimal duct

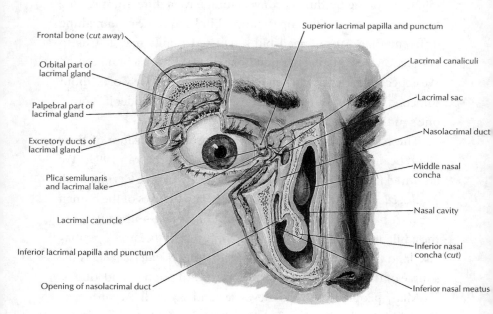

Frontal bone (cut away)

Orbital part of lacrimal gland

Palpebral part of lacrimal gland

Excretory ducts of lacrimal gland

Plica semilunaris and lacrimal lake

Lacrimal caruncle

Inferior lacrimal papilla and punctum

Opening of nasolacrimal duct

Superior lacrimal papilla and punctum

Lacrimal canaliculi

Lacrimal sac

Nasolacrimal duct

Middle nasal concha

Nasal cavity

Inferior nasal concha (cut)

Inferior nasal meatus

They show life and they show death. If we close our eyes, we can hide behind a curtain. Very few people would miss the flare of anger in another's eyes. Even fewer would miss the look of love. Men's pupils will dilate when they look at photos of sharks and female nudes; women's dilate when they see pictures of babies, mothers with babies, and male nudes; and both sexes dilate with low light, fear, surprise, joy, anxiety, loud noises, and loud music and constrict with bright light, boredom, and drowsiness. The pupils reflect our overall level of consciousness—they are the windows to our feelings and the mirrors of our responses to the world around us.

Tears—How Did They Come About?

Eyelids act like squeegees that smooth out the lubricant and thereby improve vision. They also sweep tiny particles into the gutters. (Recall that crusty junk we sometimes find in the corners of each eye upon awakening.) The lacrimal system alone suggests design. This flow of tears from the upper–outer to the lower–inner takes advantage of gravity. Without tear ducts, the tears would constantly overflow the eyelids (like the shower flooding the bathtub). Without constant lubrication, our eyes would dry up and scar; without bacteria-killing enzymes, we might have constant infections; and without the ability to blink, our eyes would be pockmarked by debris and soon blinded. The eyebrows, eyelashes, eyelids, eyeballs, lacrimal glands, and lubricating fluid all had to have come about as a whole package. Nothing less would have worked.

Tears are much more than a simple compound that can be inexpensively duplicated in a pharmaceutical house and purchased over the counter. They come in three very different forms: one geared for lubrication and protection, another associated with sadness, and another associated with happiness. Each type is secreted from a different location, contains different concentrations of salt, maintains different ratios of proteins, and flows at different rates. Emotional tears have 21 percent more proteins, suggesting they carry away chemicals that produce stress. Having a good cry and then feeling better may have a physiological basis.

Only humans seem to have tears for profoundly sad times—and for especially happy occasions. Could this be a function of survival of the fittest or a function of mutation? Hardly. It involves too many specific areas of the brain and the rest of the anatomy. The proponents of evolutionary theories never discuss how the different kinds of tears came about.

> The pupils reflect our overall level of consciousness—they are the windows to our feelings and the mirrors of our responses to the world around us.

Placement and Coordination

Further indications of purposeful design include the fact that we have two strategically-placed eyes, which give us a panoramic view and depth perception. One giant eye in the middle of the forehead could never have worked as well. One eye in the mouth to watch food go down, like the oak toad has, would be useless. Also, might two eyes allow for a spare in case one eye is blinded? Two eyes in the front (typical for predators) aid in the hunt, whereas one eye on each side of the head (typical for animals of prey) helps detect predators. Compare the wolf with the rabbit. Humans fall into the predator group.

The constant coordinating of the eyes is accomplished in part by six extrinsic muscles that—by their unique positions—can move the eyes in nearly every direction. The left eye can watch a farmhouse along the outer periphery while the other eye can watch a fire to the far right, yet these images are comfortably combined into one uniform picture. Any distortions due to angle of sight are automatically erased. Every involuntary blink is ignored. The mind can easily focus back and forth between background and foreground simply by adjusting the pupils.

The mere fact that the eyes are located near the top of the head also suggests design. This added elevation aids distance vision. Having eyes at knee level would place any animal at a distinct disadvantage. It may also be too dusty. Animals know that added elevation has benefits. Prairie dogs, meerkats, bears, and raccoons are often seen standing high on their hind legs. Eyes located on the head also minimize transmission time to the brain. And eyes need to be located above our hands to see what we are touching and above our mouths to see what we are eating.

The fact that both sides of the brain see through both eyes is another intriguing feature that suggests that both hemispheres are needed for all assessments. If the right brain were to see solely through the right eye and the left brain solely through the left eye, there might be delays in assessing relevant stimuli. If one eye were to be damaged, one side of the brain would be excluded from the visual world.

The pupil of each eye functions like the aperture of a very fancy camera, constricting to protect the retina when the light is too bright, and dilating to protect us from harm when the light is too dim. If you were to walk from the darkness of a movie theater into bright sunshine, you would be forced to squint until your pupils could constrict. That can take up to five minutes. The reverse process takes about twenty minutes.

A Path for Light

As light reaches our eyes, it passes through a transparent, protective layer called the cornea, a buffering fluid in the anterior chamber, then the lens, and finally the gelatinous vitreous body before striking the retina, where the image is collected and forwarded to the brain. The iris is the colored part of the eye, having a highly varied array of spots, wedges, starbursts, and spokes. The patterns are so varied from person to person that they can be used like fingerprints for personal identification. The iris dilates and constricts the pupil based on intensity of light or distance. An inappropriately dilated pupil can suggest serious internal disease, such as a brain tumor or a major stroke.

Just inside the iris is the bean-shaped crystalline lens, which circular and spoke-shaped muscles stretch to focus on distant objects and squeeze to see closer objects. Together, the iris and pupil function like a very sophisticated automatic camera.

The retina is a very thin and complex tissue that lines the back of the eye. It acts like a constantly changing roll of film and is made up of 7 million cone cells for color assessment, 125 million rod cells for adaptation to the dark, and 1.2 million nerve cells that collect billions of bits of information. These are instantly organized into transportable packages, and the data is then forwarded to the optic nerve in the center of the retina. When our eyes are open, a steady river of information travels to the brain. One might compare this process to a crowd of a million schoolchildren taking endless photos that self-develop and then handing them to a group of teachers who make immediate decisions about them. Even when our eyes are closed, there's a steady flow of information telling the brain that the screen is blank. The reason why movies—which are only a rapid progression of still shots—give the illusion of motion is that the retina takes a tenth of a second to see an image, while movie frames move at 24 frames per second.

Here is a vastly simplified sequence of the chemical changes that take place in just the cells of the retina:

stimulation by light
↓
structural change in *retinene* of photopigment
↓
conformational change of photopigment
↓
activation of *transducin*
↓
activation of *phosphodiesterase*
↓
decreased intracellular *cGMP*
↓
closure of sodium channels
↓
hyperpolarization
↓
decreased release of synaptic transmitter
↓
response in bipolar cells and other neural elements

Similar to the color strips in a television set, the individual cone cells are geared to assess one of the three primary colors—red, green, or yellow. They can determine any variations or mixtures of these, plus hue, intensity, and color saturation. When rod cells are exposed to normal light, they bleach out and become relatively useless. When a person moves to darkness, however, they quickly regenerate. It's your rod cells that help you struggle to find that seat in the movie theater. Older people tend to lose these cells and become increasingly blind at night. A similar problem happens to victims of famine or to those who have a deficiency of vitamin A.

Every aspect of vision suggests purposeful design. Arguments favoring evolution require giant leaps of faith to conclude that millions of steps—some in tandem, some in parallel, many quite different—could have come about randomly—steps needed to sort out colors, determine distance, assess movement, connect all the dots, give the whole image meaning, and initiate a response. Individual steps along the line would be useless, and they would not have come about by themselves without an underlying plan. Each step is so dependent on so many others that isolated mutations could never have caused all of them at the same time. Causing even a few of them would take a sequence of very lucky mutations. And lastly, jumping from a non-eye species to an eye species requires whole packages—and it should be noted that there are no transitional species, or in-between eyes found thus far in the fossil records.

Bottom-Line Points

- *The human race would not have survived without the ability to see.*

- *Visual cues are critical for nearly every action we take—or don't take.*

- *Eyes are like antennae for the brain. Millions of cells lining the interior of each eye function as photochemical receivers, converting light waves into a myriad of electrical impulses that are forwarded, at a speed of about 200 miles per hour, to the brain.*

There the impulses are sorted, organized, and analyzed in holographic ways. All of this is accomplished in milliseconds.

· *The pupils reflect our overall level of consciousness—they are the windows to our feelings and the mirrors of our responses to the world around us.*

· *Every aspect of vision, from the eyebrow to the retina, suggests purposeful design.*

God gave man two ears, but only one mouth, that he might hear twice as much as he speaks.

—A 2000-year-old axiom of Epictetus the Stoic

8

Hearing

The ability to hear depends on another extremely complex, intricately coordinated, and well-designed system. Our ears are contrived to capture a wide range of sound waves, convert them into millions of discrete electrical impulses, and forward them to the brain for in-depth rapid analysis. As with vision, the human race would not have survived (or perhaps even come about) without the ability to hear approaching danger or to carry on significant conversations. Imagine trying to make sense of a movie if your visual and auditory systems were not coordinated. Imagine not understanding the significance of specific sounds. A waiter's creaking shoes or papers shuffling might be indistinguishable. Imagine not being able to separate masculine voices from feminine ones, adult voices from children's, or happy sounds from frightened ones. The brain does this for us with ease.

Although our ears capture sounds, they cannot "hear" any more than a microphone can hear an emcee. Sounds are actually heard in the auditory lobes of the brain and then made to seem as if they were coming from some point beyond us. Having two ears— one on each side—helps us assess the location of sounds. The difference in the timing of a sound's arrival may only be 20 millionths of a second, but that slight delay allows the brain to make a determination. Some of our reactions are automatic. A screeching car will readily set off the adrenalin response; a gunshot may prompt you to fall to the ground. If someone were to scream "fire" in a movie theater, you would be on your feet and looking for the exit before you knew it.

Our ears act like satellite dishes, capturing and focusing sound waves centrally down the ear canal. Although they cannot move to better capture the sounds, our heads will automatically turn to improve reception. Notice how a hard-of-hearing person might cup a hand behind an ear. The irregular shape of our outer ears, with a broader, curled back half, acts like a cupped hand. As we age, the ears enlarge to help capture sound better. Earwax seems to protect us from mites, and tiny hairs keep out small debris. The inner ear lies within the skull, where it is protected from injury.

> The cochlea can detect every instrument in an orchestra and spot a missed note, hear every swallow and breath you take, and pick up a whisper—all at the amazing sampling rate of 20,000 times a second.

The Journey of Sound

Textbooks compare sound waves with the ripples from a rock thrown into a pond, but like light waves, sound is actually three-dimensional, a series of rapidly expanding spheres. A mere speck of these spheres is captured by our ears. These waves ricochet down the outer canal to the eardrum, set up vibrations that are passed through three tiny bones in the middle ear—called the hammer, anvil, and stirrup—to a fluid-filled apparatus called the cochlea. Ripples in the cochlea's fluid stimulate hair cells. Envision fields of hay swaying with numerous and varied gusts of wind.

The inner hair cells do most of the hearing, while the outer hair cells do most of the fine-tuning. Each ear has about 35,000 inner

Pathway of Sound Reception[5]

Frontal section

Facial nerve (VII) (*cut*)

Limbs of stapes

Base of stapes in oval (vestibular) window

Prominence of lateral semicircular canal

Vestibule

Incus

Semicircular ducts, ampullae, utricle and saccule

Tegmen tympani

Malleus (head)

Facial nerve (VII) (*cut*)

Epitympanic recess

Vestibular nerve

Cochlear nerve

Auricle

Internal acoustic meatus

Vestibulocochlear nerve (VIII)

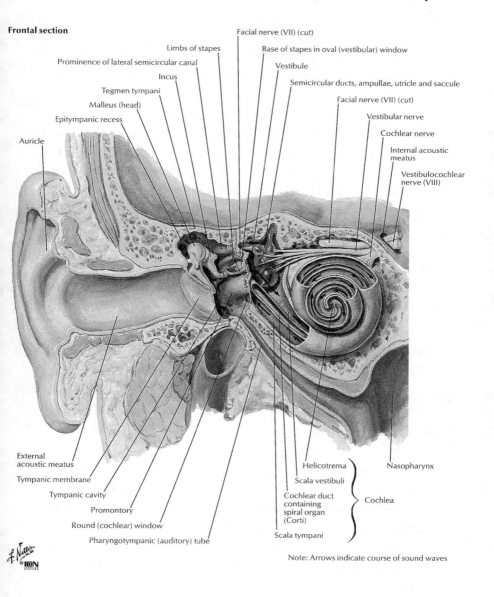

External acoustic meatus

Tympanic membrane

Tympanic cavity

Promontory

Round (cochlear) window

Pharyngotympanic (auditory) tube

Helicotrema

Scala vestibuli

Cochlear duct containing spiral organ (Corti)

Scala tympani

Cochlea

Nasopharynx

Note: Arrows indicate course of sound waves

hair cells and 20,000 outer hair cells, and each of these have between 50 and 100 *stereocilia,* or tiny hairs. The information they sense is changed into electrical impulses, and these are forwarded to thousands of nerves that combine to form the acoustic nerve going to the brain.

The cochlea does all of the "hearing" in a space that is equal to the word DOES. This apparatus can detect every instrument in an orchestra and spot a missed note, hear every swallow and breath you take, and pick up a whisper—all at an amazing sampling rate of 20,000 times a second. Your brain will immediately tell you whether a sound is familiar or not, close or far, coming toward you or going away from you, pleasant or unpleasant, loud or soft. Our ears, along with our eyes, tell us whether a comment is sarcastic or sincere, if it is threatening, or if it is a criticism or a compliment. Although much is indicated through body language, a blind person can frequently tell what is truly meant by the way words are spoken.

Selection and Recognition

The sounds that we hear best fall into the same frequency range as those we speak. Coincidence? It seems logical that speech and hearing would either have evolved together or been designed together. Imagine a species that made sounds that none of its members could hear, or vice versa.

Our ears are sensitive enough to hear a feather brushing against a cloth; yet they cannot hear blood racing through capillaries a few millimeters away from them. If we heard our breathing, saliva being swallowed, every heartbeat, joints moving, and bowel peristalsis, we would never be able to concentrate on anything else. Our body naturally muffles some sounds; in other circumstances, the brain blocks them out. Take a breath and see if you can hear it. Of course you can…but you usually don't. You took 21,000 breaths in the past 24 hours.

The auditory part of our brain acts like a security guard, listening to every sound and selectively telling us what we need to know, especially if there's a threatening sound. Auditory impulses can combine with old memories or lessons, telling us, *That's Mom calling* or, *That must be my spouse's car.* Sounds can also set up memories. Recall listening to the radio and singing along with an old song. Could you still identify the voice of a relative who died 20 years ago?

We know some of the pleasurable feelings we sense when listening to music are chemically mediated, since they can be lessened by the use of *naloxone,* an endorphin-blocking agent. There may be visual links as well. That same old song may also give you a visual image of an old date. That familiar voice will bring back a picture. A leaf rustling may remind you of a tornado and set off a post-traumatic stress reaction.

Much like vision, hearing had to come as a whole package. For humans to have had a rudimentary, partial, useless hearing organ goes counter to any logic. To have had minimal hearing capability that then expanded to our current level would have required millions of purposeful mutations—or design.

Bottom-Line Points

- *The ability to hear is another extremely complex, intricately coordinated, and well-designed system.*

- *Our ears are contrived to capture a wide range of sound waves, convert them into millions of discrete electrical impulses, and forward them to the brain for in-depth rapid analysis.*

- *Although our ears capture sounds, they cannot "hear" any more than a microphone can hear an emcee. Sounds are heard in the auditory lobes of the brain and then made to seem as if they were coming from some outside point.*

- *Some of the pleasurable feelings we sense when listening to music are actually chemically mediated.*

- *Much like vision, hearing had to come as a whole package.*

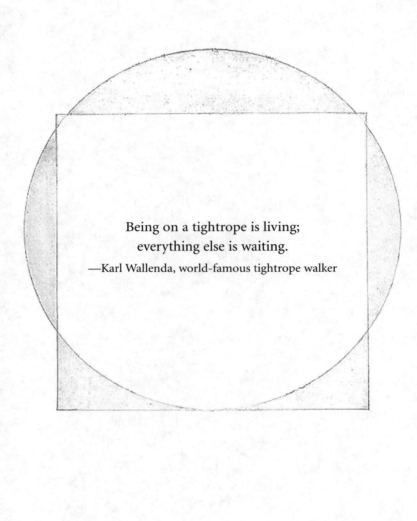

Being on a tightrope is living;
everything else is waiting.

—Karl Wallenda, world-famous tightrope walker

9

Balance

Our balance is managed primarily by three semicircular canals, called a *vestibular system,* found in each ear. These fluid-filled canals are complex gyroscopes, which respond to spinning, changes in acceleration in the vertical axis such as occur on a moving elevator, and changes in acceleration in the horizontal axis such as occur during walking. Because life works in three dimensions, every move we make is aided by at least two and usually all three of these canals. They can work separately or together, and with or without visual or auditory input; they give us unified, uninterrupted input for good balance and fine coordination. Without them, walking down a sidewalk would feel like walking across the deck of a rocking ship.

Merely turning to speak to a passenger while driving a car may seem simple, but the brain must keep track of every visual and auditory cue inside and outside the car, determine if it is safe to look right, keep track of traffic, maintain the right pressure on the accelerator, control all appropriate muscles in the head, neck, and eyes, find the words and say them, and maintain a sitting and driving balance. Billions of neurons are at work; yet unless there's an injury, every movement comes off smoothly and in unison.

Without the semicircular canals, walking down a sidewalk would feel like walking across the deck of a rocking ship.

The ability to maintain our balance can be broken down into scores of smaller steps and these, in turn, can be further divided. The sense of balance requires the whole package phenomenon and could not have come about by random genetic accidents. To suggest otherwise is to say that there were prehistoric animals with partial, therefore useless, balance apparatuses.

Receptors and Impulses

The receptors within the vestibular system are hair cells similar to those found in the cochlea. Each cell has between 40 and 70 smaller hairs, which are covered by a membrane. Picture a blanket covering the upstretched hands of hundreds of people. If some giant were to pull that blanket, every finger would sense the same motion at the same time. Each finger would also know if the pulling were to slow down, speed up, or cease. When you press down your car's accelerator, the fluid-covered horizontal membrane in each ear lags behind, bending the hairs in the opposite direction; this tells you you are moving forward. The faster the hairs bend, the faster you know you are accelerating. Slam on your brakes, and the momentum of this membrane carries it forward. Fluid in the other canals works similarly. Turn to the right and the fluid goes left; look up and the fluid goes downward. If a conveyance reaches a steady speed, the brain accommodates this, making it easy for us to ride a train or enjoy a Ferris wheel. This is the same mechanism that tells the infirm to use a cane or a toddler to hold on.

The impulses from the vestibular nerve arrive at the midbrain and cerebellum (the part responsible for coordination and equilibrium) in milliseconds, allowing us to adjust to most changes of position. Indeed, every move, no matter how minute, is coordinated. Without these mechanisms, you might push away from the table and fall backward; if you were to roll over in bed, you might keep rolling; or if you tried to catch a ball, you would most likely miss it and injure yourself with the landing. Every car ride would cause horrid motion sickness; boat rides would be out of the question; and balancing acts unheard of.

Imagine calmly drinking a cup of coffee and reading the newspaper while riding on an extremely high, widely looping amusement park ride that is spinning at a thousand miles per hour. You can even stand up on it and walk about or write a letter with ease. It's not fantasy; it's our planet. We are spinning at an incredible speed, yet if it weren't for the sun and stars moving across the sky, we might not know we were moving. And then factor in the speed at which we are traveling around the sun. Our adaptation is so good, no wonder in olden days people thought the heavens moved and we were stationary.

Bottom-Line Points

- *Because life works in three dimensions, our balance is managed in three dimensions by three semicircular canals. These complex gyroscopes respond to spinning, changes in vertical movement, and changes in horizontal movement.*

- *The sense of balance requires the whole package phenomenon and could not have come about by random genetic accidents. To suggest otherwise is to say that there were prehistoric animals with partial, therefore useless, balance apparatuses.*

- *Every move, no matter how minute, is coordinated by the balance mechanism.*

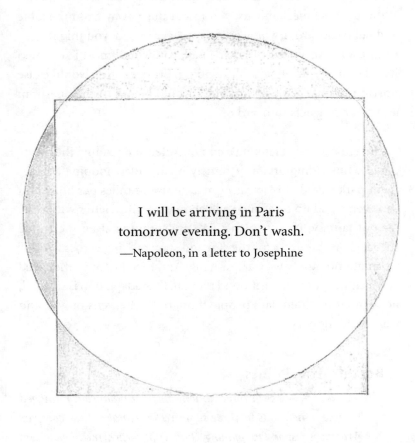

I will be arriving in Paris
tomorrow evening. Don't wash.

—Napoleon, in a letter to Josephine

10

Smell

The olfactory system is nearly as complex as those for vision and hearing. As with all the senses, it is not really the nose that identifies a smell, but the brain. The six million olfactory cells inside a nose can detect 10,000 separate odors and up to a half-million combination odors. We can diagnose disease, detect danger, identify food, recognize relatives, and probably distinguish another person's sex with our noses. Studies have shown that a two-day-old baby starts making a sucking sound, even when asleep, if exposed to the smell of its mother's milk on a breast pad. That smell will help direct him or her to the right place each time. Wherever we go, each of us carries an olfactory ID card, much like fingerprints—and though many cultures struggle to wash it away or cover it up, a dog, which has 35 times as many olfactory cells as we do, can easily sniff us out.

To get an idea how much your nose contributes to taste, pinch your nostrils together while eating. The food becomes dull. Your brain makes you think that taste comes from your tongue, but the finer flavors are identified by your nose. Contrary to most people's belief, the sense of smell is primarily responsible for taste. A person can still taste food with a damaged tongue, but a bad sinus infection will turn most food into soft cardboard. Without smell, the enjoyment in eating would be lost. Meals would vary only by volume, texture, temperature, color, and ease of chewing. Not very exciting. Perhaps not even compatible with survival. Research has shown that people who have lost their sense of smell can tell the difference between only sweet, sour, bitter, and salty. They usually lose weight.

Without the olfactory sense, we would not be able to tell spoiled milk from fresh, perfumes from poisons, the fragrance of a flower from the stench of a dead animal, Coca-Cola from 7-Up, or a gas leak from baked bread. Our eyes can deceive us. How many times has something looked good to eat and yet tasted funny? Some restaurants use realistic replicas of meals as window dressings to entice us; retail shops use certain pleasant aromas to prolong shopping. When you're hungry, the sense of smell is heightened and food becomes increasingly appealing.

Natural Odors

Some of our natural human aromas come from our three million sweat glands, far more than possessed by hairy apes or any other mammal. Under the lens of the microscope, the skin from our armpits looks like a sponge. We secrete up to eight liters of fluid per day, depending on ambient temperature and level of physical exertion. Body odor is actually not sweat, but a bacteria overgrowth. Sweat alone cannot be detected by the human nose.

Not every race smells the same. During the nineteenth century the Japanese complained that the European merchants smelled like *bata-kusai*—"sticks of butter." Vietnamese and Koreans have very few sweat glands under their arms, and 90 percent of the Japanese population lacks underarm smells. At one time, the remaining 10 percent were excluded from military service because of armpit odor.

Europeans and Africans uniformly have the largest number of sweat glands. The reasons for this are not known.

Function and Position by Design?

Without nasal passages, we would be forced to breathe through our mouths. Not only would this be a nuisance, but this air might be too dry, too dirty, or too cold. The nose warms and cleans the air for us. Without specific nasal sensors, we might not be able to find food. This may have been more important during the Stone Age, but this same sense tells us when dinner is ready. Police depend upon the sense of smell to tell whether a gun has been fired or if a body has been dead for a while. Scent tells us if another person has good hygiene. Doctors can diagnose kidney failure by the patient's odor. Detecting the smell of a gas leak or smoke can save a person's life.

The nose is shaped like an air scoop, jutting away from the face to lessen self-smells and to better sample the environment. It is strategically located above the mouth to act like a customs official that monitors all food passing beneath. If the nose were located elsewhere, perhaps on the forehead, its surveillance value would be minimal. If it were located in the armpit, it would be overwhelmed by other smells. If found along the shins, it would probably be easily traumatized. Directly above the mouth is the ideal spot...and there is no fossil evidence that noses appeared anywhere else on the body first.

> Without the olfactory sense, we would not be able to tell perfumes from poisons, the fragrance of a flower from the stench of a dead animal, Coca-Cola from 7-Up, or a gas leak from baked bread.

The idea of having two nostrils that point downward may be taken for granted, but this too represents an important feature. If the nose had begun in the inverted position, it might have flooded during rainstorms or caused our eyes to fog. Debris from a sneeze could be blinding. If the nose were beneath the mouth with upward openings, it would be cluttered with bread crumbs and lost peas; strands of spaghetti might be life-threatening. Excessive drooling might drown someone.

Where else could the nose best monitor incoming air and assess food, yet be connected to the lungs? When viewing this as a WPP, could the nose have come by chance to the proper location and have formed the complex neurological connections and the connections with mouth, throat, and windpipe by chance?

The shape of the nose is important. This shape utilizes the same principle as the ears, capturing aromas and funneling them inside to a complex, more protected area for analysis. Notice how the outer sides of the nose will flare whenever a person takes a sniff, as when checking out a bouquet of flowers. They broaden to get a better sample. We may also sample those flowers with only one side since we each have a dominant side; commonly a right-handed person will be right-nosed, too.

We have two nostrils for the same reasons we have two ears and two eyes. The duality adds perspective and location. Evidence suggests that the two sides may have slightly different functions— and for unclear reasons, the nostrils frequently take shifts, alternating about every three hours. Both nostrils rarely work to full capacity. They can affect mood and behavior.

Indescribable Sensations

Diane Ackerman, author of *A Natural History of the Senses,* calls the olfactory system a "mute" sense. Try describing the smell of popcorn to a stranger to this country. You can easily describe its color, size, shape, texture, and even the sound it makes when chewed, but you cannot tell them how to recognize the smell. One might try to explain a smell by describing how it affects them. Perhaps it is nauseating or mouthwatering—but does that truly get the point across? One can paint a picture of a red barn, but try painting a scent. Comparisons sometimes help—a tangerine smells like a cross between an orange and a lemon—but what if a person has never smelled an orange or a lemon? Try telling someone how to watch out for the smell of gas if they've never smelled gas.

Aromas are mostly identified by memories of previous encounters that are not transferable. They are also colored by experience and culture. Babies don't find feces abhorrent, and yet adults do. The lack of bathing is common, and not bothersome, in many poorer cultures; and bathing was relatively rare in prior times.

Detection Equipment

According to evolutionary theory, the olfactory system is one of the oldest sensory systems, and in some animals it has become the most developed sense. In humans, the receptor area occupies a mere square inch located deep within each nostril. The tissue is yellowish and easily distinguished. In fact, the deeper the yellow, the keener the sense. Albinos often have pale-yellow olfactory tissue and a poor sense of smell. Females have a keener sense of smell than males, presumably for reproductive reasons. As with hearing and vision, olfactory thresholds diminish with age, and by 80 as much as 75 percent of smell may be lost. Some think the nose gets bigger with age to accommodate this loss. There is no smelling aid as there is a hearing aid, but history suggests there will be.

The olfactory receptor cells have tiny hairs that pick up scents by their shape. Peppermint is wedge-shaped and fits into a V-shaped site. Camphor and musk are both spherical, yet they fit into different-sized receptacles. Ether is rod-shaped and fits into a trough; floral scents are disclike. Like the primary colors, smells tend to lump into a few basic categories—minty, floral, ethereal, camphoraceous, musky, resinous, foul or putrid, and acrid (vinegar)—and then the receptors separate shades of differences or combinations. Musk is so potent that it can be smelled at .000000000032 of an ounce. We need only eight molecules to stimulate a nerve ending, but the aroma will remain undetected unless a minimum of 40 nerves have been stimulated. A change in intensity must exceed 39 percent to be detected, whereas a change in light of 1 percent can be detected. To have aromas, substances must be volatile, meaning they emit molecules that bounce around on their surfaces. Steel and ivory lack such wayward molecules. Because many items lose their volatility under weightless conditions, astronauts lose taste and smell. Aromas are also strongly linked to memory. The smell of a barbecue may bring back family memories, and a perfume the first kiss. The smell of smoke will set off internal alarms.

> The olfactory system is a "mute" sense. How can you tell someone how to recognize a smell? You can paint a picture of a red barn, but try painting a scent.

Protection and Responses

Besides the nose's location and shape, there are several other aspects that suggest design. Air is filtered by small hairs as it is inhaled by the expanding lungs. This protects us from pollen, dander, dust, bacteria, fungi, viruses, smog, skin cells from other people, minute insects, and even specks of dog feces. On a breezy summer day, the air in every big city is cluttered with tons of invisible desiccated dog feces. These tiny particles are trapped in mucus, which drains to the outside or down to the stomach. Cool air is warmed in the nose, and dry air moisturized.

Several other mechanical responses protect us. We will automatically gag and spit something out that smells vile. The sneeze can blast irritating debris out of the system at speeds that exceed a hundred miles an hour. The cough may be the backup system if an irritant gets beyond the upper passages.

Almost all sexual behavior is set in motion by the olfactory senses. Studies suggest men are more attracted to women around the time of ovulation and that intercourse will occur more often then. A woman's sense of smell is keener around ovulation as well, perhaps to pick up the male scent better. At least 30 different hormones in the vagina can act as an attractant, and during intercourse, they may be responsible for that runny nose.

Without the sense of smell we might be less interested in sex. The human body has several natural smells, including pheromones—sexual hormones that intrigue, attract, and oftentimes stimulate others. These aromatic chemicals have been demonstrated to exist in animals and suspected in humans for years. Kissing is probably made more fun by their exchange. Lips to lips, nose next to nose, they are easily exchanged. Pheromones are what make an ovulating woman more attractive.

Evidence suggests that a tiny hole found on each side of the middle wall in each nostril, called the *vomeronasal apparatus* or *Jacobson's organ*, may hold receptors for pheromones. These sexual hormones are silently emitted from armpits, beards, and pubic areas, and are received by a partner's nose; they advertise sexual status and the intensity of sexual interest. The hairs act as wicks; the arms act like bellows.

Rudyard Kipling once said, "Smells are surer than sights and sounds to make your heartstrings crack." During Elizabethan times, a woman would peel an apple, keep it in her armpit until it was saturated with her sweat, and then give it to her lover to inhale. They were called "love apples." The impact of pheromones on the vomeronasal apparatus is not entirely male–female. They will also cause women who live in dormitories or share homes to begin having their periods in synchrony. They may play a role in homosexual relationships.

On close inspection, the vomeronasal tissues look different from other nasal tissues, but they are closely connected to the olfactory system. One-quarter of all people who lose their sense of smell lose their desire for sex. Most people intuitively know that smell plays a role in sexual attraction. Look at the money spent pushing perfumes and colognes. Ads for them portray sexually attractive people. Every company is looking for that magical formula made of pheromones; should it be discovered, the profits might exceed those from the cure for the common cold.

If the nose were the evolutionary product of trial and error, survival of the fittest, or multiple mutations, one would expect to find fossils of species with noses in varying locations, in varying degrees of completion. None such exist. Is it coincidence or an accident that the sense of smell monitors everything we eat and drink? Or inhale? Is it a mere chance mutation that the nose makes air going into the lungs safer, cleaner, and warmer?

Bottom-Line Points

- *The six million olfactory cells inside a nose can detect 10,000 separate odors and as many as a half-million combination odors.*

- *Almost all sexual behavior is either set in motion or augmented by the olfactory senses.*

- *We have two nostrils for the same reasons we have two ears and two eyes. The duality adds perspective and location.*

- *The olfactory receptor cells have tiny hairs that pick up scents according to their shape and size.*

- *Besides its location and shape, there are numerous other aspects of the olfactory system that also suggest intelligent design.*

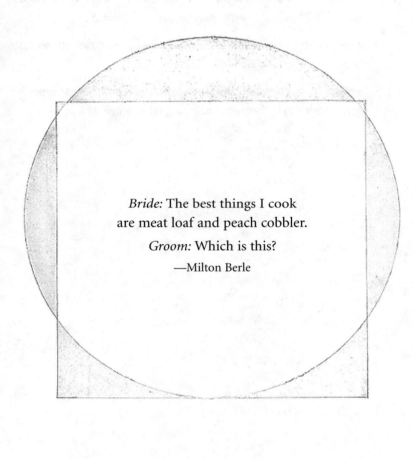

Bride: The best things I cook
are meat loaf and peach cobbler.

Groom: Which is this?

—Milton Berle

11

Taste

Stick your tongue out as far as you can in front of a mirror. You should see several bumpy growths at the rear—and if you strain a little, you might even see a V-shaped pattern of larger, button-like growths across the very back. These *papillae* contain most of our 10,000 taste buds. They are present by the third fetal month. Textbooks typically say we detect only four tastes: sweet (sucrose), salty (sodium chloride), bitter (quinine hydrochloride), and sour (citric acid)—but the tongue can actually also pick up metallic iron salts, *umami* (a meaty or savory taste—for example, monosodium glutamate), certain amino acids, and chalky tastes. Fat sensations can be sensed by the sides of the tongue, and a number of flavors, like chocolate, can be improved when pressed against the soft palate.

We begin life with a much larger number of taste buds than we have when we are older. They are widely dispersed about the tongue, inner cheeks, larynx, palate, and throat, even in the stomach. As we age, these numbers and areas lessen. There is an inherent logic to having more taste buds during the time of maximum growth. It may be the same logic that makes food smell and taste better when we're hungry.

The mouth is uniquely suited to be a tasting and preparation chamber. Bite-sized food is received, macerated, pulverized, hydrated,

chemically cleaved, partially digested by enzymes, treated with antibodies, and reanalyzed before being passed on. If any of the food
seems tainted, a built-in mechanism tells us to spit it out. After the
food passes the first analysis, it is moved to the stomach, where a
backup system will do further assessments. If a health-threatening
problem is found there, a second built-in mechanism will induce
vomiting. Diarrhea may be a third design to get rid of toxins. This
is why doctors are reluctant to give patients antidiarrhea medications.

Formation and Characteristics

The mouth is the first facial organ to form in the embryo;
because of its importance, control of its functions is allotted an inordinate amount of space in the brain. Many attributes support design.
Most obvious is its anatomical position. It faces forward, beneath
the nose and eyes, and is connected to the gastrointestinal tract.
What other location would lend itself so well to eating, smelling,
or seeing our food?

The mouth has a versatile set of muscles that allows us to open
and close, suck, bite, chew, whistle, whisper, kiss, and speak. Lips
help us sense whether food is too hot or too cold; the hard and soft
palate keep food from going into the nose; the tongue automatically moves the food along for proper chewing, tasting, and swallowing. The lips and the tongue are among the most sensitive (and
sensual) tissues in the body.

The position and shape of our teeth is deliberate. The incisors
act like adzes and can easily slice through fruits and vegetables; the
canines, situated beside the incisors, can grip and tear flesh; and
the premolars and molars can grind food, nuts, and seeds. Our
enamel is one of the hardest biological substances known; without

it our teeth would rot. Our teeth can also sense the hardness of a material, keeping us from biting something that may be damaging. There are no prehuman fossils with nonfunctional teeth, useless tooth buds, or only upper teeth.

The tongue can stretch forward to taste with a lick. It can sense if a bone is present, ferret out unwanted matter, scrape bits of food away from crevices between teeth, help form words, sense the temperature of food, shift food from cutting teeth to pulverizing teeth, help digest food by secreting enzymes, initiate the swallowing process (roughly nine times a minute), and help spit out bad food. Despite a minimum of 5000 chews per day, this organ is practically never bitten, and almost all of these functions are done automatically for us.

> The mouth is uniquely suited to be a tasting and preparation chamber.

The production of saliva is triggered by the mere anticipation of a meal, literally whetting our appetite, and is then increased when the food arrives. Over one quart of watery mucus, rich in enzymes, salts, and antibodies, is secreted each day from several strategic sites around the mouth. It keeps tissues moist and clean, food lubricated, and the inner mouth protected from injury. It helps sterilize and digest food, and the maintenance of a pH of seven protects the throat from regurgitated acid.

Tasteful Sensations

Bitter and sour are the most sensitive taste buds, possibly to lessen the chance of being poisoned. For comparison, if sweetness can be detected at one part in 200, then saltiness will be detected at one part in 400, sourness at one part in 130,000, and bitterness at one part in two million. These taste buds are augmented by 10,000 smell receptors in the nasal passages; together they can turn a meal into a gustatory symphony. Hundreds of flavors (instruments) may play a concerto in your mouth with each bite. You may taste a mushroom (hear an oboe) or taste some chicken (hear a violin). Other times, you may appreciate a sauce (hear the wind section) or stumble on a clove of garlic (a soloist). If the meal (performance) was exceptional, you may leave the table (concert hall) happy, satisfied, and relaxed. In a broader sense, every day our eyes receive a visual symphony and our ears an auditory symphony. Perhaps our noses receive an olfactory symphony.

Taste buds are made up of four types of cells lining tiny pores; the cells change every ten days. They collect passing molecules by matching their shape, size, or electrical charge and then send that information to the brain for interpretation. Other detectors determine food texture, bite size, speed of chewing, food temperature, adequacy of lubrication, the presence of nondigestible items (such as aluminum foil), the degree of irritation (hot, cold, too spicy, too gritty), and when to swallow. Those cultures that savor hot peppers seem to have cauterized the pain receptors in their tongues.

Food always tastes best when a person is hungry, and hormones encourage the person to continue eating. Body signals tell the brain there's a need for food—and the brain, in turn, makes food seem more desirable. Some of it has to do with endorphins. Notice how content some folks appear after eating a heavy meal. Certain fats and sweets can be downright sedating. Moods always improve with a "full stomach"; anger dissipates.

If evolution were responsible for our ability to procure, taste, break down, and pass food products into the gastrointestinal tract, one would think that the fossil record would show species with partial mouths, partial tongues, and partially formed teeth. It doesn't. And could the mouth be there without the tongue, throat, esophagus, stomach, intestines, and every microscopic detail of each? Or need this all have been a WPP?

Bottom-Line Points

- *We begin life with a much larger number of taste buds than we have when we are older. There is an inherent logic to having more taste buds during the time of maximum growth.*

- *The mouth is uniquely designed to be a tasting and preparation chamber.*

- *The production of saliva is triggered by the mere anticipation of a meal; saliva keeps tissues moist and clean and keeps food lubricated, and its enzymes begin the digestion process.*

- *Because of the mouth's importance, control of its functions is allotted an inordinate amount of space in the brain.*

- *Many of the mouth's attributes, like the position of the teeth and the salivary glands, the functions of the tongue, and the ability to taste and spit out spoiled food, support intelligent design.*

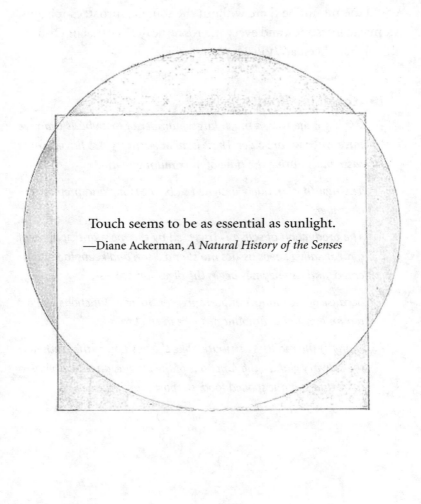

Touch seems to be as essential as sunlight.

—Diane Ackerman, *A Natural History of the Senses*

12

Touch

A network of millions of sensory receptors blankets every square millimeter of the human body. It is designed to help us carry out every function, to protect us, and to give us pleasure. A person might see hot coffee spilling in their lap, but only touch will report the severity of the injury. Touch can tell you if your clothes are too loose or too tight, if your shoes fit, if a dinner roll is too hard, if the day's humidity is rising, and if a shower is too cold. Touch often complements the other senses, but it also works alone. Without the appropriate tactile sensations, a hug or a kiss would not be the same. A back rub might be irritating, and intercourse might be traumatizing. A minor infection might become fatal if a person could not feel it festering.

Although touch is sometimes referred to as the fifth sense, it could easily be called the fifth, sixth, and seventh senses. Not only are there four major types of sensation—hot, cold, pain, and pressure—but there are numerous variations, degrees, frequencies, and combinations of each. All of us can easily distinguish between being licked, patted, bit, gnawed, slapped, wiped, fondled, scratched, kneaded, tickled, pricked, scraped, burned, tapped, pounded, brushed, pulled, stretched, twisted, cut, pinched, shaved, scratched, probed, picked, banged, and nudged without much thought. We can tell wet from dry, smooth from rough, sharp from dull, hard from soft, and differences between textures and types of vibrations. We take these capabilities for granted, yet each sensation involves multiple complex neurological pathways. In less than a second, a sensation can be identified and an action selected. Millions of inaction decisions are also made.

An Indispensable Touch

We know that touch is critical to mental health. Monkeys that are deprived of touch, yet can see and smell their mothers, suffer severely. Massaged babies gain weight 50 percent faster than unmassaged babies, and they seem more emotionally content. A number of studies have shown that infants who are otherwise well-fed and well-cared-for, but are deprived of physical contact, grow up psychologically and physically stunted. Studies of adults who grew up in orphanages where the infants were uniformly ignored have consistently yielded the same kinds of results. Touch is critical during the first few months of a child's life.

We depend upon our sense of touch for identity, comfort, affection, and protection. The entire skin surface, including mucous membranes, acts like a surveillance unit, quietly and constantly assessing every square millimeter of contact with our environment. The brain keeps track of every thread of clothing and will immediately report to you if something is allergenic, pinching, too tight, too wet, too warm, or too cold. Exposed areas of skin will keep track of ambient conditions and quickly tell the brain if the outside temperature is changing, a breeze is blowing, or (perhaps) an insect has landed. If there's a need to know, you will be informed immediately. Receptors in the feet monitor the inside of our shoes as well as the surfaces we walk on and immediately inform us if we've stepped from a sidewalk onto grass, or started up or down a hill. Your eyes may tell you there's snow on the ground, but it's the tactile senses that report whether it's freezing outdoors or the snow is turning into slush.

Receptors

Sensory receptors come in a variety of shapes and sizes. Many act like tiny frayed electrical wires, ready to fire off the instant they are touched. *Meissner corpuscles* (tactile corpuscles are located between the epidermis and the dermis, particularly in hairless, sensitive areas such as the fingertips, clitoris, penis, nipples, palms, and tongue. Every fingertip has about 9000 of these corpuscles per square inch. They can distinguish between different types of light touch, between sharp and dull, between various textures; they can detect low frequency vibrations and the size of any stimulus. *Pacinian corpuscles* respond to pressure, stretching, and vibrations in deep tissues near joints, genitals, and mammary glands. These receptors resemble miniature onions, with different layers that can decipher the type of vibration or extent of the pressure. *Merkel's disks* pick up continuous stimuli and touch. *Krause's end bulbs* pick up touch in the mucous membranes. *Ruffini corpuscles* sense heavy pressure and temperature. *Proprioceptors* in our stomach tell us if we are full, and those in the colon if we need to defecate; others scattered about the body tell us what our muscles and joints are doing and how we feel.

Receptors at the base of every hair also play a major role in tactile senses. Each individual hair can sense anything that brushes against it—merely pull a single hair on your head. You can usually feel if your hair's out of place. The average body has five million hairs, and studies have shown that down hairs (the soft, fuzzy ones) need to move only .00004 inch to trigger a nerve.

Image and Sensation

Knowing where we are and what every part of our body is doing at all times is critical, and the sense of touch plays a major role in this. Creating and maintaining this body image is similar to maintaining a moving holographic image within the brain. This requires the constant infeeding of information from millions of terminals to our brain, saying what's changing and what's not. If you enter a conference room, your brain knows the location of every part of your body in relation to the walls, doors, fixtures, windows, and occupants. As you move, your brain keeps a fix on where you are and what is happening every millisecond. We take for granted that we will know when it's time to eat, sleep, breathe, defecate, and urinate, but these activities plus many more require very sophisticated internal signals. If you were to run the 100-meter dash, would your gasping for air at the end be voluntary or enforced? Imagine how difficult life might be if we didn't know when our body needed food or drink, when to stop eating or drinking, or when to speed up breathing. What if these bodily functions merely happened at random? Specific safeguards are designed to make our lives quite bearable.

> The sense of touch plays a major role in creating and maintaining our body image—similar to a moving holographic image within the brain.

We each have five to ten times more cold receptors than warmth receptors, yet it takes a drop of about four degrees for the cold receptors to pick up a change and a two-degree climb for the warmth

receptors. The reason for the difference is unknown. Cold receptors are typically found on the face, especially on the forehead,
eyelids, lips, and tip of the nose where they might be considered
sentinels; warmth receptors are more widespread and deeper. The
tongue seems to have the most warmth receptors per unit area—
this might be a throwback to the times when we needed to eat our
prey while it was still warm, rather than cold and possibly tainted.
Wanting hot meals nowadays may be a carryover. Consider the
bone-cracking sensation of eating potato chips. A throwback too?

Emotion and attitude can easily color the sensation of touch.
Picture yourself standing on a crowded sidewalk, and then add in
a cute toddler who bumps into the back of your leg. Not an unpleasant thought? Now picture yourself on the same sidewalk and add
in a vicious-looking dog that bumps the back of your leg in exactly
the same way. Feel different?

The Gift of Pain

Perhaps the most important purpose of the sensation of pain
is to alert the body to an injury. This is a gift. Obviously, pain is
far from a wonderful present for those who chronically suffer, but
it can be a gift in acute situations. A sudden burning pain will make
us pull our hand away from a hot stove or teach a child not to play
with matches. The nerve endings at the injured body part seem to
be shouting, "Look down here right now and do something about
this immediately!" The sudden worsening of a pain when one moves
an injured knee may be the body's way of telling the person they
are making a mistake. The lessening of pain tells us an injury is healing.

Whenever a tissue is injured, it releases certain chemicals—such
as prostaglandins, serotonin, histamines, and bradykinin—that

initiate healing and protect the wound. The bradykinin seems to cause most of the pain that draws our attention. Without the prohibitive sensation of pain, we might make old injuries worse. Try lifting something heavy. If your hands say it's too heavy, you will stop. Try throwing a ball if your shoulder hurts. The body frequently tells us what we can do and what we can't.

Although a pinprick is not terribly painful, we sense this kind of pain the fastest. The sensation travels to the brain at 98 feet per second. A six-foot-tall person would feel a sudden pain in the big toe in less than a twentieth of a second. Burning and aching pains travel slower, averaging about six-and-a-half feet per second.

Visceral pains emanate from internal organs. A sharp pain in the upper right quadrant of the abdomen may signal gallstones, a pressurelike pain over the left side of the chest may portend a heart attack, pain in the right lower quadrant of the abdomen could be appendicitis, pain in the left lower quadrant might be diverticulitis, a burning pain beneath the sternum may suggest acid reflux or an ulcer, and pain shooting down the back of a leg may mean a lumbar disc is pressing against a nerve root.

The sensation of pain tends to be graduated—meaning the larger the injury, the greater the pain—but there are a number of psychological and physiological issues that affect this. A similar back pain may send one person to bed, while another person may stay at work with an ice pack under their belt. Some people who have survived near-death experiences, such as multiple stab wounds, will deny having ever felt pain, whereas the same people might stub a toe and be in agony. We seem to have a built-in mechanism to blot out memories of massive injuries. Soldiers who sustain dreadful, gaping wounds will sometimes turn down morphine, saying they don't need it. Athletes who are "hyped" will ignore serious pain so they can continue playing. Endorphins and enkephalins are partly responsible. These are nature's internal pain remedies, and studies have shown that levels of these in the blood and the brain increase under times of excitement, extreme exercise, and extreme pleasure. Women who are delivering babies will have very high levels of enkephalins. Otherwise, the pain of childbirth would be completely intolerable.

It is doubtful that a single species could ever have existed without tactile senses. Microscopic organisms seem to know when they bump into each other, and they go out of their way to avoid obstacles. The more complex an organism becomes, the more complex its senses—but is that an accident? If tactile receptors evolved through survival of the fittest or random mutations, why are there different receptors for slices, pinches, pricks, burns, freezes, and bruises, not a simpler, all-in-one sensory receptor? Is pain a gift comparable to a loving touch?

Bottom-Line Points

- *A network of millions of sensory receptors blankets every square millimeter of the human body.*

- *Touch is designed to help us carry out every function, to protect us, and to give us pleasure.*

- *A minor infection might become fatal if a person could not feel it festering.*

- *The entire skin surface, including mucous membranes, acts like a surveillance unit, constantly assessing every square millimeter of contact with our environment.*

- *Touch is critical to mental health.*

I entered biology to understand the beauty of life.
I started with the ecology of animals,
but that wasn't quite right, so I went one
level deeper, to the study of tissues, then to
chemistry, and finally even dabbled in the
depths of quantum mechanics. Yet when I got
there, I saw that the wonder of life had somehow
slipped through my fingers along the way.

—Albert Szent-Györgyi, 1937 Nobel Laureate in Biology

13

Skin

Our skin is the largest organ of our body, and it is designed to serve a number of functions. It weighs six to ten pounds; in the average adult it covers an area of 22 square feet. For the most part it is only one-seventh of an inch thick, but it comes much thicker in places where we need more protection, such as the bottom of our feet, and thinner where we need increased sensory perception, such as our fingertips and our lips. Without this exterior covering we could not survive. Needless to say, we would also look rather horrid, having the color and texture of raw steak. We would freeze to death in the winter and cook in the summer; we would turn into prunes in the desert. We might even rot.

We arrive dressed in a birthday suit far superior to anything one can buy off the shelf. It is waterproof, antibacterial, antiviral, antifungal, elastic, flexible, self-repairing, toxin-resistant, insulating, self-cleaning, supportive, sexual, sensual, washable, self-replenishing, capable of absorbing some chemicals and rejecting others, porous, self-lubricating, scented, capable of making vitamins, sensitive to painful stimuli, and able to detect changes in temperature, vibration, and pressure. It functions as a duffel bag, keeping all of our truly personal belongings contained—and it clearly has aesthetic aspects. Without it, attraction between lovers would take on a new meaning. Skin is the medium a newborn uses to sense its new environment. This is where a mother feels her child suckle, and the baby feels the nipple. This is where the magic of a lover's touch is felt.

A Triple Covering

There are three layers: *epidermis, dermis,* and *hypodermis,* of which the epidermis is outermost. It consists mostly of dead cells that are constantly being sloughed. Shedding is a cleaning mechanism that rids us of dirt, grime, parasites, and bacterial overgrowth. We each lose ten billion skin cells per day, mostly in bed, inside our clothes, or in the bathtub; if one could look extremely closely at a naked person walking, one would see a cloud of cells, like an aura, surrounding them. When this cloud falls on our shoulders, it is called dandruff. It also falls in our food, on our desks, and even, with hugs, on our family members. Wrestlers exchange billions of skin cells, as do lovers. Our epidermal slough becomes a feast for bed mites. Curiously, when one person looks another in the face, they are looking at billions of dead cells. Fortunately, it's a microscopic phenomenon.

As the outermost cells are lost, newer cells grow up from beneath. Every two weeks we get a totally new covering. You can time this by watching a tan disappear. Despite constant turnover, though, everyone's exterior remains the same. A white person will not slowly become a nonwhite person; a pug nose remains a pug nose; and knees don't show up on elbows. The deepest skin cells are designed to reproduce every pore, freckle, dimple, ding, shade, and variation. Oddly, a bump on the scalp will remain a bump on the scalp. Even those fine lines in a fingerprint or toe print will retain

Skin: Cross-Sectional View[6]

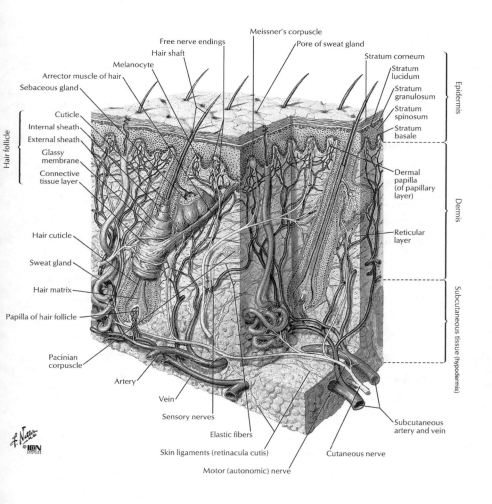

Meissner's corpuscle
Free nerve endings
Hair shaft
Pore of sweat gland
Melanocyte
Stratum corneum
Arrector muscle of hair
Stratum lucidum
Sebaceous gland
Stratum granulosum
Stratum spinosum
Stratum basale

Epidermis

Cuticle
Internal sheath
External sheath
Glassy membrane
Connective tissue layer

Hair follicle

Dermal papilla (of papillary layer)

Dermis

Hair cuticle
Reticular layer

Sweat gland

Hair matrix

Papilla of hair follicle

Subcutaneous tissue (hypodermis)

Pacinian corpuscle

Artery
Vein
Sensory nerves
Elastic fibers
Subcutaneous artery and vein
Skin ligaments (retinacula cutis)
Cutaneous nerve
Motor (autonomic) nerve

the same pattern for life. And this genetic plan for the skin is executed ten billion times a day.

Sweating It Out

The middle layer of skin, the dermis, is much thicker than the epidermis. This is where the nerves, capillaries, and glands reside. The most familiar glands are the sweat glands, which come in two types: *merocrine* (or *eccrine*) and *apocrine*.

Merocrine glands are typically found in the palms, soles, armpits, and forehead. Each of us has two to three million of them, and they are as unique to human beings as speaking, walking on two feet, and handling complex ideas. No other animal sweats like we do; most do not sweat at all. These glands secrete a half-quart of relatively imperceptible sweat daily, but under circumstances of excessive heat, stress, or exercise they can pump out one or two quarts per hour. After being stimulated, the glands' tiny, wraparound muscles squeeze millions of minute bulbs that release a diluted version of serum. It coats the body and then cools it by evaporation. No one knows why we don't pant like most other animals. This feature is unique to us; although it is in place to maintain body temperature, it may also be present to make us slippery when under attack by a predator. Because there are an inordinate number of sweat pores on our fingertips—approximately 2000 per square inch—sweat may also aid in grasping things, as does wetting a fingertip to turn a page.

Apocrine glands are also found in the dermis, and although these bulblike structures look similar to merocrine glands, they act quite differently. They secrete a scented—often subliminally scented— material which may be entirely related to sexual arousal. In contrast to all other primates, these glands are found only in the armpits, pubic area, nipples, and men's beards. In many ways they are the olfactory broadcast centers, aided by thousands of wicks (hairs). These glands show up at the time of puberty. In some cultures these smells are welcome—sometimes considered a normal part of courtship.

The reason these scents become bothersome is that their fatty-acid components linger if a person doesn't bathe or change clothes, and then malodorous bacteria readily proliferate. Encouraged by advertising, we may scrub away the good with the bad, though. The same type of thing happens with *sebum* on hair. Sebum is a naturally occurring oily product secreted by the *sebaceous glands* at the base of every hair follicle. It is designed to keep our hair moist and nonbrittle, but few people in western cultures want this naturally oily look. Instead, they use shampoos to get rid of the natural oils. Further, only mammals have hair. We have approximately 100,000 hairs, and we can grow our pelts ten feet long (although three feet is the usual maximum). Monkeys do not have this ability.

Another interesting group of cells found in the skin are the glands that make earwax. The purpose of this wax might be to discourage mites and other parasites from taking up residence in the ear canals. Apparently, the stuff tastes bad (at least to mites). The wax may also play a protective role, shielding the eardrum from loud noises.

The Importance of Fat

Situated below the dermis is the hypodermis. This layer is mostly fat tissue. It is responsible for insulation, cushioning, and keeping the skin attached to the muscles beneath. It keeps us warm, like an internal body suit. Since it absorbs substances well, it is one level where many medications can be injected. The loss of skin fat through aging causes older folks to always feel cold and bruise easily. This is why teenagers can walk around in t-shirts in winter weather and the elderly need a heavy wrap. The loss of elasticity with age causes skin to droop.

Elaine Morgan wrote in *The Scars of Evolution* that human skin more resembles the skin of aquatic animals than grassland animals. The nakedness, underlying fat, elasticity, the wealth of apocrine glands, and the proliferation of sebaceous glands are undeniably unique to humans and not present in other primates. When one compares the fat level in human skin with that of a chimpanzee, it becomes readily apparent there is a major structural difference that is not dietary. Our exterior more resembles that of whales, seals, and dolphins—and barely, if at all, resembles monkeys. In fact, Caroline Pond writes that "an exceptionally obese monkey resembles a lean human being."

We accumulate fat tissue in the skin quite differently from other animals. According to Elaine Morgan, many species in captivity (meaning they're well-fed) will never double or triple their weight, unlike successive generations of humans who are well-fed. People are much bigger than they were a century ago. A nonhuman primate may develop a rounder abdomen, but it will never develop bloated cheeks, fat buttocks, flabby arms, a large bust, and fleshy thighs.

Elastic, Sensitive, Protective, Scented

Our skin can shrink to fit a person with anorexia or comfortably accommodate someone who tops a thousand pounds. It can stretch and retract as joints flex and extend—hundreds of times a day for our entire life. We are cooled by, in addition to millions of sweat glands, a myriad of blood vessels that can hold or release heat by constricting or dilating. Women flush more than men because they have more of these surface blood vessels. Women also tend to be warmer, and this may be why they tend to faint more often—more surface blood vessels mean more blood can be diverted away from vital organs. If we are cold, these vessels constrict to retain heat. If outdoor conditions are severe, the fingers, toes, and tip of the nose will turn an intense white color, protecting the inner body.

Goose pimples lessen heat loss by raising hair and creating tiny pockets of warmer air (in the more hairy individuals). Shivering increases heat production, as if a billion tiny heat lamps were turned on.

> We arrive dressed in a birthday suit far superior to anything one can buy off the shelf.

Skin contains melanin to help protect us from sunburn. It also maintains a specific pH to repel bacterial invaders, and it absorbs sunlight to make vitamin D for our bones. Without the sun's effect on our skin to make vitamin D, our bones would crumble long before we reached adulthood.

The most sensitive skin of the body is found on the lips, nipples, anus, and fingertips; these sites have increased nerve endings and a special blood supply. Not only do the lips check food for temperature and texture, but they are also a major source of sexual arousal. Only the skin on our feet, hands, and certain other select areas where pressure may be applied can develop calluses to increase protection. Fingertips come with ridges for grasping, like tiny tire treads, and fingernails are sharp for scratching, fighting, and scraping away parasites. We all have unique pore prints, just as we have unique fingerprints.

The color and texture of our skin reflects our internal health. Anemia or a drop in the red blood cell count from bleeding is readily evident by pallor. Jaundice, or the yellowing of skin, shows up with liver disease. If there is a blood-clotting defect, the skin may show bruising. If there's a fever, the person looks flushed as the body tries to lower its core temperature. If there's been violence, the skin will tattle as to where the injuries occurred. If there's kidney failure, the skin will take on a characteristic odor. Old-time physicians could actually diagnose kidney failure and diabetes by smelling their patients.

The sweat glands can act as thousands of miniature kidneys, excreting a number of medications, certain salts, and some toxins. Skin can also act like the gastrointestinal tract and absorb a number of medications, such as nitroglycerin, hormones, and blood pressure medications, as well as deodorants and perfumes. Cells within the skin know how and when to constrict local blood vessels after an injury to lessen bleeding, and how to summon helpers to heal a wound or fight an infection. An abscess will be brought to the surface to drain.

Although 350 scents are known to emanate from the skin's surface, there may actually be more than 1000. Some of these may depend on what we have recently ingested, some are universal, and some are unique to an individual. A bloodhound can find a criminal after sniffing the person's belongings. In the future, we may be able to pick up a scent from fingerprints. There is evidence that certain human scents attract chiggers, lice, mosquitoes, and bot flies. Other scents repel them.

We think a human baby knows its mother, in part, by her smell. Human baby hair has a scent that is a natural opiate—it promotes interest, protection, and relaxed parenting. One often hears adults comment on how much they like the smell of a baby. Were babies designed to be cute, adorable, liked, cuddled, loved, protected, and nourished?

Bottom-Line Points

- *Skin is thickest where we need more protection.*

- *Despite the constant turnover of cells and sloughing of skin, everyone's exterior remains the same.*

- *Only mammals have hair.*

- *Skin is responsible for insulation, cushioning, and keeping the skin attached to the muscles beneath.*

- *The most sensitive skin of the body is found on the lips, nipples, anus, and fingertips; these sites have more nerve endings and a special blood supply.*

- *Although 350 scents are known to emanate from the skin's surface, there may actually be more than 1000. Each one of us has a distinct, unique odor.*

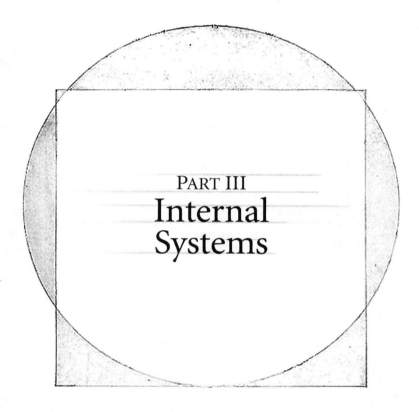

PART III
Internal
Systems

Bones, physiology, the nervous system—the body has thousands of consummate designs that elicit our wonder and admiration.

—Randolph Nesse and George Williams,
Why We Get Sick

14

The Endocrine System

The endocrine system includes the pituitary, thyroid, and adrenal glands, the testes and ovaries, and numerous smaller islands of tissue located in the pancreas, heart, lungs, brain, kidneys, stomach, liver, and placenta. Each gland produces specific hormones that carry messages to target cells, telling them what to do, when, and how. To date there are more than 40 hormones known, and the production of each one is controlled by a feedback loop. Many work in parallel or tandem, some compete, and some have double and triple feedback loops. The overall complexity, the necessity for the WPP—whole package phenomenon—and the need for all systems to be in place simultaneously strongly challenge evolutionary theory.

The concept of a feedback loop may sound intimidating, but each of us operates with similar models every day. Many large corporations and government agencies make major decisions based on feedback. Picture a person who is responsible for keeping the daily supply of cookies for New York City at a constant number. Not only does he keep track of every cookie consumed on a microsecond-to-microsecond basis, but which types are preferred; he can adjust to every change. No one wants a backlog of stale cookies. If, for example, the supply of macaroons drops precipitously, every baker in town is immediately told to increase production. If the Chinese restaurants cut their orders of fortune cookies, appropriate bakers are told to slow production. If a huge Boy Scout convention comes to town, the bakers might be told to increase manufacture of chocolate-chip. If the convention is then canceled due to bad weather, production is stopped. Actions depend on reactions and vice versa.

A Cookie Counter in the Brain

And so it goes with the pituitary gland, our biological cookie counter. This tiny, tear-shaped organ is strategically located near the center of the brain, where it can monitor varying hormone levels (numbers and types of cookies) that are made by the various glands (bakers). As the concentration of a particular hormone (macaroons) drops in the bloodstream, the pituitary notes the change and quickly sends its hormones (messengers) to the responsible glands (bakers). Once levels are back up to normal, the messenger system quiets down. If a certain hormone level becomes too high, the appropriate messenger system shuts down.

The brain and pituitary gland determine the various needs throughout the body and pass that information on to the appropriate gland. Most of the changes are proportional—a 10 percent

Example of Simple Feedback System

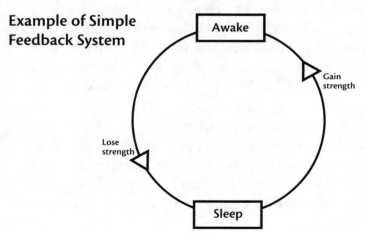

Actual Endocrine Feedback Loops

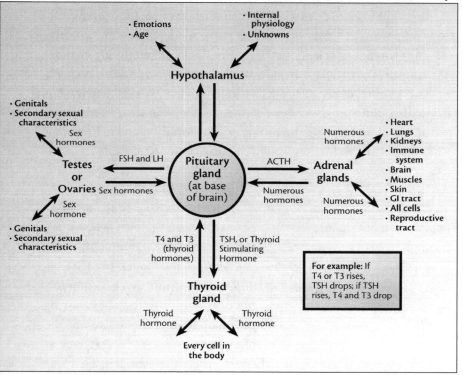

decrease of supply in the periphery is typically matched with a 10 percent boost centrally—but occasionally the pituitary gland will change the rules and tell a gland to increase or decrease hormone levels based on a person's emotional state, anticipated activity, ongoing activity, or failing health. During times of famine, the pituitary will tell a woman's ovaries to stop producing female hormones, probably to prevent ovulation and pregnancy when it might be hard to care for a baby. We know that during times of food shortage, animals will have fewer offspring, and during good times, more. Happy, sad, and stressful times have distinct impacts on most hormone production.

Under most circumstances, this feedback system works very smoothly; however, as with the manufacture of cookies, trouble can come from a variety of sources. There might be starvation causing an iodine deficiency (a shortage of flour), an interfering medication (a labor strike), an infection or toxin (industrial sabotage), carrier-protein deficiency (a flat tire), birth control pills (a new CEO with a different agenda), or a clogged artery (a huge traffic jam). If there's a shortage, the pituitary will steadily increase hormone messenger production until it gets the response it wants.

Mail for Mailboxes

The pituitary gland, our biological cookie counter, monitors varying hormone levels (numbers and types of cookies) that are made by the various glands (bakers).

Every hormone acts as a messenger with specific instructions for specific cells. For example, follicle-stimulating hormone, or FSH, is designed to stimulate cells found in the ovaries and testes; it cannot be picked up by any other cells along the bloodstream. When FSH arrives at the ovaries, the ovarian cells start producing estrogen. Thyroid-stimulating hormone (TSH) goes to the thyroid; growth hormone (GH) goes to bones and muscles.

To be sure the proper target cell receives the correct message, the different hormones (mail) come in different sizes, shapes, wrappings, electrical charges, and configurations. For example, certain pituitary hormones that carry male-related messages will only fit into male-related receptacles (mailboxes) located inside the testes. The hormones produced by the testes will fit into receptacles in the beard, muscle bundles, voice box, and sperm factories. Female hormones will mostly go to female receptacles. These messages are very convoluted compounds, twisted and turned and resembling a tangled ball of yarn, yet each type fits snugly inside the appropriate receptacle. At any moment, millions of these hormones are in circulation. Envision a windstorm blowing all of the mail for Chicago down a five-mile stretch of the Outer Drive in that city, yet every letter and package is able to sort itself out and end up in the correct mailbox.

Triiodothyronine and *thyroxin*, abbreviated T3 and T4, are two hormones (cookies) from the thyroid that are regulated by TSH from the pituitary gland—the cookie counter. T3 and T4 act like a foot on an accelerator of a car—but in the human body there is at least one accelerator per cell, or a total of at least ten trillion accelerators. The speed and efficiency of everything we do is affected by the concentration of thyroid hormone. If levels are too low, the body's engines slow down; if the levels are too high, the engines speed up. This is clearly reflected in diseases of the thyroid. An excess of hormone will make a person "hyped"—with a fast heart rate, constant anxiety, insomnia, and a fast metabolism with weight loss. A shortage of hormone causes lethargy, somnolence, and weight gain. Most of the time the TSH goes up or down in response to increasing or decreasing T3 and T4 production. There could not easily have been multiple intermediate prehistoric systems leading up to this hugely complex system of feedback loops. One either has the whole system, or one has nothing.

Message Sources

The parathyroid gland is made up of four to six separate islands of tissue embedded in the thyroid gland. They monitor calcium levels in the bloodstream and regulate it by secreting *parathormone* (PTH) which increases the absorption of calcium from the bones and from foods we eat. Calcium regulation is critical for maintaining good health and bone structure. It involves billions of chemical reactions every second. Too much PTH will leach the bones of their calcium; too little will lead to low calcium levels and muscle spasms, even death.

Glucagon and *insulin* are secreted by the pancreas and play vital roles in the metabolism of glucose, amino acids, and fats; their levels usually rise and fall based on food intake and activity. A shortage of insulin leads to diabetes—with the blindness, kidney failure, and heart attacks so commonly caused by high sugar levels.

An adrenal gland is located over each kidney. Its product *cortisol* helps us heal wounds, maintain strength, produce glucose, metabolize fats, break down proteins, and cope with stress. Under emergency circumstances, cortisol levels will shoot up to help us respond; when we're laughing, cortisol levels will plummet. Levels fluctuate from minute to minute, morning to night, day to day, and season to season—depending, in part, on experiences, thoughts, fears, stresses, and level of activity. These levels are modulated by *ACTH,* another hormone from the pituitary, whose secretion can be affected by forces in the brain still unclear to us. Cortisol levels commonly peak between 4 and 10 A.M., just before we wake and afterward. This is the time when we are typically most stressed—eager, in a sense, to gear up to tackle the day. Muscle strength is at its peak, heart rates are hastened, blood pressure climbs, and most people think their clearest. This is also the time that most heart attacks occur. As the day wears on and anxieties are overcome by fatigue, the body settles down and cortisol levels fall.

Another hormone manufactured by the adrenal cortex (outer part) is *aldosterone.* This chemical helps us regulate the balance of salt and water in the body. Imagine how your life might be if there were no way to tell whether the concentration of salt in your body was too high or too low—and furthermore, you had no means to adjust it. On any given day you might shrivel up like a prune; another day you might bloat up like a waterlogged corpse.

The inner core of the adrenal glands functions more like nerve tissue. It secretes two hormones, *adrenaline* and *noradrenaline* (also known as *epinephrine* and *norepinephrine*) that play an additional role in controlling blood pressure. Under cold conditions these hormones will cause the blood vessels in your hands to constrict (your hands turn blue, or even white), shifting blood away from the cold and keeping the inner body warmer. These hormones can quickly prepare the body for flight or fight. The pupils will dilate, allowing more light in for better vision or showing the enemy that the person is angry or both; heart rate and blood pressure increase while blood is shunted to the muscles to fight or run away; superficial blood vessels constrict, presumably to lessen blood loss if there's a wound; bowels and bladder evacuate, perhaps to lessen

Simple Glucose–Insulin Feedback Scheme

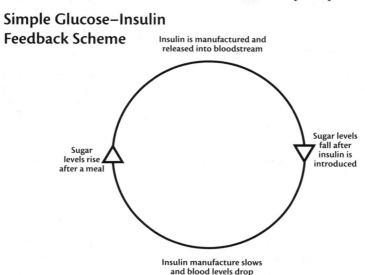

Insulin is manufactured and released into bloodstream

Sugar levels rise after a meal

Sugar levels fall after insulin is introduced

Insulin manufacture slows and blood levels drop

The Manufacture and Use of One Molecule of Insulin

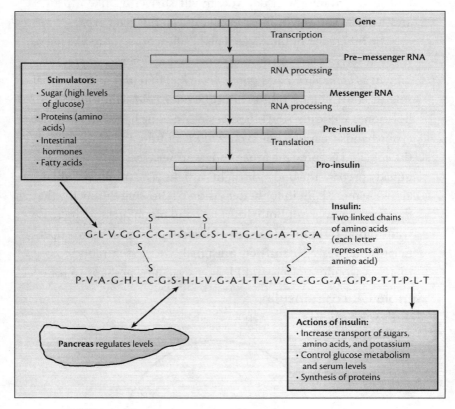

the load or make the individual less desirable prey; sweat pours out to make the person more slippery if attacked; areas of the brain are stimulated for increased arousal and focused attention; and glucose and fatty acids are mobilized for instant energy.

We frequently endure some form of the flight-or-fight reaction in our daily lives. Stage fright is a good example; social phobias are another. Just before giving a speech or sitting down in the dentist's chair, some people will sweat profusely, their blood pressure will increase, their bowels may become overactive, and their heart rate will quicken. They will act as if they were under attack and needed to flee.

Growth and Maturing

Growth hormone comes from the pituitary. It enhances protein synthesis, fat breakdown, sugar metabolism, and salt balance. A shortage results in dwarfism, and an excess causes giantism. Somehow the body knows, under normal circumstances, to grow symmetrically. Most of us grow in similar ways and rates, and we all stop growing at very predictable times.

Prolactin is another pituitary hormone; it plays a role in menstrual cycles and controls milk production in lactating females. It carries information to increase production when it's time to nurse, and it knows when it's time to stop. *ADH* controls water balance. Damage to the part of the pituitary producing it can result in severe dehydration, with the loss of a quart of urine per hour.

Nearly every aspect of our sex life is regulated by the pituitary hormones *FSH* and *LH*. During puberty, they tell the ovaries to increase secretion of female hormones, which leads to breast development, pubic and axillary hair, and menstrual periods. (Humans appear to be the only animals who also go through menopause.) The same hormones in men will cause an increase in testosterone secretion which, in turn, causes voice changes, pubic and axillary hair, and beards. Without pituitary control, there would not be any eggs or sperm; the desire for sex would vanish.

> Every hormone circulating in the bloodstream will fit snugly inside the appropriate receptacle. Imagine a windstorm blowing all the mail for Chicago down a five-mile stretch of the Outer Drive in that city, yet every letter and package is able to sort itself out and end up in the correct mailbox.

Hundreds of different feedback loops are at work in the human body, crisscrossing, overlapping, and interacting with each other all day long. They involve millions of compounds that know exactly how to find their target cells. These cells know what to do with each message. A single cell might receive TSH, GH, LH, and FSH multiple times in the same hour. The endocrine processes often interact with each other. A marathon runner would never finish a race if his insulin–glucose system was working but his pituitary–adrenal gland system was not—nor would a woman ever produce an egg or a man a sperm. Could there have been prehuman species without growth hormone? Could there have existed useless protein molecules that were destined to become testosterone over the next billion years? Or insulin? Nearly all of these hormones had to have appeared simultaneously, along with their target cells and the feedback loops.

Bottom-Line Points

- *Each gland produces specific hormones that carry select messages to target cells.*

- *There are more than 40 hormones, and each one is controlled by a feedback loop.*

- *Many hormones work in parallel or tandem, some compete, and some have double and triple feedback loops.*

- *The pituitary gland is strategically located near the center of the brain where it can monitor all hormone levels.*

- *The body knows how to regulate hormones. Growth hormone is one example: Most of us grow in similar ways and at similar rates, and we all stop growing at relatively predictable times. Both legs match; both hands match.*

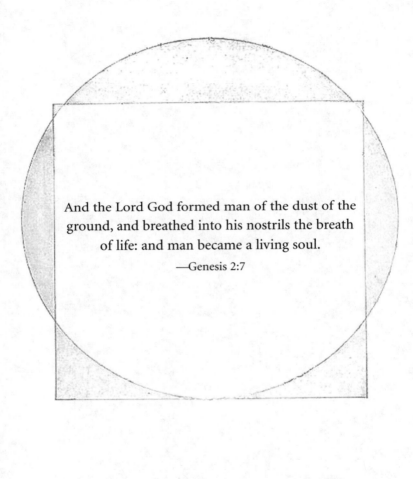

And the Lord God formed man of the dust of the ground, and breathed into his nostrils the breath of life: and man became a living soul.

—Genesis 2:7

15

The Respiratory System

We each breathe about 20,000 times a day, or about eight million times a year. Each breath moves about a half-liter of air; over a day's time that approximates the amount of air in a high-rise building. Over a year's time a person will have sampled all of the air found in their extended neighborhood; during an average lifetime, a person will have inhaled the equivalent of all the air in a small city. A significant amount of what we breathe in is the same air that someone else has exhaled. Theories suggest that we will each breathe, drink, and eat molecules that once belonged to Rembrandt, Einstein, and Magellan.

Plants and trees create a nice balance of oxygen for us; they use carbon dioxide, our metabolic output, for their metabolism, and release oxygen for our metabolism. Without this complementary system, the human race would not have come about—and as the trees around the globe diminish, some scientists are worried this balance may be altered.

Although each person can consciously take in a few extra breaths, hold their breath for a minute, or even exercise some control over breathing during calisthenics, meditation, childbirth, and singing, most of our breathing is automatic. Other than sea mammals and penguins, we may be the only beings that can hold their breath. If this is accurate, why did the primate family lose this ability—or why did we develop it? Why (or how) did the larynx move upward for monkeys, or downward for us?

The brain manages our breathing needs based on whether we are resting or exerting ourselves. Rates increase whenever more oxygen is needed and decrease whenever less is required. If breathing were not automatic, making it happen would monopolize our thoughts. To hike up a hill, we would have to calculate how much faster we would have to breathe, or how deeply, and for how long. And then there would be other calculations for the descent. Every three seconds or so we would have to take in and let out a breath. Even if that were possible during the day, one wonders how a voluntary system could be carried out during sleep. Design?

Physical conditioning plays a role. Healthier people breathe more slowly. That's mostly because strong muscles need less oxygen. A well-trained athlete might run six miles and breathe barely 20 times a minute, whereas a sedentary office worker might find himself gasping for air at 40 breaths per minute after the first mile. If there's a chronic deficit of oxygen, such as exists at a high altitude, the kidneys compensate by secreting a hormone that stimulates the production of more red blood cells. In that way, more oxygen can be carried to the tissues. It's like recruiting extra people to carry a heavy load.

Out with the Bad, In with the Good

The primary role of the respiratory system is to exchange bad air (low in oxygen and high in carbon dioxide) for good air (high in oxygen and low in carbon dioxide)—new logs for the fireplace. Oxygen is critical for almost every chemical reaction in the body.

A partial drop in its level can make a person feel panicky; a sudden, major drop can cause a heart attack; and a prolonged drop can lead to coma and death.

The respiratory center is located in the brainstem and functions using a feedback system. Too little oxygen, it speeds up; too much, it slows down—but the feedback loop is further complicated by internal changes in pH balance. If the kidneys leave too much acid in the bloodstream, the lungs will compensate, blowing off more carbon dioxide, and vice versa.

Evident purposeful design? The air is sucked in by a bellows system—a vacuum created by the contraction of the diaphragm and chest-wall muscles—and then it is exhaled by the recoil elasticity of the lung tissues. Like stretching a rubber band and then letting it go back to its original shape. Air enters through the nose, where it is filtered by nasal hairs (cilia), cleaned by antibodies and killer cells, tested by smell sensors, humidified by mucus, and warmed by the sinus corridors. All of the captured pollen, dirt, bacteria, viruses, fungi, and smog particles are dropped down the esophagus. Cold weather stuns the cilia and causes the typical runny nose.

On average an adult will breathe 12 to 16 times a minute. After the air passes the nasal passages and enters the trachea, it travels outward through Y-branching tubes of decreasing size until it reaches the 150-million-plus alveolar cells and ten billion pulmonary capillaries, where oxygen is exchanged for carbon dioxide. Red blood cells need only one to three seconds to complete the exchange.

> During an average lifetime, a person will have inhaled the equivalent of all the air in a small city.

From the Tip of the Nose to the Tips of the Lungs

There are several appropriate bells and whistles throughout the respiratory system, such as sighing. We all sigh every few minutes. These large boluses of air are needed to pop open sticky air sacs. Millions of cells lining the windpipe catch particulate matter; our windpipe closes whenever we swallow. If the tongue didn't help cover the trachea, we'd choke on every bite of food.

Although yawning signals that someone's tired, it might have a greater purpose. As we fatigue, we don't breathe vigorously, and the yawn makes up the deficit. Sneezing is another automatic response; it explosively eliminates irritating substances at a speed of 100 miles per hour or more. Coughing and choking help expel larger foreign objects that are inhaled by accident.

As air moves down through the trachea or windpipe, it passes through several tough rings of cartilage, among which is the Adam's apple. These rings keep the windpipe from collapsing whenever we inhale. To demonstrate how important this feature is, try sucking a drink through a paper straw with a kink in it. The harder you suck, the worse the kink. Yet the rings are relatively soft and flexible. Were they bone, the human neck would not bend.

As air travels down through the bronchial tubes, it is further cleansed by cells with hairlike cilia, which form a slowly moving escalator service that brings debris back up to the top of the windpipe and dumps it over the side into the esophagus. *Dust cells* traveling within the smallest tubes digest the tiniest particulate matter, then they, too, hop on the same escalator. Scientists estimate that as many as 50 million of these dust cells are sacrificed each day to keep our lungs clean.

Eventually, the inhaled air reaches the air sacs—millions of microscopic bundles of lung cells with capillaries, where the exchange of carbon dioxide for oxygen is easily conducted. Each one of these cells knows how to conduct the exchange. The average adult has a total exchange surface of 70 square meters.

Purposeful design seems evident when one studies the respiratory system. From the moment we take in a breath to the moment we let it go, every aspect of respiration is controlled, monitored, and corrected on a microsecond-to-microsecond basis. With rare exceptions, your body realizes your needs and is constantly adjusting bodily functions. If it were not automatic, your first night's sleep would be fatal.

Bottom-Line Points

- *The body is designed to exchange carbon dioxide, a product of metabolism, for oxygen, the fuel of metabolism.*

- *Oxygen is maintained at very specific concentrations throughout the body.*

- *The epiglottis covers the larynx (windpipe) when we swallow so we won't aspirate our food.*

- *Breathing speeds up when we need more oxygen and slows when we need less. Most of our breathing is automatic; this frees us up for other conscious activities.*

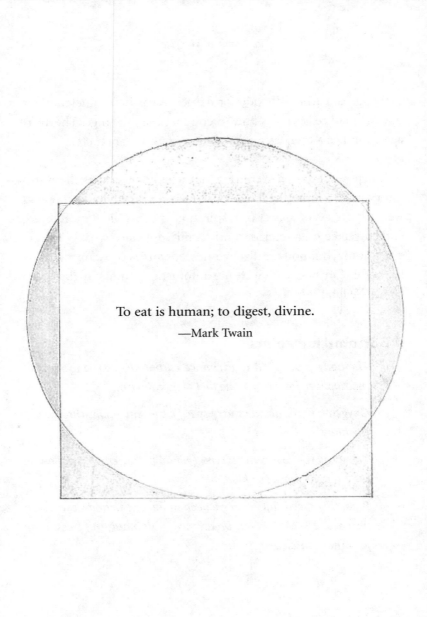

To eat is human; to digest, divine.

—Mark Twain

16

The Gastrointestinal
System

We each spend about three-and-a-half years of our lives eating 25 tons of food, all of which is pulverized, hydrated, analyzed, sanitized, sorted, processed, organized, absorbed, packaged, loaded, modified, distributed, and eventually eliminated by a 30-foot-long flexible cylindrical factory. This seemingly short length is very deceptive. The lining of the small intestine has thousands of *villi* (tiny, fingerlike projections), each of which has scores more of tinier villi. This villi system gives the GI tract the equivalent area of half a basketball court.

The workings of the digestive tract may seem simple. You feel hungry, you eat a meal, you stop eating when full—and later, whatever isn't needed will be eliminated. This description is like saying the Milky Way is a bunch of stars. The breakdown and absorption of all foods and liquids is handled by billions of worker cells—which are regulated by more than 100 million nerve cells and make use of a very long list of chemicals, including ones with such odd names as CGRP, CCK, endothelin-2, and enkephalins. Another 30 enzymes change sugars, proteins, carbohydrates, and fats into their most basic units. All of these compounds and workers know when to start and stop, how and where to work, and how to stay out of each other's way. Hundreds of different kinds of food units are acted upon by millions of chemicals and enzymes, oftentimes in less than a second.

The Gastrointestinal System[7]

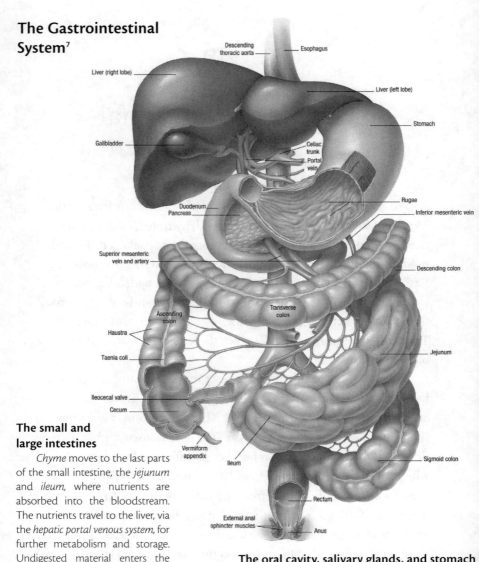

Descending thoracic aorta
Esophagus
Liver (right lobe)
Liver (left lobe)
Stomach
Gallbladder
Celiac trunk
Portal vein
Rugae
Duodenum
Pancreas
Inferior mesenteric vein
Superior mesenteric vein and artery
Descending colon
Transverse colon
Ascending colon
Haustra
Jejunum
Taenia coli
Ileocecal valve
Cecum
Vermiform appendix
Sigmoid colon
Ileum
Rectum
External anal sphincter muscles
Anus

The small and large intestines

Chyme moves to the last parts of the small intestine, the *jejunum* and *ileum*, where nutrients are absorbed into the bloodstream. The nutrients travel to the liver, via the *hepatic portal venous system*, for further metabolism and storage. Undigested material enters the colon, where water and electrolytes are absorbed. The remaining waste is stored until eliminated.

The oral cavity, salivary glands, and stomach

Digestion begins in the mouth as food is mixed with saliva. Saliva breaks down the starch in food into smaller sugars. After moving to the stomach through the esophagus, food is further broken down by enzymes and hydrochloric acid. A layer of mucus protects the stomach lining from damage by the hydrochloric acid.

The smaller units of food are absorbed into the body by diffusion or complicated transport mechanisms. Many nutrients are repackaged and then moved into the bloodstream. Some fats travel alone, and some have carriers. Certain sugars may go directly to the liver or to muscle cells; some absorbed products, like iodine, go to the thyroid; and others, such as water and minerals, go to every cell.

Although every process has multiple, interacting steps, digestion is handled very smoothly. Food substances vital to life are readily recognized and quickly absorbed; unwanted items are passed on as waste; regulated amounts of water are absorbed; and toxic or irritating substances are quickly eliminated.

The stomach secretes about two-and-a-half liters of gastric juice per day, including the very caustic hydrochloric acid and several potent enzymes. This acid can corrode zinc and blister skin, yet the stomach lining remains impervious to it. To protect the stomach itself from being digested, cells along its inner wall secrete a barrier of mucus. There are proteins within this gel that resist degradation also. Could this have come about by mutation?

Eat, Drink, and Make Your Brain Merry

The mere fact that our bodies tell us when we are hungry and when we are not is a very useful design. Imagine how it might be if you couldn't tell you were hungry. You might go days without a clue until you became too weak to feed yourself. What if you lacked a way to know you were full? You might gorge yourself beyond capacity. How would you know if you needed a drink? Lift your skin up to see if it tents?

Knowing when it's time to eat is a given for us, yet the process is very elaborate. Chemical and neurological signals constantly bombard the brain with information about nutritional status. If the signals indicate that sugar or fat levels are low, the brain will create hunger sensations. Over time the desire to eat intensifies, driven by further chemical cues and eventually by stomach cramps. Once hunger is satisfied, the pangs are replaced by the much more pleasant chemical feelings of satiety.

Everyone knows the hungrier you are, the better food tastes. Grocery-store owners prefer hungry shoppers; restaurants count on hungry people ordering more than they can eat. The faster the service, the greater the chance the customer will want dessert. It takes a minimum of 20 minutes to feel full. This delay also causes obesity. Is it poor impulse control, purposefully delayed satiety, or a throwback to prehistoric times when eating too slowly might put one in jeopardy?

The brain constantly monitors the body's state of hydration and relays all changes to the thirst mechanism. No one can consciously sense that their kidneys are not getting enough water or that their blood pressure is dipping, but we all know when we're thirsty. During water shortages, the brain will initiate water-sparing programs, concentrating urine and absorbing every speck of water from feces.

Simple Digestion Feedback Loop

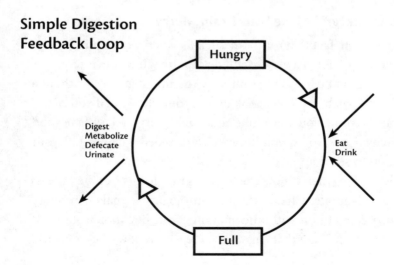

Same Digestion Feedback Loop, Still Simplified

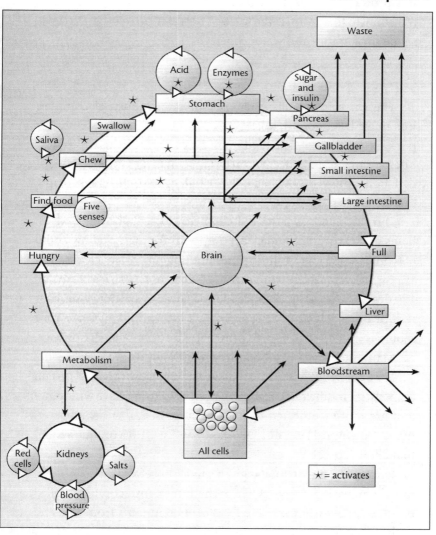

People who try to diet quickly learn that the first few days might not produce any losses. A built-in mechanism purposely slows metabolism to minimize the losses. This reaction may be a survival mode for famines and water shortages.

Can You Stomach It?

The gastrointestinal system acts like an industrial complex. Before we take food in, it is assessed by our security systems. If it passes inspection, it is loaded onto the conveyor belt, where large bites are made smaller, fibers are ripped apart, casings are shredded, bones are crushed, bacteria are killed, seeds are cracked, and everything is pulverized.

Our teeth and jaw are situated in very logical positions, which helps us tightly grasp and crush our food. We each swallow about 600 times a day, half of those times nothing more than clear saliva. We can tolerate temperatures from 10 degrees F. (like ice cream) to 170 degrees (hot soup). Notice that you cannot swallow with your mouth open. This restriction protects the windpipe. Once your mouth is closed, the windpipe is protected by the tongue sliding back.

Many mammals can breathe while they eat. We can breathe while we chew, but not as we swallow. Human newborns and certain animals, including our presumed monkey cousins, have windpipes that are more connected to their nasal passages. Ours, however, moves downward later during infancy and sets up a unique system that allows speech.

Once in the throat, food is given a little shove, and the esophageal muscles move it downward. These rhythmic contractions are called *peristalsis;* they will carry the food or its remnants from one end to the other, always going in one direction. Some of these contractions are so strong that they can overcome gravity, as with a person drinking while standing on their head.

The entrance to the stomach acts like a trapdoor. It opens as the peristaltic waves bring food and water and then closes to keep acid and partially digested food within. Factors such as eating too much, obesity, peppermint, chocolate, and taking certain medications can weaken this trapdoor and lead to heartburn. Under normal circumstances, this door is protective. In similar fashion, the valves in the heart prevent blood from backing up, and those in the legs keep blood from pooling around our ankles.

Seeing, smelling, and even thinking about food will cause the mouth to water and the stomach to secrete gastric juices. They are getting ready. Juices increase as food enters the mouth. Smokers often have stomach problems because putting something up to the lips sends a false signal. When the food actually does arrive, it is mixed with hydrochloric acid and several powerful enzymes that break it down into a mushy, somewhat slimy collection of proteins, fats, sugars, carbohydrates, and vitamins called *chyme*. At the same time, the stomach secretes a hormone to alert the pancreas, small intestine, and gallbladder to begin preparations. It then churns and squeezes this semiliquid material through another one-way valve into the small bowel, where most of the digestion and absorption occurs. The stomach acid and enzymes are also quickly neutralized there.

Nausea is the signal there's something wrong with the food. The trapdoor at the gastric–esophageal junction opens, the esophagus relaxes, and the muscles of the stomach violently contract to cause vomiting. This is a coordinated, well-designed function to quickly rid the body of something it views as dangerous. To think that vomiting is a result of mutation or survival of the fittest is a statistical overstretch—the changes in the brain, stomach, esophagus, and mouth had to have come about together. It is doubtful that a species existed that could partially vomit or that vomited bad things on some days and not on other days. Examples could go on ad nauseum, but it should be noted that vomiting may also be a community protective mechanism. Whenever one person in a group vomits, nearly everyone else vomits or feels like doing it. Presumably, this is an alerting process, telegraphing others nearby that they too may have eaten something dangerous and need to get rid of it. The inner body doesn't know that everyone else may have eaten other places. Design? Coincidence? There are other reasons why we vomit, such as encountering the smell of decaying flesh or certain chemical odors, and because of head injuries.

An Absorbing Topic

When the chyme begins to arrive, the small intestines go into a heightened state of activity. An enzyme called *CCK* is immediately secreted, which helps keep the back door of the stomach, the *pylorus,* tight and causes the gallbladder to contract. Fat-digesting bile cascades down the bile duct and mixes with the food. Further along, 90 percent of this same bile is absorbed and recycled to the gallbladder for another meal. At the same time, digestive juices begin pouring out of the pancreas. They contain bicarbonate to neutralize stomach acid and very powerful enzymes that can break food materials down to their simplest molecules.

The thousands of villi (those tiny finger-shaped brushes with thousands more microvilli) act like millions of hands kneading a long, gooey loaf of bread; they move the chyme along as they tear it apart. Every type of mineral, salt, carbohydrate, protein, and sugar has its unique way of entering the body. For the most part, bacteria were killed in the mouth and stomach, rendering the food safe for the small bowel. A few bacteria are strong enough to survive and make us ill, like salmonella and shigella. We react with vomiting and diarrhea to rid ourselves of them.

Once digestion and absorption are complete, the chyme moves into the large intestine through another valve. It is now called feces. This valve prevents any fecal material from backing up into the small bowel, and the appendix, a much-disputed item in evolutionary theory, might be a sentinel to watch for fecal contamination. Peristalsis slowly moves the thickening feces toward the anus. En route, water is removed, and the fecal material is packaged into little bundles for elimination.

> You feel hungry, you eat a meal, you stop eating when full—and later whatever isn't needed will be eliminated. This description is like saying the Milky Way is a bunch of stars.

Final Issues

Everyone has a reflex that tells the GI tract to have a bowel movement after a meal, typically after breakfast. Children often have to go during meals. Babies will defecate after a bottle. Food stimulates the off–on switch on the conveyor belt, and the old stuff must go to make room for the new.

A newborn baby's colon is void of bacteria—that's why their bowel movements are not smelly. Even the most sensitive of people can usually change a newborn's diapers. That smell changes rather drastically in the ensuing months, however, as bacteria populate the intestines. Most of these organisms probably come through the rectum, but many may arrive with mother's milk. This process may seem to be a random event, but the types of bacteria that ultimately take up residence are quite specific, and a delicate balance is maintained.

Individually, some kinds of bacteria in the bowel can be extremely dangerous, such as the group that causes gas gangrene, but somehow they all keep each other in check. We depend upon many. Bacteria are responsible for making some of the B vitamins needed for good health, and vitamin K for clotting. (Without K we would bleed to death.) Microorganisms also break down indigestible plant products and help absorb cholesterol, which, contrary to media hype, is a necessity. If survival of the fittest is a fact, one might ask why humans evolved away from making their own vitamin K.

The major content of feces is bacteria, quadrillions of them. They turn stools greenish brown, and their byproduct (gas) gives it a foul odor. That repulsive stench may be purposeful, designed to alert us to contaminated food or water. Most human beings can detect the smell of feces diluted one billion times.

A noticeable byproduct of bacterial work is flatus. We pass about one quart of gas per day, in variable volumes and about 14 occurrences. Some styles of release are legitimately labeled—by investigators—*slider, pooh,* and *staccato*. A few people have been shown to pass 20 liters per day, presumably due to an overgrowth of certain bacteria in their colon. Although gas may seem like an absolute waste product, it helps propel fecal material.

The act of defecation is another well-designed, purposeful function, obviously best accomplished by using an independent, rear exit so as not to interfere with other activities. Over a lifetime, a person will defecate four-and-a-half miles of feces (somebody actually calculated this)—30 percent bacteria, 20 percent inorganic material, 20 percent undigested roughage, and the rest fluids. Unlike birds and most other animals, humans can retain stool for extended periods and evacuate it at planned locations. This process may seem simple enough, but it requires the coordination of several muscles. Not only does the stool need to be moved to the rectum and packaged properly, but its presence needs to be sensed; the sphincter, or opening, must remain tight until voluntarily relaxed; and then another set of muscles must expel the waste material. The accumulation of waste material or gas or both needs to exceed 18 millimeters of mercury (.35 pounds per square inch) of pressure. A person can walk around at 17 millimeters (.33 psi) and not know it.

The first part of a meal reaches the end of the small bowel in four hours; undigested portions may enter the colon within eight hours. Today's BM could easily be yesterday's meal. Stress, caffeine, certain food allergies, and an overactive thyroid can expedite the transit time. Medications such as narcotics might lengthen transit times, and antibiotics that kill off certain bacteria can shorten them, but barring a serious illness or an injury, the conveyor belt keeps moving, day and night, slowed or hastened by meals, emotions, and daily habits.

Bottom-Line Points

- *Each of us spends about three-and-a-half years of our lives eating 25 tons of food, all of which is pulverized, hydrated, analyzed, sanitized, sorted, processed, organized, absorbed, packaged, loaded, modified, distributed, and eventually eliminated by a 30-foot-long flexible cylindrical factory.*

- *The breakdown and absorption of all foods and liquids is handled by billions of worker cells—which are regulated by more than 100 million nerve cells.*

- *The appropriate nutrients always find their way to the correct destinations, billions of times a day.*

- *The brain constantly monitors the body's state of hydration and makes second-to-second corrections.*

- *The stomach secretes about two-and-a-half liters of gastric juice per day, including the very caustic hydrochloric acid and several potent enzymes; yet the lining of the stomach is protected from digesting itself.*

- *Vomiting is a coordinated, well-designed function to quickly rid the body of something it views as noxious or dangerous.*

- *We depend upon colonies of 500 or more types of bacteria that individually total in the quadrillions in the small intestine; all of these are controlled, contained, and properly utilized.*

- *The act of defecation is another well-designed, purposeful function.*

- *With the exception of the use of artificial intravenous lines, the body cannot exist without a gastrointestinal tract.*

The best and the most beautiful things in the
world cannot be seen or even touched. They
must be felt within the heart.

—Helen Keller, famous lecturer and teacher
who was deaf and blind

17

The Circulatory System

In your lifetime, your heart valves will open and close more than three billion times. Trillions of red blood cells, white blood cells, and platelets will cycle through this four-chambered organ every day, yet very few will be damaged or sent the wrong way. The blood will be propelled through a complex set of pipelines that will eventually deliver oxygen, water, nutrients, vitamins, hormones, and antibodies to every part of the body—and then, a similar set of pipelines will return the same blood, now bearing carbon dioxide and waste products to the heart. This cycle is repeated every second of life; proper function is critical. There's no dropping off the heart for maintenance every year like a car. This machine fixes itself on the run.

The heart knows to speed up with exertion, stress, or illness, and to slow with rest. It knows how much blood to pump and for how long, and it can make adjustments between beats. Anything less than a perfect response leads to shortness of breath or excessive fatigue. A seven-second pause will result in a loss of consciousness; a four-minute pause is uniformly fatal.

The arteries carry oxygenated (red) blood to every cell, and the veins return deoxygenated (blue) blood to the heart. They travel beside each other like a four-lane highway, interconnected by crisscrossing avenues, streets, alleyways, and paths. The arteries (avenues) come off the aorta (highway) and flow into *arterioles* (streets),

The Vascular System[8]

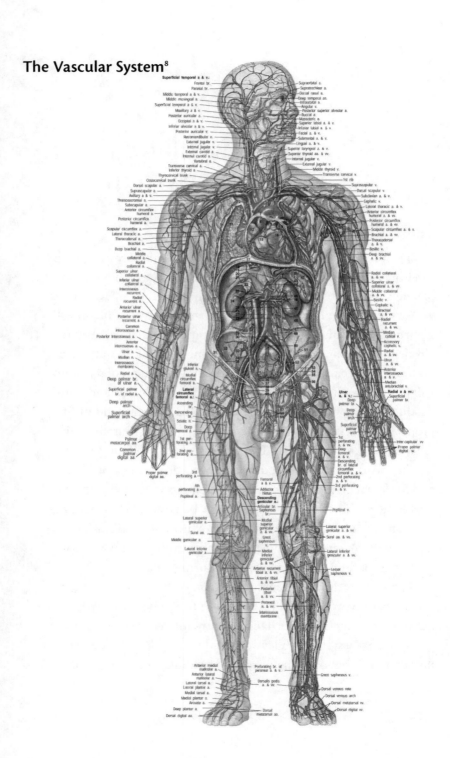

which in turn deliver blood to the capillaries (alleyways) that service individual cells (homes). After red cells have passed through the narrowest channels (paths), they start back through *venules* (streets), which connect to veins of increasing size, then proceed to the huge *vena cava* and ultimately to the heart and lungs again. As the blood is being recycled, the spleen removes old or damaged red blood cells and the bone marrow makes new ones.

As with metropolitan traffic control, some channels can be closed while more-needed routes are widened. There are detours, roadblocks, entrance ramps, exits, underpasses, and overpasses. Even rerouting. After a large meal, blood will be shifted from the extremities to the stomach to aid digestion. During exercise blood will shift to the active muscle groups. If there's been an injury, the body will close nearby blood vessels and reroute the blood to lessen its loss.

The heart has often been conceived as the seat of romance, yet feelings of love probably emanate more from the nose and brain, as noted earlier. Valentine cards suggest that the top of the heart has a derriere shape, but the heart's real shape and size more resembles a person's fist. This is an incredibly resilient organ, withstanding enormous strain day in and day out. It is controlled by interacting mechanical, electrical, and hormonal input. It has multiple backup systems and feedback loops within feedback loops. All accidental?

The Pump That Never Stops

The embryonic heart starts beating by the third week of life. Blood can be seen flowing through blood vessels by the fourth week. By the time a person is grown, this organ will pump 75 gallons of blood per hour and beat at

There's no dropping off the heart for maintenance every year like a car. This machine fixes itself on the run.

least 100,000 times a day. Because it is so critical to life, it is cushioned by the lungs and protected by the rib cage.

The right side of the heart receives blood from the body and pumps it through the lungs to exchange carbon dioxide for oxygen. Blood then returns to the left side, where it is pumped to the body. Each organ will receive a prescribed amount. Both sides of the heart simultaneously squeeze and relax together, acting like a powerful suction bulb; the four valves keep blood from backing up. The heart is also wrapped in a lubricated, cellophane-like sack that keeps it from rubbing against the lungs.

Every squeeze of the heart is initiated by an electrical impulse originating in the upper right chamber. As it travels downward through the tissues, the muscle cells contract in unison. If the brain senses a need for more blood, oxygen, or both, perhaps following an injury, it tells the heart to pump harder and faster. During extreme conditions, a normal heart can reach a pace of 200 beats per minute (usual is 60 to 100 beats per minute). In the "cath lab," electrical wires can race the heart at 600 beats per minute; during times of sleep, the rate may drop below 60. If the origin of the electrical impulse is damaged, another area downstream will automatically take over. If that area is damaged, a third, and even a fourth, backup system is available.

Oxygen needs are controlled by complex feedback systems that know what an individual needs at all times. A marathon runner at rest may be comfortable with a heart rate in the thirties, whereas an elderly person may pass out at this rate. The pulse tends to be faster in children because of growth needs, and slower in adults.

The heart also delivers oxygen and nutrients to its own muscles through the coronary arteries. If one of these vessels becomes blocked by a clot, the muscle downstream dies, causing a heart attack. If, however, the blockage builds up slowly, over months or years, the heart can sometimes make new vessels. It can also shunt blood to another coronary vessel to service some of the same muscle from the other side.

Pipelines to Every Location

Blood vessels carry a variety of nutrients from the gastrointestinal tract to many specific sites in the body: water and salts to every cell, metabolic products to the kidneys, clotting and anticlotting factors to injuries, white cells to infections, and hormones to target tissues. The vascular system also plays a major role in regulating body temperature. Whenever you go outdoors in the winter, your surface blood vessels will constrict, keeping the warmer blood protected deep inside and making your fingertips paler. On a hot day the same surface vessels will dilate, causing you to flush and thereby lose heat. This flushing response is often seen with high fevers as well. Heat literally radiates from one's body. This amazing, self-regulating, life-sustaining, highly complex system requires input or cooperation from nearly every cell.

The smallest blood vessels are the capillaries. They are so narrow that red cells have to pass through in single file. They offer about 6300 square meters of interior surface; if one could split them open and lay them side by side, their absorptive surface would equal the size of a football field. They are semiporous, allowing millions of different-shaped, different-charged, and different-sized particles to pass through holes called *fenestrations*. Specific docks have different shapes and varied unloading equipment. Sodium has a certain way of entering a cell, which is different from that of calcium; cholesterol will pass through a loading dock differently than thyroid hormone; and water passes back and forth by a separate mechanism. When white cells are needed to fight an infection, they slip between the cell walls to attack the intruders. Gas exchange—oxygen and carbon dioxide—follows natural law, passing from higher concentrations to lower concentrations.

Once the nutrients, hormones, vitamins, and oxygen have been absorbed and the cells have dumped their waste products into the bloodstream, the blood starts back to the heart. Some of the return flow is from pushing by the cells behind, but it is mostly due to the suctioning effect of the heart and the contraction of muscles. Every time a person moves an arm or a leg, those muscles squeeze the blood along. Valves inside the veins prevent it from flowing backward.

The lymphatic system is a relatively unknown hero of the circulatory system. It is responsible for draining excess fluid from tissues and for fighting infections. Its channels might be likened to a city sewer system with drains at every corner and a complex underground pipe system. Many lymph channels run parallel to blood vessels; all together they may return as much as four liters of serum-like fluid per day to the bloodstream. Strategically placed lymph nodes guard the channels like sentinels; they harbor infection-fighting white cells that are ready to be launched at a moment's notice. If a cat scratch were to get infected, a nearby lymph node would swell. For unclear reasons, lymphatic channels tend to be favorite routes for cancer.

Contents of the System

There are three main types of cells circulating within the blood vessels: *red blood cells, white blood cells,* and *platelets.* The red blood cells are primarily responsible for transporting oxygen. Stem cells in the bone marrow produce 200 million per day, while the spleen continually removes a comparable number of old and defective cells. (Old is 120 days.) These cells are biconcave spheres—like tiny donuts with indentations rather than holes. They collect oxygen in the lungs, deliver it to every cell in the body, and then bring carbon dioxide back. After they are broken down, they are converted to bilirubin, which is excreted with bile to digest fats, reabsorbed further down the small intestine, and then recycled by the liver.

There are compensatory and feedback mechanisms with blood cell production. If one were to move to a higher altitude like that of Denver or climb a mountain where oxygen concentrations are less, the bone marrow would compensate by making more red cells. Climbers often stay at several base camps at gradually increasing altitudes for up to a week, to allow their bodies—mostly their red blood cell count—to adjust.

A stem cell in the bone marrow goes through several steps to become a mature red blood cell, and if this process were halted at any point, the intermediate cells (stages) would be useless. Can evolution explain how thousands of genes and millions of new proteins might have changed together in such a coordinated man ner? Can survival of the fittest or random mutations explain how a *hemocytoblast* (the first stage) could change into a *proerythroblast,* whose only apparent job is to change (mature) into an *erythroblast,* whose only job is to become a *normoblast* and then a *reticulocyte* and finally a red blood cell that is sent out into the bloodstream? A similar question applies to the manufacture of hemoglobin, the 465-amino-acid oxygen-carrying molecule found with in each red cell. It not only needs a way to grab hold of oxygen (turning blood red), but a mechanism to release it (turning blood blue). Any error in its very complex makeup could render it useless or dangerous. Add in the mechanisms that incorporate into the red cell such critical items as iron, folic acid, and vitamin B-12. All of these systems would have had to evolve at the same time, or else we would have useless red cells floating around in our arteries.

We also have millions of white cells traveling in our circulation. They come in three basic types—*granulocytes, lymphocytes,* and *monocytes*—and each plays a different role in our body's defense system, sometimes acting solely and sometimes in concert. In a case of appendicitis, the number of granulocytes may double or triple as the bone marrow increases production to carry on the fight. In viral infections, such as infectious mononucleosis, the number of lymphocytes may skyrocket.

Neutrophils are the most common kind of granulocytes, and these cells are among the most important warriors. Since their life span may be only six hours, the body is constantly making millions of them. They can function as sentries, combatants, cleanup crew, or all three. Whenever an infection begins, these cells, acting like fire engines, hurriedly leave their stations (the bone marrow) or converge from other blood vessels, penetrate capillary walls by squeezing between blood vessel cells, and go directly to the site of infection. They are drawn by biological 9-1-1 calls (chemical signals) and arrive with a host of biological torpedoes, bullets, and nets. Many are capable of both hand-to-hand combat and chemical warfare. Pus is their battlefield.

Monocytes react in a similar way. Once distress calls are sent out, they pass through the capillary walls, change into macrophages, and begin eating (engulfing) bacteria. These cells can secrete more than a hundred different substances that impact the inflammatory response and clot formation. Some of these cause the pain and inflammation.

Lymphocytes primarily reside in the lymph nodes, spleen, and bloodstream. They are responsible for antibody formation, fighting certain infections, like viruses and fungi, and destroying tumors. Some are called *natural killers;* without them we would not survive to adulthood. Like Doberman pinschers they stand guard at every lymph node, including our tonsils. They monitor changes in all cells and quickly eliminate any abnormal ones, probably protecting us from cancer many times a day.

Cancer Attacked by Killer Cells

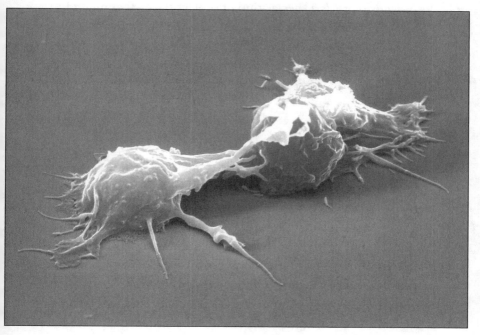

Scanning Electron Micrograph (SEM) of two human *natural killer* (NK) cells attacking a cancer cell. The NK cells have numerous long fluid projections, which are beginning to flow around the cancer cell. NK cells are a type of white blood cell known as *T-lymphocytes*. These have the ability to destroy virus-infected cells and tumor cells. On contact with the surface of a tumor cell, the NK cell recognizes certain proteins called *antigens*, which activate its cell-killing mechanism. The NK cell then binds to and destroys the cancer cell using toxic chemicals. Magnification: x2800 at 6x6 cm size.

A *dendritic cell* is a special kind of protective cell that might be a white-cell derivative; it works closely with the immunity process. These newly discovered cells with very long arms are found in the skin and mucous membranes. Like an octopus they reel in invaders, chop them into tiny pieces, and hand them to the antibody-making cells for easier analysis.

Damage Control

There are trillions of platelets in our circulation at any one time. These are breakaway products from much larger cells called *megakaryocytes*. They function like the little Dutch boy who put his finger in the dike to stop a flood. Without them, the smallest cut could cause us to bleed to death. Their turnover is rapid, with a shelf life of only seven days. Their unique keylike projections fit into specific locks whenever a blood vessel is injured. Less than a second after the injury occurs, platelet keys will be snagged by these locks. This, in turn, sets off a series of very fast-moving events. Nearby platelets become sticky, releasing chemicals that attract more platelets, which join in the pileup of dike-plugging material.

At the same time *fibrinogen* forms a lattice-like structure that captures additional platelets, white cells, and red cells to form a blood patch (an internal bandage). Meanwhile a clotting *cascade*—sequence of linked events—starts. Clots fill in the holes; the whole bandage hardens and pulls the wound together. Within hours to days, work crews arrive to remove the clot, clear out debris, and replace damaged structures with normal tissue. Wide, gaping wounds will fill in with muscle and skin tissue.

The reason why aspirin works to prevent heart attacks is that it interferes with that lock-and-key connection between platelets and the wall of the blood vessel; essentially, the platelets become

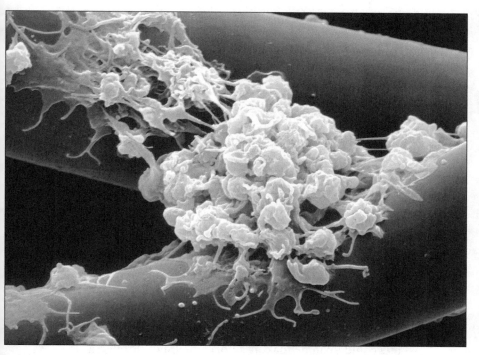

Scanning electron micrograph (SEM) of activated platelets on a cellular filter. Platelets, or *thrombocytes*, are a constituent of the blood formed in the bone marrow. When they encounter a damaged blood vessel they become activated and secrete chemical mediators, including *serotonin*, which cause the blood to clot. The mediators convert soluble *fibrinogen* to the insoluble protein *fibrin*. The resulting fibrin mesh traps platelets and red and white blood cells, forming a plug that seals the damaged vessel. A cellular filter removes cells and other small particles from fluids. Magnification: x2000 at 6x7 cm size.

less "sticky." No one knows how the body is able to confine the clotting process to where it's needed, but without this safeguard, the body would suffer runaway clotting.

The complexity and mutual interaction of injury recognition, bodily responses, clot formation, and wound repair cannot be explained by mutation or survival of the fittest. Everything is just too interdependent. Just the fact that a platelet adheres only to an injured blood vessel is something to marvel at. Also, any blood vessel can spasm shut to lessen blood loss. Without these systems, every mother would hemorrhage to death during childbirth. A paper cut might require transfusions. Tackle football could be a fatal sport. And how does the body know to clot in a selected area only? Proponents of evolution point to clots causing heart attacks and strokes as flaws (meaning not designed), but no one knows if diet, stress, and lifestyle may truly be responsible.

Delivering the Goods

If one could imagine making a horizontal slice through a capillary and then magnifying it ten-thousandfold, the view might resemble the most congested street in Bombay at the busiest hour—yet the carts, cars, trucks, buses, birds, animals, and pedestrians are odd-shaped packages that know where to go and how to get there. A simplified list of passersby at any one moment could include hundreds of white and thousands of red cells, tens of thousands of platelets, millions of oxygen, carbon dioxide, and nitrogen molecules, scores of antibodies to old infections and previous vaccinations, every component of the clotting cascade, anticlotting factors, erythropoietin to stimulate red-cell production, iron, calcium, magnesium, manganese, cobalt, chromium, copper, zinc, nearly every vitamin, numerous proteins and amino acids, salts like sodium and potassium, ammonia, sugar, insulin, uric acid, liver enzymes, prostate enzymes, cancer markers, genetic markers, thyroid hormone, adrenal hormones, ACTH, TSH, GH, FSH, LH, vasopressin, parathyroid hormones, pancreas enzymes, glucagon, somatostatin, all the types of cholesterol, fatty acids, blood pressure–regulating chemicals, muscle enzymes, brain enzymes, hormones that communicate between the stomach and the gall bladder, hormones that communicate between the kidneys and the thirst mechanism, adrenalin, noradrenalin, and albumin. This list is far from complete. Each component is regulated, controlled, and maintained at very specific concentrations. As with an orchestra playing a symphony, every instrument, every note, every pause is perfectly coordinated.

The walls of every blood vessel are lined with millions of biological workers that capture, unload, transport, and modify passersby. There are triangular docks to receive triangular compounds, specific tangled-web ports for specific tangled-web compounds, convoluted ports for convoluted compounds, and electrically charged ports for electrically charged compounds. Some docks are involuted and some protrude. Some have Velcro-like hooks. Some ports are open 24/7, and others only when there's a need. Some items pass through by themselves; others need help.

Evolutionary development would have had to account for each of the circulatory system's characteristics separately and simultaneously to explain the human species. There could not have been blood vessels without a heart to pump the blood or a brain to monitor the heart's work. There could not have been a human being without a circulatory system capable of delivering its goods to every cell. There could not have been blood without bone marrow to produce it or a spleen to remove aging cells. There could not have been a viable human (or indeed any animal) without a way to deliver cellular waste products to the kidneys. The human species could not exist unless millions of extremely unlikely occurrences came about at exactly the right time and in exactly the right manner.

Bottom-Line Points

- *Trillions of red blood cells, white blood cells, and platelets will cycle through the heart every day; yet very few will be damaged or pumped in the wrong direction.*

- *Blood is propelled through a complex set of pipelines that will eventually deliver oxygen, water, nutrients, vitamins, hormones, and antibodies to every cell in the body—and then, a similar set of pipelines will return the blood, now bearing carbon dioxide and waste products, to the heart.*

- *The heart knows when to speed up with exertion, stress, or illness (and how much) and when to slow down during times of tranquility or rest.*

- *The lymphatic system, another complex set of pipelines, is responsible for draining excess fluid from tissues and for fighting infections.*

- *The circulatory system maintains a constant flow of nutrients, minerals, vitamins, waste products, red blood cells carrying oxygen or carbon dioxide, white blood cells for fighting infections, platelets for clotting wounds, and numerous clotting factors. None interfere with each other.*

What is a man, when you come to think
upon him, but a minutely set, ingenious
machine for turning, with infinite artfulness,
the red wine of Shiraz into urine?

—Isak Dinesen (Karen Blixen), *Seven Gothic Tales* (1943)

18

The Excretory System

We drink more than 7000 gallons of fluid in our lifetime, which adds to the total of 2000 liters of blood passing through the kidneys each day. All of this amounts to about 52 million liters over an average life span. Every time the heart contracts, the circulatory system sends 25 percent of the blood directly to the kidneys. This continuous cycle slows at night to allow sleep; it speeds up when we're overhydrated and slows down when we are low in fluids.

Imagine your plumbing dumping all your sewage into your living room. Every biological species has ways to rid itself of its waste products. Or, imagine a city water system that kept re-using the same bath water. If your kidneys were to shut down, you would die within one to two weeks. Diseased kidneys can lead to lethargy, vomiting, confusion, muscle twitches, convulsions, and coma.

Much More than Simple Filters

The two kidneys are located on each side of the spine just beneath the diaphragm. They are about the size of a man's fist and are shaped like a kidney bean. An evolutionist might view these organs as simple filters, but their complexity rivals any other system. They maintain proper hydration and proper salt concentrations, eliminate toxins, clear out wastes, and help control red blood cell production.

Each kidney has 1.3 million filtration units; each is a microscopic ball of twisted blood vessels—miniature pipelines that bring in the "dirty" blood and return "clean" blood. These cells know what to filter, what not to, what should be reabsorbed, and what shouldn't. Some items pass through freely; others are actively removed. In this way, the body's balance of water and salts is tightly regulated. If sodium levels drop, a person may go into a coma. If potassium levels rise too high, a person might die. If a person becomes dehydrated, signals travel from the brain to the colon and kidneys, telling them to absorb every molecule of water. If a person has had too much to drink, the extra water is eliminated. Everyone knows the more you drink, the more you will urinate.

> Imagine a city water system that kept re-using the same bath water. If your kidneys were to shut down, you would die within one to two weks.

The kidneys also monitor red blood cell levels and notify the bone marrow with a hormone called *erythropoietin*. If there's been a blood loss, erythropoietin levels rise. Kidney disease is often associated with anemia because this hormone diminishes. The kidneys are also partly responsible for maintaining calcium and phosphate levels. Too much calcium can lead to kidney stones.

The kidneys and liver are responsible for eliminating toxins (note—many medications are viewed as toxins). The body recognizes they don't belong there and works hard to get rid of them. Researchers and doctors sometimes make use of this function; a kidney infection can be more readily treated if the antibiotic goes out via the urinary system.

If your blood pressure were to fall, your kidneys would release a hormone to retain salt and raise blood pressure. If it were too high, the opposite would occur. This feedback loop is often the target of antihypertensive medications. The kidneys also work with the lungs in maintaining the body's internal pH.

After the blood is filtered, urine collects in the bladder for temporary storage. After 300 to 400 cubic centimeters accumulates, the brain receives a signal (from stretch receptors) that the bladder is full. The message may tell you that you can wait a bit longer, or it may tell you to seek out a bathroom immediately. When you urinate, you may think that you are in control, but the only control you have is giving the okay. The spinal cord and bladder muscles do the rest. If the bladder is infected, it sends out signals (burning sensations) to urinate more frequently, presumably to rid the body of the infection.

Like any factory, cells have their waste products, too—and every organism needs a way to eliminate them. The human race would not have lasted long without a way. All of these complex eliminatory systems had to have developed in parallel, in tandem—not sequentially or in useless forerunners.

Bottom-Line Points

- *About 52 million liters of blood are cleansed by the kidneys during an average life span.*

- *This continuous cycle slows at night to allow us to sleep; it speeds up when we're overhydrated and slows down when we are dehydrated.*

- *The kidneys constantly monitor and control salt concentrations, red blood cell production, and variations in blood pressure.*

- *Without proper waste elimination a person would succumb to coma in a matter of days and die soon thereafter.*

Muscular contraction is one of the most wonderful phenomena of the biological kingdom. That a soft jelly should suddenly become hard, change its shape, and lift a thousand times its weight, and that it should be able to do so several times a second, is little short of miraculous. Undoubtedly, muscle is one of the most remarkable items in nature's curiosity shop.

—Albert Szent-Györgyi, 1937 Nobel Laureate in Biology

19

The Musculoskeletal System

Whether you are walking, talking, or merely moving your big toe, your every action involves a complex array of interacting nerves, muscles, ligaments, tendons, joints, soft tissues, blood vessels, and bones. The brain determines in milliseconds which group of muscles and which support systems are needed and then tells each component what to do, when to do it, for how long, and how to coordinate with the other groups. Every action, in a healthy person, is accomplished with the least waste of energy.

Each movement requires several helper systems to deliver nutrients, remove byproducts of metabolism, maintain balance, measure fatigue, and monitor for safety. It takes several million cells just to move a single finger, and several more million to use a simple tool. Increase that number to a billion or so if one were to use both hands, and then add in another billion for coordination. To know if you can make it through a yellow traffic light, jump into a conversation or catch a thrown ball requires a skill called timing; without it, life would be impossible. No one could play sports; all conversations would be simultaneous talk.

We are born with the eye–ear–brain–hand coordination to read, listen, smell, and feel stimuli and then transpose them into coordinated actions, such as eating a meal or driving a car. When one plays the guitar, the tendons, ligaments, muscles, joints, and nerves

The Muscular System[9]

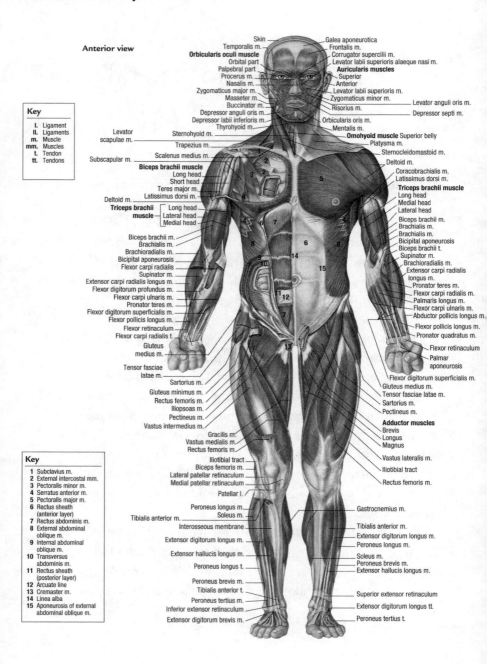

Anterior view

Skin
Temporalis m.
Orbicularis oculi muscle
Orbital part
Palpebral part
Procerus m.
Nasalis m.
Zygomaticus major m.
Masseter m.
Buccinator m.
Depressor anguli oris m.
Depressor labii inferioris m.
Thyrohyoid m.
Levator scapulae m.
Sternohyoid m.
Trapezius m.
Subscapular m.
Scalenus medius m.
Biceps brachii muscle
Long head
Short head
Teres major m.
Latissimus dorsi m.
Deltoid m.
Triceps brachii muscle
Long head
Lateral head
Medial head
Biceps brachii m.
Brachialis m.
Brachioradialis m.
Bicipital aponeurosis
Flexor carpi radialis
Supinator m.
Extensor carpi radialis longus m.
Flexor digitorum profundus m.
Flexor carpi ulnaris m.
Pronator teres m.
Flexor digitorum superficialis m.
Flexor pollicis longus m.
Flexor retinaculum
Flexor carpi radialis t.
Gluteus medius m.
Tensor fasciae latae m.
Sartorius m.
Gluteus minimus m.
Rectus femoris m.
Iliopsoas m.
Pectineus m.
Vastus intermedius m.
Gracilis m.
Vastus medialis m.
Rectus femoris m.
Iliotibial tract
Biceps femoris m.
Lateral patellar retinaculum
Medial patellar retinaculum
Patellar l.
Peroneus longus m.
Tibialis anterior m.
Soleus m.
Interosseous membrane
Extensor digitorum longus m.
Extensor hallucis longus m.
Peroneus longus t.
Peroneus brevis m.
Tibialis anterior t.
Peroneus tertius m.
Inferior extensor retinaculum
Extensor digitorum brevis m.

Galea aponeurotica
Frontalis m.
Corrugator supercilii m.
Levator labii superioris alaeque nasi m.
Auricularis muscles
Superior
Anterior
Levator labii superioris m.
Zygomaticus minor m.
Levator anguli oris m.
Risorius m.
Depressor septi m.
Orbicularis oris m.
Mentalis m.
Omohyoid muscle Superior belly
Platysma m.
Sternocleidomastoid m.
Deltoid m.
Coracobrachialis m.
Latissimus dorsi m.
Triceps brachii muscle
Long head
Medial head
Lateral head
Biceps brachii m.
Brachialis m.
Brachialis m.
Bicipital aponeurosis
Biceps brachii t.
Supinator m.
Brachioradialis m.
Extensor carpi radialis longus m.
Pronator teres m.
Flexor carpi radialis m.
Palmaris longus m.
Flexor carpi ulnaris m.
Abductor pollicis longus m.
Flexor pollicis longus m.
Pronator quadratus m.
Flexor retinaculum
Palmar aponeurosis
Flexor digitorum superficialis m.
Gluteus medius m.
Tensor fasciae latae m.
Sartorius m.
Pectineus m.
Adductor muscles
Brevis
Longus
Magnus
Vastus lateralis m.
Iliotibial tract
Rectus femoris m.
Gastrocnemius m.
Tibialis anterior m.
Extensor digitorum longus m.
Peroneus longus m.
Soleus m.
Peroneus brevis m.
Extensor hallucis longus m.
Superior extensor retinaculum
Extensor digitorum longus tt.
Peroneus tertius t.

Key

l. Ligament
ll. Ligaments
m. Muscle
mm. Muscles
t. Tendon
tt. Tendons

Key

1. Subclavius m.
2. External intercostal mm.
3. Pectoralis minor m.
4. Serratus anterior m.
5. Pectoralis major m.
6. Rectus sheath (anterior layer)
7. Rectus abdominis m.
8. External abdominal oblique m.
9. Internal abdominal oblique m.
10. Transversus abdominis m.
11. Rectus sheath (posterior layer)
12. Arcuate line
13. Cremaster m.
14. Linea alba
15. Aponeurosis of external abdominal oblique m.

to the fingers, hands, wrists, forearms, upper arms, shoulders, and neck work in unison. If a person were to sing along while playing the guitar, a few more billion neurons would be called into service. The number of neurons, muscle cells, chemical reactions, and electrical impulses used during a concert is beyond calculation.

Boats and Anchors

Forty percent of the body's weight is made up of muscle tissue, and there are more than 600 different muscle groups, which can be divided into millions of muscle fibers, which can be further subdivided into billions of muscle cells. These fibers work primarily by contracting and relaxing together. Picture a huge boat with a billion oarsmen pulling a barge in one direction while another boat with a billion oarsmen pulls in the opposite direction. They all work in unison, and they can move at speeds of 70 miles per hour. Nearly every muscle group in the body has such an ongoing tug-of-war between *flexors* and *extensors*. The goal is not to win, but to make the action happen in a balanced and smooth manner. To make a fist, you need to tightly flex all of your hand muscles—but without extensors, you could never open your fist again.

Most voluntary muscles are anchored by tough, fibrous cords called tendons. As they sink into bone, they slowly blend into calcified tissues. It takes enormous strength to break these bonds. In fact, a tendon is more likely to rip than be torn from its anchor. Many tendons are very short, but those connecting to the hands and feet stretch from high up, making our fingers and toes act like puppets on strings.

Both Power and Finesse

Think about lifting a button off the floor. Your action begins with identifying it, deciding if you want it, and judging the work needed—all within a few milliseconds. Millions of neurons are involved before you make the slightest move. Then comes the bending, reaching, and grasping—another billion neurons. Note that you don't fall over, either.

Muscles help us move food through the GI tract, breathe, pump blood, urinate, and defecate. The amazing tongue can shorten, lengthen, fold, narrow, and move side-to-side to lick, move food to the appropriate teeth, and move food to the throat; it also helps shape sounds into comprehensible words. The gluteal muscles are interesting in that they extend the legs for walking and also serve as padding for sitting. Leg, back, and arm muscles all tell us when they are tired and when they are ready to work.

> When one plays the guitar, the tendons, ligaments, muscles, joints, and nerves to the fingers, hands, wrists, forearms, upper arms, shoulders, and neck all work in unison.

There are three kinds of muscle fibers: slow-twitch fibers, fast aerobic fibers, and fast-contracting fibers. They each contract, tire, and use oxygen differently. An Olympic sprinter will have a preponderance of the fast-contracting fibers, which reach maximum speed quickly—whereas a successful cross-country runner will have more of the slow-contracting fibers that are fatigue-resistant.

A motor unit or single nerve controls the action of a specific number of muscle fibers. In larger muscles such as the leg, where action is not so fine, there may be one nerve per 500 muscle fibers. The face, however, requires many more; here, the ratio drops to one nerve cell per 23 muscle fibers. These motor units overlap in muscle bundles, and as one set of fibers is working, others are resting, much like the British soldiers during the Revolutionary War battles; the front lines shoot, and then as they kneel to reload, the second line shoots.

Think about walking, anatomically. As you flex one hip, you need to keep the other leg stiff and well-planted for counterbalance. You then flex the knee, ankle, and foot while pointing the toes. When you start to move forward, you swing your pelvis, swing your arms, and twist your back. Try keeping track of every muscle and joint while you are running or dancing. You can't, but fortunately your brain is designed to do it for you.

The miracle of fine muscle work can be seen in the hands. They are built to grasp a granule of salt, to lift a boulder, and to shave with a razor. Our hands can gesture, sign, defend, injure, kill, save, pull, push, lift, write, scribble, print, pick, scratch, type, play music, tap out rhythm, squeeze, stroke, and caress. If it were not for the opposing thumb, many of these functions would be limited. Curiously, there are no intermediate thumbs in the fossil record.

Expressive Muscles

When Darwin's ten-year-old daughter, Annie, died in 1851, he mourned the loss of "her dear joyous face." For each of us a person's face is their most memorable part—and although each of us can readily recognize someone we know, we all have difficulty describing another person to a stranger. The nose, of course, can be small or large, the lips red or pink, the hair long or short, and the eyes brown or blue, but try describing the face to someone else well enough so they will be able to find this person in a large crowd. Unless there's something very distinctive, like a huge scar, a cultural difference, or giantism, it is virtually impossible. Yet, you would still recognize an old friend or relative after a 40-year separation.

More than 50 muscles about our face and scalp help us express our feelings, protect our eyes, chew our food, swallow the food, whistle, and say whatever. It takes 12 of the 32 muscles in the face

Muscles of Facial Expression[10]

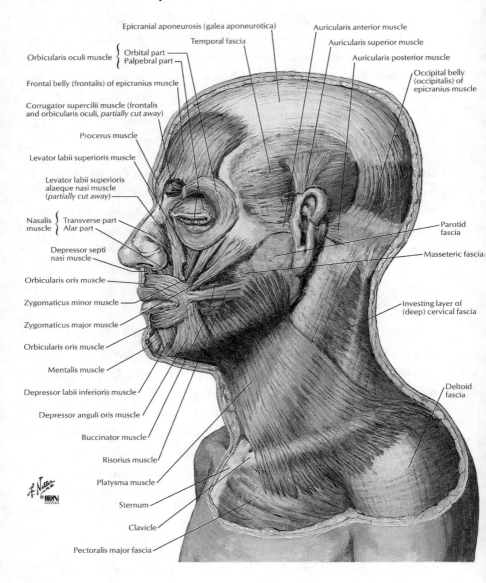

Epicranial aponeurosis (galea aponeurotica)

Temporal fascia

Auricularis anterior muscle

Auricularis superior muscle

Auricularis posterior muscle

Occipital belly (occipitalis) of epicranius muscle

Orbicularis oculi muscle { Orbital part / Palpebral part

Frontal belly (frontalis) of epicranius muscle

Corrugator supercilii muscle (frontalis and orbicularis oculi, *partially cut away*)

Procerus muscle

Levator labii superioris muscle

Levator labii superioris alaeque nasi muscle (*partially cut away*)

Nasalis muscle { Transverse part / Alar part

Depressor septi nasi muscle

Orbicularis oris muscle

Zygomaticus minor muscle

Zygomaticus major muscle

Orbicularis oris muscle

Mentalis muscle

Depressor labii inferioris muscle

Depressor anguli oris muscle

Buccinator muscle

Risorius muscle

Platysma muscle

Sternum

Clavicle

Pectoralis major fascia

Parotid fascia

Masseteric fascia

Investing layer of (deep) cervical fascia

Deltoid fascia

to create a smile—that's two to furrow the brow, two to raise the eyebrows, two to pull one corner of the mouth up and out, two to pull the other corner of the mouth, two to raise the upper lip and flare the nose, and two to pull the lower lip down. Twelve muscles move our eyes.

There are six basic types of facial expressions: enjoyment, anger, fear, surprise, disgust, and sadness—and these, like the primary colors, combine into more than 30 additional possibilities. According to Daniel McNeill in *The Face,*

> These signals emerge in infancy and on a reliable timetable. The smile and surprise appear at birth, disgust and distress (sadness) between day one and three months, the "social" smile at one and a half to three months, anger at three to seven months, and fear at five to nine months. They are almost certainly unlearned. Thalidomide babies born blind, deaf and armless show them.

Much of life's communication is nonverbal, also aided by the musculoskeletal system. The fist is a good example. Held in a certain way it may be grasping that button you picked up from the floor; poised like a boxer's, it can be a threat; held high over the head, it makes a political statement; closed at one's side, it can suggest anger; or held straight out, it can be part of a magician's game. The eyebrow may speak of concern or pleasure. Arms crossed in front of oneself may suggest defiance.

—⟋⟍—

Each person is born with 270 bones, but that number drops to 206 by adulthood, as many of them fuse. Depending on need, bones may be long, short, flat, or irregular. Pound for pound, they are stronger than steel, yet they are much lighter, for mobility purposes. Like steel girders in a skyscraper, their role is mostly for support, but they also have the functions of protection, movement, blood formation, electrolyte balance, pH corrections, and detoxification.

Bones are thickest where the greatest pressures occur, and the most flexible where give is needed. Unlike steel girders, they are capable of self-repair. Some are rounded at their ends to rotate within joints; some are grooved to conduct blood vessels and nerves; some are beveled, like the skull, so that the pieces fit perfectly together; some are centrally porous to contain bone marrow, where blood cells are made (the biological nurseries). The bones in the fingers come in small links that taper down to aid in gripping, the vertebrae increase in width as they descend the back to where the load is the heaviest, and specially shaped structures protect the lungs, heart, brain, and spinal cord. There are no fossils with false starts or bones in the wrong place.

Growing into the Perfect Pattern

Around the fifth week of an embryo's life, pockets of cartilage not much larger than a dot form tiny outlines—matrixes—of each bone. These soft, durable, fast-growing templates act like scaffolding. A DNA blueprint tells the cartilage what shape to form, when, and how fast—and how to coordinate growth with the rest of the body. Growth in the right leg keeps pace with the left, the skull remains symmetrical, the rib cage fits perfectly around the heart and lungs, and the humerus (upper-arm) bone knows which end is which.

The placenta determines how much calcium and phosphorus the embryo needs 24/7 and may actually deplete the mother's reserves if she is not taking supplements. By the twelfth week, calcium can be seen in the cartilage matrixes. The process of adding calcium is called *ossification*, and it will continue until the late teens. The growth plates located on the ends of long bones will know how fast to grow, how to connect to other bones, and how much calcium they need. Growth hormone will determine size and symmetry. An abrupt cessation of growth hormone results in dwarfism, but short stature can also be the result of poor nutrition or injury to the growth plates. An excess of growth hormone can lead to giantism. Goliath may have had an overactive pituitary.

If it were not for the support function of bones, each of us would be an amorphous mound of useless protoplasm worth pennies. The musculoskeletal system keeps us erect so we can reach for fruit on a tree, chase a rabbit, or flee a tiger. Our organs and muscles hang from the skeleton like clothes inside a biological closet, neatly packed into specific corners.

The vertebral column, or backbone, is the central support structure where most of the strength is needed, but pelvis and legs play pivotal roles. Our two-leg version seems to be an ideal design. Three legs might improve balance, but the third appendage would be very cumbersome when walking and carrying out bodily functions. If we had one leg, getting around and maintaining balance would be quite a challenge. A similar logic applies to arms. Where are one-legged predecessors or the one-armed ones? Where are the three-legged failed-species fossils?

Although we lack the durable exoskeleton of a crab, we do have armor. The brain is surrounded by the skull and cushioned by cerebrospinal fluid. This keeps us from banging our brain against the bony interior every time we turn our heads. The heart and lungs are surrounded by a flexible, barrel-like collection of semicircular bones that can expand and collapse with each breath; a woman's reproductive organs are protected by her pelvic bones; and our spinal cord travels through the vertebrae. Nearly every vital organ has a cushion, an overlying bony structure, is located in the least vulnerable area, or enjoys a combination of these features.

The size and shape of feet seem designed for planting on the ground, maintaining balance, and gripping so that the next step can proceed. The specific combination of the hip, knee, and ankle is ideal to step forward or back, hop, jump, skip, limp, slide, dance, climb, turn, and descend. One merely needs to decide what one wishes to do (within reason), and the muscles, joints, and ligaments will do the work.

> Pound for pound, bones are stronger than steel, yet they are much lighter, for mobility purposes.

Mechanical Specialization

There are five basic types of joints: ball-in-socket, hinge, gliding, pivoting, and fixed—and each type is very specifically appropriate for its particular motions. Joints are also protected from wear and tear by softer cartilage interiors and buffering fluids.

The hip, a ball-in-socket joint, allows us to move forward and back, up and down, and side to side, and to rotate. Any other arrangement would not have allowed these options. Hips are not just for walking, however. External rotation and the spreading of the legs allows for frontal sex, ease of urination, and delivery of babies. Flexion allows us to sit; extension gives us the ability to kick or push. The shoulder is another ball-in-socket joint. Without its structure, one could not bring food to their mouth, comb their hair, bathe, play ball, scratch a back itch, hug someone, zip up the back of a dress, or tie a tie. We can reach more than 180 degrees in several directions.

The elbows, knees, fingers, toes, and jaws are hinge joints that open and close like a door. The elbow gives us enormous capabilities to lift and twist items. Imagine how difficult running might be if the femur (upper leg bone) extended from the hip to the ankle. Life itself depends on our jaws opening and closing. The fingers and the opposable thumb would have required major evolutionary jumps. Hands are refined biological tools.

The ankle and wrist are gliding joints, and they complement all actions of the hands and feet. The jointlike attachments that fasten the ribs to the backbone and sternum allow the lungs room to inhale and exhale. Joints and spaces between vertebrae allow us to twist and bend. These spaces are actually flexible discs that also cushion the vertebrae with every step we take.

Each joint is very meticulously suited for particular actions. Imagine a gliding joint at the hip—and how it might give way with every step. If we had a hinge joint at the neck we could look only forward, up, and down. Try writing with stiff fingers. The mechanically correct joint is always found at the correct place.

Bones grow into very specialized shapes. The foot has 26 bones, 31 joints, and 20 intrinsic muscles that work together perfectly and can support up to five hundred pounds. By the age of 85, even an average sedentary individual will easily have clocked 100,000 miles. A farmer may have walked double that distance. Is it only chance that every heel has a built-in cushion?

The skull is a good example of millions of worker cells following a blueprint for growth. What begins as a speck of cartilage becomes a bony casing with properly sized spaces for eyes and nerves, two vertical spaces for the nose, semienclosed areas for the sinuses, temperomandibular joints (TMJ) for the jaw, a tiny hole in the middle for the pituitary gland, a large hole in the back for the spinal cord, and enough space inside for the brain. Nearly every skull is made like a house—with windows, doors, pipes, and grooves. Its shape is very durable—yet if injured, it usually cracks like an egg so as not to damage the brain inside.

Compared to other primates, human newborns have the largest ratio of the skull to the pelvis outlet. Two built-in characteristics help compensate for head size. The baby's eight, nonfused skull bones can be molded, while the ligaments in the mother's pelvis stretch. Both features prevent brain damage to the child and injury to the mother. Later on, the skull bones recover shape and fuse.

Repair, Production, Design

Bones are constantly being remodeled. If a fracture occurs, specialized cells are summoned to repair the injury. Special cells line up along bone surfaces and build bone while other cells secrete enzymes that dissolve unwanted bone.

Bones like the femurs have a hollow center where bone marrow is housed. These are the biological nurseries for red and white blood cells. Stem cells produce offspring by dividing which, after several steps, mature and enter the bloodstream. If there's a dire need, the production rates can rapidly increase.

Every aspect of the musculoskeletal system suggests design—much like a skyscraper reflects the architect's blueprint or a garden showcases the gardener.

Bottom-Line Points

- *Every action involves a complex array of interacting nerves, muscles, ligaments, tendons, joints, soft tissues, blood vessels, and bones. Millions to billions of cells work in unison.*

- *The brain determines in milliseconds which group of muscles and what support systems are needed and then tells each component what to do, when to do it, for how long, and how to coordinate with the other groups.*

- *Every action, in a healthy person, is accomplished with the least waste of energy.*

- *We are born with eye–ear–brain–hand coordination; one could break this down into thousands of components.*

- *Pound for pound, bones are stronger than steel, yet they are much lighter, for mobility purposes.*

- *The DNA blueprint tells the embryo's cartilage templates what shape to form, when to grow, how fast, how to coordinate growth with the rest of the body, and when to change into bone.*

- *Every joint is very specifically suited to particular motions, and all joints are protected from wear and tear by softer cartilage interiors and buffering fluids.*

- *All actions seem to go smoothly.*

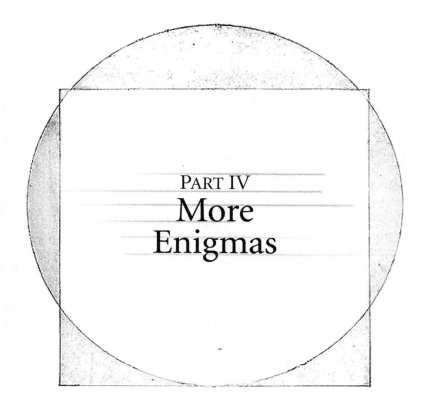

PART IV
More
Enigmas

If it could be demonstrated that any complex organ existed which could not possibly have been formed by numerous, successive slight modifications, my theory would ultimately break down.

—Charles Darwin, 1872

20

Self-Protection

The human body is constantly under attack from within and without, but like a well-built fortress, it is extremely well-defended. The brain acts like a command center, and our senses act like sentries. It takes mere milliseconds for the brain to determine if incoming reports need to be acted upon, stored away, or cast aside. A few more milliseconds, and an action, if needed, is initiated. A hiker, for example, may be enjoying walking through a forest, but his senses will quickly draw his attention to a barking dog or a falling tree. He may be attentive to birds singing, but his focus will immediately be drawn to the sound of approaching ATVs. With rare exceptions, none of us consciously look for danger, but our brain does 24/7.

Multilayered Defenses

A multitude of characteristics enhance the early warning systems, many of which have been noted previously in this book. Just the idea of raising our hands to protect our face, or the fact that we stand erect with our eyes located nearly at the highest point to see farther, are good examples. The eyes help us assess our food and drink. The six eye muscles and a flexible neck give us a near-360-degree horizontal and a near-180-degree vertical view. Our nose and taste alert us to dangers in our food, and our ears warn us of impending, yet not visible, danger. Tactile senses relay pain. Sixth senses tell us if something isn't right and what time it could be.

Our ability to learn from mistakes protects us. Faster than an eyeblink, the brain can analyze "what's wrong with this picture?" If danger is truly at hand, the body goes into biological red alert. Adrenaline is secreted to enhance motor activity as the body prepares to duck, jump, brace itself, kick, punch, or run away. (During shootings, bystanders will automatically fall to the ground. Victims of earthquakes will reflexively run outdoors. Panic, in select instances, can be a very protective response.)

According to Gavin de Becker in *The Gift of Fear,* we all have an innate ability to sense something we should fear. His example of a woman waiting on the fourth floor of a parking structure for an elevator is a good one. When the door opens, a lone man is standing inside. Even though he may be nicely dressed and seem harmless, she senses something—maybe fear—and doesn't enter the elevator.

In most situations, we avoid trouble by talking our way out of it. We all have a gift of gab (some of us more than others). We also have the ability to compromise, bargain, beg, promise, threaten, bribe, make jokes, and raise prayers. We know when to raise or lower our voice; when to add a gesture for emphasis or an action to back up what we say. We know how to consult advisors and research decisions.

Interlocking, Cooperative Systems

Many defenses can be considered a gift, such as the eyes watering so that an irritant will be diluted and washed away, or blinking to keep particles out and squinting in bright light. The nose rids us of irritants by running or sneezing and by trapping particles.

Tonsils trap or kill invaders from the start. The cough is used to get rid of deeper irritants. Antibodies in saliva help kill bacteria (we have 500 different types of bacteria in our mouth). A hiccup may dislodge food stuck in the esophagus. We vomit or endure diarrhea to rid ourselves of tainted food. Excessive urination may be a defense mechanism in a bladder infection. Excessive chatter may be a defense against fear.

We commonly inhale treacherous bacteria, viruses, and fungi, but most of these are trapped by the hairs and sticky mucus in the upper respiratory tract, disabled by antibodies, and eliminated. Harmful bacteria may enter our gastrointestinal tract every time we eat, but most are promptly destroyed by the hydrochloric acid in our stomach. Those that pass are either controlled by residing bacteria or destroyed by antibodies in the small intestine. Any child who picks his nose or sucks her thumb may be inoculating dangerous bacteria, yet the body destroys these organisms before they get a foothold. Every time we brush our teeth, we inoculate bacteria through the broken gum surface into the bloodstream, but they are dispensed with rather quickly. Intercourse traumatizes mucous membranes, but the surface bacteria never penetrate deep enough to cause problems.

> A hiker may be enjoying walking through a forest, but his senses will quickly draw his attention to a barking dog or a falling tree. He may be attentive to the birds singing, but his focus will immediately be drawn to the sound of approaching ATVs.

We protect ourselves from low oxygen conditions by quickening our heart rate and increasing production of red blood cells. If there's been a fluid overload, the heart secretes a hormone that makes the kidneys eliminate more fluid. If we're low in fluids, the kidneys lessen excretion and the bowels absorb more fluid.

To protect us from overheating, the body sweats, redirects blood flow to the surface to lose heat, and stimulates a person's thirst mechanism in compensatory ways. The body seems to know how much water to drink without formally calculating water deficit. When it's hot outdoors, we sweat—and this, in turn, cools us as it evaporates. Sweat may also make us slippery and less vulnerable to prey—part of the biological alert system. Cold temperatures are handled by shivering, which produces heat, and the constriction of blood vessels to keep heat inside.

If we touch something that is too hot, too cold, or too sharp, pain sensors immediately inform us and we reflexively pull away. If cells are injured, they secrete *bradykinin*, which irritates nerve endings, causing intense pain. Bright light causes our pupils to constrict, and dark conditions cause them to dilate so we can find our way more safely. Eyebrows protect us from glare, and the orbital bones protect us from potentially blinding blows to the eye. Earwax may protect us from mites and loud sounds. Hair on the top of our head may protect us from sunburns and keep us warmer in the winter.

If there's been an accident and major blood loss, the body causes the injured blood vessel to spasm, closing it to lessen bleeding, and it simultaneously shunts blood to vital organs for survival. One can live with a poorly perfused extremity or a nonfunctioning kidney for an extended period, but not with a nonfunctioning (poorly perfused) heart or brain. The body seems to have different levels of defensive reaction to various kinds of injuries and different degrees of damage, protecting the most important centers until the last.

Neutralizing the Enemy

Toxins are another threat to the body, and a mere list of harmful chemicals could fill a book. They are carried by food, drink, or air; they can also be secreted by microorganisms living in our intestines or within a wound. Those that enter through the gastrointestinal tract are usually neutralized and eliminated by the liver. Others that make it into the circulatory system are neutralized by bony tissue, excreted by the kidneys, or exhaled by the lungs. The toxins produced by microorganisms may be neutralized by antibodies found in the nose, saliva, stomach, small bowel, skin, lymph nodes, bone, liver, or blood vessels.

Unchecked, some toxins, such as that of tetanus, can be fatal, but most of the time we can neutralize the problem. How the body recognizes a toxin it has never seen before and then disposes of it remains a mystery. The same is true for medications. Digitalis is a common heart medicine—and the kidneys, never having seen this compound before, know how to dispose of it. That's why heart patients have to take digitalis pills every day to keep blood levels up. Nearly 100 new medications are approved each year by the FDA, yet the body seems to have some way to deal with each one.

As with a well-defended fortress, internal security also needs to be maintained. Instead of wearing photo IDs, however, our cells carry *major histocompatibility complexes* (MHCs) on their surface. These essentially say "I'm self." If a tumor cell lacks the right MHCs, it will, under most circumstances, be destroyed by the immune system. If viruses or bacteria enter a wound, they are immediately recognized as nonself and will be attacked. Every kidney or heart transplant would be rejected if it were not for medications that block the immune system.

The placenta lacks these MHCs, and so the mother's immune system does not attack the embryo. Instead, she passes on her own immunity as well as "herd" immunity—immunity shared by the entire group. These antibodies can protect the child for three to twelve months. Mothers who breast-feed will also pass on a type of antibody that helps protect the baby's intestine.

Our skin (the fortress wall) acts as a protective barrier from infections. Trillions of potentially dangerous microorganisms are present in the environment, yet the vast majority merely linger on our skin like passengers sunning themselves on the deck of a cruise ship. Pathogens are kept in check by antibodies, sealed entries, and constant sloughing. Uncountable numbers of bacteria reside in the nose, mouth, colon, rectum, and vagina, yet they are kept in check by cellular defense mechanisms, pH balance, and layers of mucus. A breakthrough by certain organisms could be fatal, but this rarely happens. We live within a structural and chemical fortress.

> Trillions of potentially dangerous microorganisms are present in the environment, yet the vast majority merely linger on our skin like passengers sunning themselves on the deck of a cruise ship.

If intruders penetrate the skin or a mucous membrane, they face a second, a third, and sometimes a fourth line of defense. If a person were to cut herself with a dirty blade, bacteria from the skin and knife would be injected. They could quickly cause a very serious infection, but nearby cells would readily recognize the danger and send out distress signals. White cells would come by the millions from all over the body. If the invaders were known, antibodies would follow. If they were new, a new set of antibodies would be made. If they were certain viruses, interferon might be secreted to block their replication.

If intruders are relatively harmless, the white cells can usually dispense with them quite easily. If they are virulent, a war ensues. An abscess is a kind of battlefield, strewn with cellular and bacterial casualties. For unknown reasons, the body knows how to point an abscess toward the surface to drain properly. A pimple is a common example.

Destructive Memories

Our immune system has an incredible, protective memory, but who wants to suffer from a disease if immunization will spare us? Vaccines make use of normal immune function, simulating the disease with a toned-down version of an infective agent. A child who has had whooping cough or the DPT vaccination ought not contract the disease again (there are exceptions). The same is true for measles, mumps, rubella, polio, and certain kinds of hepatitis.

The immune system also watches out for cancerous changes. Every day, cells mutate into pre-cancer or cancer cells, perhaps due to aging, toxins, or radiation, but they are quickly recognized and destroyed. The reason why a rare cancer cell may gain a foothold is a subject of controversy, but present theories suggest there is some failure of the surveillance system. Perhaps the immune system has aged.

The memory to make antibodies resides in the *B-lymphocytes,* which, like sentry soldiers, stay on constant alert. They patrol the entire circulatory system but tend to gather in the lymph nodes in the neck, armpits, midchest region, abdomen, and groin. Once an intruder breaks through, lymphocytes make antibodies. They can recognize up to one million different types of invaders, like a talented group of musicians who know the scores to a million songs. The moment the first three notes are heard, one of them can play the rest—and soon, the other musicians join in.

B-lymphocytes are only one facet of the guard system. *T-lympho-cytes* also help destroy invaders. *Neutrophils* do the hand-to-hand combat; *macrophages* engulf and digest bacteria; and they all communicate with walkie-talkie chemicals called *cytokines.* They can send for reinforcements and report their status. A fever will lessen the bacteria's chance of survival since certain invaders can live only within a very narrow temperature range. The body also withholds iron, presumably to slow bacterial growth.

The hand-to-hand combat involves a type of chemical warfare that can make use of many inflammatory compounds. The white cells also carry *complement,* which, like microscopic grenades, can punch holes in the sides of invaders.

Mental Defenses

On a psychological level, we have multifaceted, complex mental barriers to threats. We can rationalize that a person didn't mean it. During a crisis, denial helps some folks. *If it didn't happen, it can't hurt me.* We blame our troubles on someone else, such as thinking our debts were really caused by our business partner. We can physically and mentally withdraw from something that may seem too painful. We can try to befriend a perceived enemy, try to bargain, try to compromise. Some of us can find peace in prayer, or tranquility through meditation, an exercise program, or helping others. We can run away, stand up and fight, threaten action, or put on a poker face and act as if we are not at all worried. Our minds and bodies tell us when it's time to rest or take a vacation.

The body can anticipate, respond to, and destroy most pathogens (bacteria, viruses, fungi), most cancerous changes, and most toxins in an orderly and decisive way. Responses are complex and sustained. Immunological memories of these intruders can last for one's life. Could the presumed evolving species preceding man have learned to respond to each of these separately? How does the body know how to eliminate one medication through the kidneys and another through the liver, when most medications (toxins) are twentieth-century discoveries (100,000 years after man is thought to have arrived)?

Bottom-Line Points

·   *The human body is constantly under attack, but like a well-built fortress it is extremely well-defended.*

·   *The brain is the command center, and our five-plus senses act like sentries.*

·   *A myriad of features enhance, monitor, and support the early warning systems.*

·   *We are protected by a number of automatic reflexes—such as pulling a hand away from a burning object or blinking an eye when a ball comes too close—long before the thought of action has consciously registered.*

·   *The immune system constantly monitors for intruders and quickly goes into a destruct mode.*

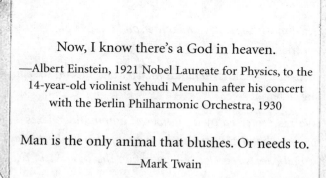

Now, I know there's a God in heaven.

—Albert Einstein, 1921 Nobel Laureate for Physics, to the
14-year-old violinist Yehudi Menuhin after his concert
with the Berlin Philharmonic Orchestra, 1930

Man is the only animal that blushes. Or needs to.

—Mark Twain

21

Gifts

Bob Barron, an artist, can make you look like me and vice versa with silicon molds, real woven hair, color-perfect makeup, and a magical artistic touch. After working 20 years in the CIA as one of their premier disguise experts, he turned his talents to helping people with disfiguring injuries. He can restore any congenitally malformed nose or ear, make damaged hands or fingers look normal, replace a lost eye with a real-looking eye, and give people with terribly burnt faces a mask that very closely resembles their previous appearance. Some of these injured people have been recluses and suicidal; after his work, they have been able to return to reasonably normal lives. When ABC's *Primetime* featured his talent, they showed how, with prosthetics, he had changed a Pakistani woman who had been blinded and whose face had been mutilated by an irate, jealous husband into her normal pretty self. His work is unmatched by anyone in the country. This is not something he merely learned to do. If so, there would be many Bob Barrons. Instead, there had to have been an underlying genetic ability—a special gift.

Jeanne Boylan is another gifted artist. She is known for profiling the faces of America's deadliest criminals. After interviewing people who have been victims of horrible crimes, getting to know their thoughts, and analyzing what they say they have seen, she is able to draw the faces of the perpetrators with incredible accuracy. She is known for the uncanny drawings of the Unabomber, the Polly Klaas murderer, and John Doe II in the bombing of the federal building in Oklahoma City.

According to Kenneth Jon Rose in *The Body in Time*, Truman Henry Safford, born in Royalton, Vermont, in 1836, was the kind of child prodigy who is known as a lightning calculator. Safford could sweep his eyes across a countryside and, in a flash, count every fence post—sometimes totaling in the hundreds. He once multiplied 365,365,365,365,365,365 by itself in his head, and at the age of 18 he graduated from Harvard with honors. He also discovered several nebulae because he could remember the positions of all the stars in the *Nautical Almanac*.

Contradictory Abilities

In *Extraordinary People*, Darold Treffert described several *idiot savants*,* including an "idiotic musical genius" called Blind Tom, who had a vocabulary of fewer than 100 words and a musical repertoire exceeding 5000 pieces. His story began at a slave auction in 1850, when his mother was sold to a Colonel Bethune. Tom was her fourteenth child and, being "useless" (blind and retarded), he was part of the deal for no cost. By age four, Tom could play complex pieces on the piano after overhearing the Colonel's daughters playing their lessons. By six, he could listen to any musical piece and then play it through note for note, accent for accent, without error and without interruption. At age seven, he began performing

---

* According to Webster, "A person affected with a mental disability (as autism or mental retardation) who exhibits exceptional skill or brilliance in some limited field."

concerts and made $100,000 for the Colonel (many millions of dollars in the present-day equivalent). A contemporary panel of 16 music experts in Philadelphia said he had a capacity ranking him among the most wonderful phenomena in musical history. At age eleven, he performed at the White House.

Alonzo Clemons is a master at sculpting. His works sell for as much as $45,000. He was normal at birth, but in 1959 he suffered a severe head injury. He was three then, and the accident left him with a subnormal IQ of 40. No one knows if his talent was genetic or acquired, since he had shown some unusual skills with Play-Doh previous to his injury. As an adult, Alonzo's talent is readily evident. According to Dr. Treffert, "In a single setting he can produce a horse, gorilla, and wildebeest. He kneads and presses the clay with his hands to initially form the sculpture and then uses his fingers to create the finer features and his fingernails for the minute etching and markings that characterize his works." He can copy almost any two-dimensional picture into three-dimensional sculpture and has never had an art lesson. Whenever he is asked how he does his sculptures, he always replies "hands," or "God gives talent."

And then there's Leslie Lemke, born in 1952 and adopted out. Treffert says this man is the most remarkable idiot savant he has ever met. Although Lemke suffered from blindness, cerebral palsy, and retardation as a child, he could play thousands of songs on the piano from memory and sing in multiple languages. He never practiced and never needed lessons. For years he played concerts and recorded albums. He was called a *prodigious savant,* a term that is used whenever a retarded person's skills far exceed those of normal prodigies. He was featured on shows such as *60 Minutes;* he could repeat an entire day's conversations, word for word, inflection for inflection. Every song he had ever learned was stored in memory for life, and notably, he played with only nine fingers. The last digit on his left hand was useless.

What Do We Mean by "Gifts"?

Where do these gifts come from? No one knows. There are theories about one side of the brain being larger than the other, or that we all have these potentials and they emerge in only some people following trauma or illness. Another pertinent question is, who is gifted? The answer to this question may vary from generation to generation, culture to culture, race to race, religion to religion, and even hobby to hobby. Some of the most gifted people from the past include Michelangelo, Beethoven, Mozart, Rembrandt, da Vinci, Galileo, Lincoln, Einstein, Ansel Adams, and Martin Luther King.

> Where do these gifts come from? No one knows.

Those from the present include Itzhak Perlman, Tiger Woods, Bobby Fisher, Stephen Hawkings, Celine Dion, Andrea Bocelli, the Williams sisters, Kitaro, and Yao Ming.

Then again, what are gifts? Are they heightened intelligence, ability to act or sing, or agility on the playing field (plus a little publicity)? Can ordinary people be gifted too? If a car mechanic is the best mechanic in the state, is he gifted? If a CEO can take a corporation from red to black ink honestly, is she or he gifted? Is a person who jumps into a raging river or runs into a burning building to save another person's life gifted? Are the scores of firemen and policemen who raced into the World Trade Center towers after the 9/11 attack gifted? Many would think that they were. I certainly do. Gifts may vary from being a professional gem cutter to being a terrific mom to simply being kind to strangers.

Many of us use the word *gift* rather loosely. If my child draws pictures well in school, I might call her skills a gift. You might not.

If a young man sings beautifully in the church choir, we might all agree he has a gift. Are good looks and a shapely body gifts? Is the ability to counsel emotionally damaged children a gift? Who's to truly say who is gifted—where's the standard? In my mind, each of us has a large number of unlabeled gifts.

Far Beyond Mere Survival

If becoming a "gifted" painter is merely the luck of the genetic lottery, then one must wonder why people can paint at all. Being able to paint a water scene, sing an aria, win a debate, or test a complex hypothesis cannot easily be attributed to survival of the fittest. The human race has gone beyond competition for mere survival. If one were to assume that gifts came about by a genetic accident, then one would have to explain how millions, if not billions, of extremely compatible neurological changes simultaneously came about in the brain and spinal cord. According to Dr. Richard Restak in *The Secret Life of the Brain,* during the first few weeks of life, 250,000 neurons form in the brain every minute and then migrate farther and farther out to find their niches. The distance, and the precision with which each neuron travels, are comparable to a person walking from Los Angeles to New York City and finding the correct office suite, all without benefit of a map. Within a few weeks at this stage of growth, billions of neurons arrive at their correct addresses, at the right time, and make thousands of connections. Our cross-country traveler would also have to have known everyone within a square block of downtown Manhattan. Extraordinary skills like these don't seem to be the results of accidents.

The encyclopedia is full of the names of people who have or had exceptional gifts, yet the question lingers as to whether we all have gifts. Other mammals don't harmonize, draw portraits, or paint murals. No living species, as far as we know, celebrates another's accomplishments, mourns the dead (except maybe elephants), discusses politics, or contributes to charity. No untrained animal would jump into a raging river or race into a burning building to save a total stranger's life. Yet some of us who are not paramedics or firemen may jump into a river or race into a burning building to rescue strangers. Aren't these gifts?

Gavin de Becker's *The Gift of Fear* strongly argues that fear is a gift that keeps us out of danger. Can love be a gift too? Can deriving an insight or offering assistance be gifts? These are abilities that widely separate us from animals.

Anatomical–Physiological Gifts

There are an extensive number of anatomical and physiological attributes that may also be considered gifts. The five senses stand out. Without them, our survival as a species would be in peril. The ability to run and hide or to stand up and fight is a skill that might be a gift. Survival depends on these, too. What about the ability to hold our breath—when underwater, or to avoid inhaling foul or dangerous scents? We seem to be the only land animals that can do this. As far as we know, only humans have the ability to converse abstractly, and according to Ian Tattersall, "Humans had a vocal tract that could produce the sounds of articulate speech over a half million years before we have evidence our forebearers used language." If true, then how would one explain speech on the basis of survival of the fittest? Our flat, naked faces seem to make conversation and communication much easier.

Among the numerous examples of anatomical gifts, the eyes, ears, and nose are commonly cited. The hymen is not. Its purpose is to protect the birth canal and reproductive organs from injury or infection, yet this membrane is constructed in such a way to allow the loss of menstrual blood. Could there truly have been any in-between models? The rectal and bladder sphincters are also overlooked. These are not simple open-and-close orifices. Without them we could never control urination or bowel movements. Are compatible genitals and pleasurable sex gifts? Without genitals that interact perfectly and the sensory–hormonal pleasures that encourage intercourse, would the human race be here? Is mother's milk a gift? Through it a child is given immunity to diseases and a very balanced meal for growth and development, much more so than anything man has yet to come up with. Was there such a thing as an intermediate breast milk?

What about menopause? With the exception of the pilot whale and maybe the elephant, which stops having babies at age 55, this change is uniquely human. Menopause could be considered a gift, not because a woman will be free of periods, but because she won't have to raise children at an advanced age. Grandparents will readily admit that sending their grandchildren home at night is a relief. Raising children requires enormous amounts of time and energy— something the younger folks have. This inability to conceive also benefits the children too. Having older parents lends itself to being prematurely orphaned.

Menopause is clearly programmed into all women's genes and occurs around age 52, when the ovaries stop making estrogen. It may be a progressive change. At 34, women are 85 percent less fertile than they were in their 20s, and this percentage slowly changes with the years. In their 40s women will notice changes in stamina and sleeping patterns. By 52, on average, most menstrual periods cease. Men undergo a similar phenomenon, which is called *andropause.* Not only do sperm counts drop, but by 40 many men suffer from erectile dysfunction. That number steadily increases with advancing age. Are we purposefully designed not to bear children at a later age? There's some logic to it.

Can the capacity to feel pain, just as with fear, be considered a gift? On the surface one might argue that anything that hurts can't be good, but a closer look reveals much more. If you were to touch a candle flame, you would quickly pull yourself back to prevent further damage. You would also forever remember that fire hurts. If you were to step on a tack, you would quickly retract your foot to lessen the depth of the wound. What if you were to look directly at the sun? Does eye pain warn you to look the other way and never do it again? Does a loud siren tell you to cover your ears? What valuable lesson is learned if steaming hot soup burns your tongue? Are these warning signals gifts?

> During the first few weeks of life, 250,000 neurons form in the brain every minute and then migrate farther and farther out to find their niches. The distance, and the precision with which each neuron travels, are comparable to a person walking from Los Angeles to New York City and finding the correct office suite, all without benefit of a map.

Our body uses pain in a variety of ways. It tells us if a body part is damaged and warns us to take precautions. For example, a sprained ankle or a sore knee tells you to stay off that limb. Different bellyaches may indicate you're hungry, you need to have a bowel movement, you have gas, or you need to see a doctor. Pain catches our attention and demands a response. Without it, we would not know which part of our body is in danger or already injured. Pain is also weighted with meaning. Having a kidney stone and giving birth to a child bring comparable degrees of pain—and yet no one wants another kidney stone, but a woman might want another pregnancy.

And what about endorphins? Chemically, they resemble narcotics (pain killers), and they are brought into play with every painful event. Stress will reduce their concentrations; humor will elevate them. Athletes get a "high" or sense of well-being with exercise that is due, in part, to increased endorphins.

Intangibles

We share many anatomical gifts with other creatures. But even though we all have the capability to breathe, pump blood, extract oxygen, exhale carbon dioxide, chew and digest food, eliminate waste, fight or run away, gain muscle strength through repetitive use, grow with symmetry, reproduce, resist infection, heal wounds, and use the five senses to track down food, human beings have so much more.

Laughter is one of these. Even though an explanation of the phenomenon has been tackled by many texts, articles, research projects, and professional comedians, the causes of laughter (and the reasons why we laugh) remain complex and quite elusive. Researchers have, however, shown that women, on average, laugh more at men than men at women; we laugh more when something obnoxious happens to someone we dislike than to someone we like; speakers often laugh more than their audiences, using laughter for punctuation; without realizing it, people often add laughter to their speech at points that are not funny. Humor can be malicious or comforting. It can lessen pain. Women laugh more than men, but men can get laughs easier.

Is insight a gift? It may be uniquely human. When your child acts lethargic, is it helpful to wonder if they might be ill and you should check their temperature? If production has slowed at the factory, does insight into a variety of potential problems lend itself to a fix? Does insight help psychologists and pastors counsel troubled families?

What about language? By the age of two, a normal child knows 20 words; by three, 100 words; and by six, 20,000. By age three, children can make plurals and use tenses correctly. By five, they have learned the general rules of a language.

Paralanguage is another gift and a very strong component of communication. The term refers to what we say or communicate without actually saying it, or how we augment whatever we're saying to give it a different connotation. Consider word substitutes, inflections, talk coordinators, semi-noise, a smile, a tilt of the head, a wink, a glance in the other direction, a glare, eyes rolling up, a sigh, pauses, false smiles, snorting, moving closer, moving back, pinching, shaking a hand, a finger wave, hands on hips, crossed arms, the victory signs, pouting, yawning, stares, clapping, lip biting, lip smacking, jaw clenching, and fist-making.

What does a shrug tell you? Or a shrug with a smile? Or a shrug with a sneer? What does a wink mean from an admirer, or a loud sigh from a child you are chastising? Eyebrows can express anger or doubt. A smile can be friendly or threatening. According to psychologist Simon Baron-Cohen, the eyes can convey interest, calm, trouble, tenderness, callousness, certainty, uncertainty, reflection, thoughtlessness, seriousness, play, sadness, happiness, attention, inattention, dominance, submission, friendliness, hostility, desire, hate, trust, distrust, alertness, fatigue, sincerity, surprise, knowledge, anger, and forgiveness. According to Daniel McNeill in *The Face*, the eyebrow is the great supporting player of the face, and its work generally escapes notice. It helps signal anger, surprise, amusement, fear, helplessness, attention, and many other messages we usually grasp at once.

Our face and our different ways of communication are gifts. The face is the most identifiable part of each of us, and although we can readily recognize a familiar face by skin color, texture of hair, and certain features, we mostly recall expressions.

To communicate or emphasize messages we often use props such as lipstick, powders, orthodontics, dermabrasions, Botox, collagen injections, surgery, tattoos, jewelry, colognes, perfumes, hats, brief-cases, biking apparel, flashy cars, and clothes. We use these props to hide self-perceived ugliness or enhance beauty. Our exterior is a message. What's the message when a woman wears a revealing top—or a high-button blouse? What is a muscular man who wears short sleeves in the winter telling us? What's the message when a very obese woman eats only salad for lunch? Is she on a diet, show-ing us that even when eating low calorie meals she has remained overweight—or just that she likes salads for lunch?

According to Bruce Bower in *Science News* magazine from July 7, 2001, within a few hours of birth, babies will copy smiles, frowns, and other expressions. Newborns will stare at pictures of their mother much longer than at pictures of strangers. Within days they will prefer attractive faces over unattractive faces. There's no partial-ity if the faces are turned upside down, but there is a preference for visual novelty—as if the child has learned when it's time to move on. Babies also prefer human head silhouettes over animal silhou-ettes. A small area in the brain behind the right ear seems to hold the key to remembering faces. A person with an injury in that spot will not recognize old faces or remember new ones. And it's not just faces. This area helps us distinguish between different cars and between various bird species. The nature of face recognition remains a heated subject among neuroscientists.

Is it a gift that we all look almost alike? Is it a gift that we don't look exactly alike? How much fun would a basketball game be if every player on the court looked and played alike? And what if their parents and everyone else in the audience looked alike? We need

strong similarities and relatively minor but distinctive differences
to enjoy life and give it some variety. If every male were Tiger Woods
or Michael Jordan, these sports would be boring.

No one can prove that human anatomy, physiology, attributes,
or skills are gifts. The answers lie in one's own belief system. If that
belief system is evolution, then one needs to ask if all of these attributes could have come about easily—or at all—through tandem
mutations, simultaneous genetic changes, or survival of the fittest.
If so, millions of simultaneous coincidences had to have happened
millions of times.

Some Possible Gifts

Here are a number of characteristics and abilities that might
be considered gifts. Some are captured or modified from previous
chapters, others are newly added. A few appear to be uniquely
human; many are shared with the animal kingdom.

1. Complex communication skills, including speech, paralanguage
    (body language), lip reading, and sign language. (Noted, some
    butterflies may communicate with ultraviolet reflections from their
    wings, whales by loud moans, ants by touching antennae, bees by
    dancing, monkeys by vocalizing and learned signing, and
    elephants by subsonic means.)

2. To imagine; to have the ability to fantasize or marvel. According
    to Mark McGinnis, imagination was given to us to compensate
    for what we are not; a sense of humor was provided to console
    us for what we are.

3. To have a conscience and to display morals, ethics, decency, and aesthetics. To obey laws or commandments. To postpone gratification if an action might injure another.

4. To make use of humor. No animals tell jokes or laugh spontaneously in a way we can observe.

5. To recognize achievement and have pride in one's work.

6. To offer sympathy, feel compassion, or cry for another's tragedy.

7. To fear, to proceed with caution, to hesitate; to have suspicion or apprehension.

8. To dismiss the day-to-day, unimportant details from our memory and yet retain important information.

9. To celebrate, to toast, to roast, to tease, and to be jovial.

10. To remember pleasant events and forget the acute events in major trauma.

11. To enjoy happiness, joy, gladness, bliss, cheerfulness, and to remember with fondness.

12. To draw, to doodle, to paint, to recognize colors, and to sculpt.

13. To coordinate colors or textures.

14. To mimic or pantomime.

15. To smile. This is the most easily recognized human expression. Smiles and surprise are the only expressions recognizable from 150 feet away—and from 300 feet only a smile is. There are different kinds of smiles, which, we believe, only other humans can distinguish—such as those of contempt, fear, compliance, flirtation, grin-and-bear-it; the smirk, the qualified smile, and the embarrassed grin. (A chimp's smile is actually a grimace and reflects pain.)

16. To postpone pleasure, such as having dessert at the end of the meal, not the beginning; or intercourse after wedding vows.

17. To have faith, hope, and charity.

18. To plan for the future, such as for a trip or a party. To schedule events. To show up for events previously scheduled.

19. To organize our life or our living quarters.

20. To set priorities.

21. To appreciate someone or something. To offer respect, do favors, and feel satisfaction.

22. To compete, unrelated to mating or food gathering. There is no evidence that any other mammals have scheduled sporting events, debate clubs, or beauty contests.

23. To show passion and enthusiasm, to be inspired, to rejoice, to show concern, and to get excited about an upcoming event.

24. To love, to show affection, to adore, to care about.

25. To display benevolence, altruism, and self-sacrifice. Some animals show altruism, like the narwhale when it purposefully breaks the tip of its tusk off inside the painful, broken tusk of another whale. Presumably, this act protects the wound and lessens the pain.

26. To enjoy non-estrus sex (intercourse unrelated to ovulation). Bonobos (a rare ape of the Congo region) seem to be the only other primate that shares this trait.

27. To be considerate, patient, and understanding.

28. A sense of time, timing, and punctuality. How would we hold meetings, have guests in our home, know when to speak and when not to, when to swing the bat at a baseball, or when to shoot at the hoop without some internal timing mechanism? (Noted, plants

and animals know—and react to—the time of day and the season of the year. Timing has an impact on all living things.)

29. To be responsible for or commit to a project or an idea.

30. Speech, singing, humming, whistling, shouting, screaming, and teasing.

31. To be brave, plan strategies, and plan contingencies. If plan A doesn't work, to go to plan B or C or even D.

32. To use reasoning or exercise self-control.

33. To anticipate, such as guessing what the other team might do or what another person might say. No one knows if animals think about their eventual death and what will happen to their offspring.

34. To feel sadness and have the ability to overcome it.

35. To dance, perform, act, sing alone or in a group; to play an instrumental solo or play with an orchestra; to direct actors or work behind the scenes.

36. To play, to pretend, or to fake. Humans can pretend they are having a good time when they are not. They can pretend they are full when they are starving. They can pretend they like a present when they do not. They can even pretend to pretend.

37. To put one's life on the line for an ideal, another person, or one's country.

38. To issue orders or follow orders.

39. To write or print, to read, and to recite. To understand the deeper meaning or read between the lines.

40. To compromise, barter, or bargain.

41. To feel the sense of nostalgia. To enjoy the past and to predict the future. To reminisce.

42. To learn and teach complex ideas.

43. To use common sense in everyday decisions.

44. To enjoy an event vicariously, such as watching the hometown team win or your nephew take first place.

45. To follow a complex recipe, understand a map, or give directions.

46. To supervise the work of another individual.

47. To promise, to vow, to warn, and to fulfill an agreement.

48. To talk, gab, debate, argue, hint, suggest, or agree.

49. To save and cherish items like a high school sweater (things that are not related to survival).

50. To pray, to have faith, to join others with similar feelings, to sing hymns, to believe, and to worship.

51. To have those nagging feelings, hunches, gut feelings, and insight.

52. To doubt and to hesitate; those actions that keep us out of trouble.

53. To wonder, to dream, and to relax.

54. To admire and to emulate.

55. To wish for something good.

56. To share, to be happy for another person, or to be proud of someone.

57. To be able to make various facial expressions and gestures.

58. To regret and to apologize.

59. To know what to disregard—or whom.

60. To show contempt for an individual or a rule.

61. To seek justice. To trust one another.

62. To have grace.

63. To have guilt feelings—so you won't do it again?

64. To feel disgust. Does this feeling protect us from eating feces-contaminated foods, drinking urine- or chemical-tainted water, sharing drinks, and avoiding people who are ill? Gagging, spitting, and vomiting may save our lives.

65. To maintain or strike up a friendship.

66. To long for someone or something.

67. To deceive. We all use opacity or camouflage—with window shades, sunglasses, clothing, closed doors, PINs, poker faces, white lies, and military fatigues.

68. To have the ability to recall a smell, vision, sound, or emotion in a split second.

69. To care for the ill or lame, protect and help the elderly, donate time or money to charities. Not only do some of us take care of the less fortunate, but we also take care of ailing animals. With very rare exceptions, an animal will not care for another species.

70. To share and cooperate. If survival of the fittest were our driving force, one would have to explain how the Pilgrims survived when they first came to America or how a soccer team wins the World Cup. Mutual aid: we often help protect and help support one another.

71. To have wisdom and knowledge; to calculate, deduce, analyze, theorize, and speculate.

72. To be embarrassed or chagrined.

73. To do things in moderation; to plan future compromises or sharing.

74. To do multitasking or be multilingual.

75. To recite poetry.

76. To be curious beyond that which is needed for survival, such as performing scientific inquiries and experiments.

77. To show humility, self-discipline, and generosity.

78. To suffer anxiety. Is this a modified form of fear—a gift when appropriate and in moderation?

79. To worry—another gift? We often take worry too far, but these feelings might be there to make us aware of potential adverse consequences.

80. To forget. Could retrograde amnesia be hardwired into place so we won't fear death when it is upon us and will blank out horrendous experiences? Many have suffered horrendous accidents— knife stabbings, wheat-combine manglings, and motor vehicle accidents—yet the victims frequently cannot recall a single thing about the incident. This form of amnesia can stretch back from several minutes to a number of hours before the event. Recall the surviving bodyguard in the accident that killed Princess Diana. How could he remember other times of his life and yet not recall the worst moment of all?

81. To suffer. Is that a gift? Apparently Mother Teresa, the 1979 Nobel Laureate for Peace, thought it was when she said, "Suffering opens up space within that otherwise would not be there—so that God can come in and fill it."

82. To remember.

83. To endure a near-death experience? There are numerous reports of NDEs in which people saw bright lights, deceased loved ones, or Christ. Are these designed reassurances?

84. To change our ways—plasticity.

85. To be in sync. To dance, march, play a musical instrument, or sing in sync. Like millions of fireflies that simultaneously light up (oscillate) in the meadows, our heart cells squeeze, and our brain cells fire off electrical impulses or brain waves in synchrony. And our muscle cells pull at the same time—and our five senses work together.

86. To heal physically; to heal emotionally.

87. To hope.

All plants and animals have these timepieces:
living clock control is ubiquitous
throughout the organic world.

—John D. Palmer, *The Living Clock*

22

Biorhythms

Every aspect of our life is controlled by an internal clock and internal calendar; instead of depending on revolving hands, digital readouts, or pages with numbered squares, however, we are run by specialized neurons in the brain. Every species has its own built-in timekeeper or timekeepers; even microbial organisms need rest periods. Specialized cells tell a cat when to sleep, a plant when to sprout, a flower when to bloom, a leaf when to turn red, a raccoon when to fatten up, a bird when to migrate, a bear when to hibernate, a marmot when to wake, and a deer when to give birth.

The daily cycle is called the *circadian rhythm*—taken from the Latin words *circa* (about) and *dies* (day)—and it reflects that our biorhythms will approximate, but not precisely follow, the solar night–day cycle. Our day-to-day, month-to-month, season-to-season, and year-to-year activities require flexibility since some winters can be longer, food shortages happen, or we may move to a different area. The circadian rhythm of an infant changes as it grows; a night worker will have a different biorhythm than a day worker; a person's rhythm will change under stress; and a male's rhythm may differ from a female's. It's as if your wristwatch could slow down when you were running late or your calendar could flip ahead if the weather becomes unseasonably hot. Hormones will wax and wane from hour to hour or week to week; chemicals can change concentrations; and cellular metabolism can vary, based on external stimuli and preprogrammed plans.

The human race marches in unison. Each of us is conceived within a specific time of the menstrual cycle, and most of us are delivered during the fortieth week after conception; our embryonic heart starts beating at four weeks; we form fingers by the seventh week, and fingerprints by 24 weeks; we begin to roll over, crawl, walk, and talk at practically the same ages; we pass through puberty in our early teens and stop growing in our late teens; we are the most sexually active as young adults; women cease having menstrual cycles in their late 40s; men go through a male menopause close to 50; and most of us shrink in height, turn gray, and become forgetful around the same age.

Our biological calendar makes adjustments in hormones and bodily functions based on age, season, nutrition, and stress. It knows when it's time for a child's baby teeth to fall out, beards to start, and breasts to appear. Like a video recorder, it dates every memory so you can recall an event and connect it to an approximate time of the day, month, season, and year. Can you recall where you were and what time it was when the World Trade Center towers were struck? Or when JFK was shot?

The Timing of Our Functions

Roughly three times a day, our biological clock reminds us it's time to eat. We are told when it's time to go sleep and when to rise. Our temperature drops in the morning and rises in the afternoon. We have a sense of timing in our conversations, social gatherings, and sporting events. The ears of an 80-year-old usually match up with his or her 80-year-old nose, wrinkled skin, and joint pains. One rarely sees skin out of synch with the rest of the body, such as old ears and a young nose. Certain hormones peak as we wake to give us more energy, and wane as we settle down at night to sleep. Every cell in our body has some idea what time it is. The liver is never in a daytime mode while the lungs are in a nocturnal mode.

Death typically occurs in the early morning hours, peaking at 5 A.M. Birth also tends to occur in the early hours, often around 4 A.M. Certain times of the day are better for athletic events and spelling bees; certain times are better for treatment with cancer drugs. Toothaches are worse in the morning, presumably due to increased sensitivity to pain.

It seems as if every aspect of the human body has an expiration date stamped on it, a kind of planned obsolescence and cadence that all cells follow. People may live longer these days on average, but the limit of human longevity remains about 120 years. The average adult makes ten billion new cells a day and removes just as many dead ones. We lose 40 to 50 hairs a day. After age 40, we lose about 1000 nerve cells per day. Red blood cells have a life expectancy of 120 days in males and 109 days in females. Platelets live seven to ten days. Human skin totally replaces itself every two weeks. Toenails, fingernails, and hair grow at very specific rates. Eyelashes last three to five months. Liver cells turn over every five months. Gums are replaced every one to two weeks. The inner lining of the blood vessels renews itself every six months. Intestinal cells turn over every three days. And so on.

> Every aspect of our life is controlled by an internal clock and internal calendar; instead of depending on revolving hands, digital readouts, or pages with numbered squares, however, we are run by specialized neurons in the brain.

Internal functions are timed. The feeling of satiety (that full feeling after a big meal) occurs 20 minutes after the stomach is actually full—that's why some folks eat more than they should. Swallowing takes 4 to 8 seconds. Food lingers in the stomach for four hours while stomach waves mix it every 20 seconds. The pancreas needs about 45 minutes to get the digestive juices flowing, and then chyme moves a quarter of an inch per minute through the small intestine, taking three to ten hours to reach the large colon. The elimination of waste typically occurs within the first hour after waking. To get ready for the day?

Kidneys slow down at night. Nicotine from cigarettes reaches the brain in seven seconds. Once a drug leaves the gut, it is evenly distributed in about 60 seconds; alcohol metabolism varies with time of day. A knee jerk takes four-tenths of a second. White cells ooze through blood vessels and move three times their length per minute. It takes about 60 seconds for blood to circulate through the entire body. Small arteries contract every 2 to 8 seconds. The testes produce a thousand sperm a second. It takes two months for sperm to mature; they can propel themselves at a speed of 4.2 inches per hour (like a swimmer at 12 yards per second); and they reach the site of fertilization in an average of 50 minutes.

Sleeping and Waking: Still a Mystery

The sleep–wake cycle remains one of the most interesting of the cycles, and the reason why we sleep is one of the most baffling questions. Superficially the answer may seem quite simple: We need to rest. If that's the case, however, why do insomniacs not feel rested after lying awake in bed all night? Surely their muscles and joints would have recovered—but more often these people feel worn-out, weak, and pain-ridden. Something more is needed than merely lying down. Volunteers who are kept awake for several days and nights begin to hallucinate and have trouble concentrating. Maybe the main purpose of sleeping is to rest the brain, yet the electrical activity of the brain is typically very high then. Perhaps sleeping is the time for the body to repair itself—but metabolic studies have shown that protein synthesis actually slows during this time. If anything, body repair work is a 24/7 phenomenon.

Overall, modern science knows very little about this activity that takes up a third of our lives. Every living, visible animal sleeps. Some animals sleep upside down like the bat; others sleep with one eye open like the dolphin; and nocturnal animals sleep during the day. We know that infants require more sleep than adults and that if we don't sleep long enough, we accumulate a sleep deficit. The average adult needs between six and eight hours per night, yet Napoleon slept only four hours and Einstein slept ten hours. No one knows why people have different requirements. Most Americans watch late-night television and function with a sleep deficit of 20 hours per week. Many of us can whittle this down on weekends, and sometimes we can eliminate it on vacations, but many of us quickly sink back to the 20-hour deficit within two weeks back at the job.

We know that the pineal gland—a small, pine cone–shaped gland found in the middle of the brain—has a lot of control over sleep. It secretes a sedating hormone called *melatonin*. In lower-order animals, this gland can sense the light changes from day to night and adjusts the secretion of its hormone accordingly. In humans our adjustments might be mediated through the eyes, but the data suggests there are other factors as well.

After we fall asleep, blood pressure falls, heart rate slows, body temperature drops as much as two degrees, hormone levels change, blood vessels constrict to retain body heat, cold receptors shrink, smell seems to shut down, the three bones in the ear loosen up, taste buds dry up, and urine output slows. All senses are set to their lowest notch. Does urine output slacken because there is less blood passing through, or do we sleep better when we don't have to empty our bladders so often? Either could be in place by design.

The body knows when it's had enough sleep. The signal to wake is not just the rising sun, the sound of a neighbor's car, or birds singing—any more than a sunset and the sound of crickets is the signal to sleep. Experiments on people living underground for weeks have shown they will lose their usual circadian cycle yet wake when they are rested. In the hour or two before we wake, our body begins secreting more cortisol and adrenaline in preparation for the stresses of the world again. Blood pressure is the highest, platelets the stickiest, and heart attacks most likely.

> Is sleep some form of mini-hibernation, electrical restoration, or hormonal regeneration, or a time for our body to reassess its internal status in some unexplained way? We have lots of questions and many theories, but few facts.

What Is Sleep?

Is sleep some form of mini-hibernation, electrical restoration, or hormonal regeneration, or a time for our body to reassess its internal status in some unexplained way? Are daydreams representative of night dreams, or are they built-in portable television sets for entertainment? Is this how the brain works out problems? We have a lot of questions and many theories, but few facts.

Is sleep a function of evolution? One could argue that the first living entities did not sleep and that rest slowly evolved as the complexity of the animal increased and sleep became an increasing requirement. To the contrary, one could also argue that sleep is far too complex to have come about by mere mutation or survival of the fittest. It involves every cell, tissue, gland, and organ. It results in major changes in brain electrical activity and causes changes in body hormone levels. From a design perspective, it's extremely interesting that sensory systems ramp down to aid sleep and yet remain vigilant; that swallowing and kidney function decrease; that the body automatically continues to breathe and carry on necessary functions; that it will automatically shift its position to avoid pressure injuries; that complex preparatory changes begin occurring as early as two hours before rising; and that we go to bed exhausted and wake up refreshed.

Aging

Aging is an entirely different biorhythm. Every step in child development, every facet of puberty, and every stage of personality development is present in the DNA blueprint long before birth. Diet, stresses, and often environmental factors can impact the stages, just like ink can spill on a drawing board, but the plans are there. How large a role environment plays remains a heated debate, but it is readily apparent that the supposedly blank slate we all begin life with comes outfitted in different colors, patterns, and sizes.

A number of theories place the beginning of dying in the mid-20s. As the years pass, our skin becomes more fragile, our bones soften, our hearing worsens, our joints show wear and tear, our capacity to exercise diminishes, and our bowels slow down. Not uncommonly, we need bifocals at age 40 and trifocals at 50, and 20 percent of us need hearing aids by 70. The heart eventually wears out, the kidneys start to fail, and the brain shrinks 11 percent. The capacity for rote memory lessens, but there is evidence that wisdom increases.

No one knows why we age or why some of us age better than others. Genetics and environment play a role. If parents live to 100, their offspring are more likely to live long. Sun-exposed skin is going to age more quickly, athletic trauma to a knee will lead to a worn joint, and overuse of certain medications or exposure to industrial chemicals may harm internal organs. We think *telomeres* play a role. These are tiny segments of DNA that clip themselves off with each generation of cell division—like firing a gun and not reloading. Once the DNA strand is void of telomeres, the cell line dies. The number of telomeres ranges from 40 to 60 per cell.

Whether we realize it or not, we all march to the same drummers. Most of us are born at 40 weeks, have children between the ages of 15 and 40, and die in our 70s or 80s (though we all have the potential for 120 years). Night and day, summer and winter, sun and shade all play roles in regulating our internal clocks. One needn't wear a wristwatch to be biologically on time.

Bottom-Line Points

- *Every aspect of our life is controlled by an internal clock and internal calendar; every species has its own built-in timekeeper or timekeepers.*

- *Our daily cycle, or circadian rhythm, has built-in flexibility because weather (and many other factors) can change and food shortages occur.*

- *No one knows why we sleep, but we know it's critical to survival.*

- *Nearly all of us get hungry at the same times of the day and feel tired at the same time in the evening. Internal monitors tell us what we need.*

- *We begin aging (or maturing) the moment conception occurs, and all of us go through the same stages in the same ways at approximately the same ages.*

Our Heavenly Father invented man because he was disappointed in the monkey.

—Mark Twain

23

The Differences Between Man and Monkey

Are we basically monkeys or not? Scientists say that human DNA and chimp DNA are between 95 and 98 percent the same. Yet our blueprint allows us to do calculus, compose poetry, build cathedrals, and walk on the moon, while chimps pick bugs off of each other and eat them. It's obvious there is a physical resemblance, but does similarity prove that both species descended from the same ancestor? If so, why have we progressed over 500,000 years, and they haven't? Why are there so many hard-to-explain differences, like facedown deliveries rather than faceup, bipedalism (walking on two feet), and speech? Why is it that monkeys never need a haircut?

Even if we were truly identical in 98 percent of all our genes—the maximum possible percentage—that still leaves 120,000,000 chemical bases in which we differ. Listed below are just a few characteristics. In each case the genetic gap is monumental.

Humans vs. Other Primates

1. Chimpanzees' feet and big toes are prehensile, able to grab nearly anything. Without a great deal of training, humans can barely pick up a folded napkin with their toes. They have long arms and short legs; we have short arms and long legs.

2. Most animals, including chimps, have wraparound mouths. When a monkey shows its teeth, it is either angry, feeling threatened, or hurting. We have a narrow mouth to articulate better, and showing our teeth usually denotes friendship.

3. The chin is unique to humans. It is thought to have showed up about 150,000 years ago.

4. Humans require a prolonged childhood. (Survival of the fittest should logically require a shorter childhood.) Chimps and gorillas are emancipated by 11 or 12 years of age.

5. The human gestation period is also the longest among primates. One might think that this, too, would be contrary to survival of the fittest.

6. Tails—where did they go? There are no in-between tails.

7. Monkeys and apes rarely linger more than a few seconds over intercourse. They can always tell when a female has ovulated. We usually can't. Face-to-face intercourse is rare in the rest of the mammal world.

8. Gorillas have 48 chromosomes, and we have 46. Curiously, potatoes have even more.

9. With the exception of the pilot whale, only humans are known to go through menopause.

10. The human body is relatively naked, and there are no known intermediate, partly hairy species.

11. Apes lack the fatty inner layer of skin that we share with aquatic mammals like the whale and hippopotamus.

12. Humans are the only primate with breasts that are apparent when not nursing.

13. A newborn human arrives plump and naked; a newborn chimp is hairy and cadaver-like. Our newborns are helpless, whereas newborn monkeys can cling and move about. Gorilla babies stand at 20 weeks; humans stand at 43 weeks. Is that an advancement?

14. According to Elaine Morgan in *The Scars of Evolution*, "The really indispensable pre-adaptation for speech is the enhanced degree of conscious breath control which we share with all diving animals and no purely terrestrial ones."

15. Monkeys have a bone in their penis called a *baculum*.

16. Humans may be the only creatures who weep, although paired giraffes seem to shed tears when they are separated.

17. Many primates and most mammals make their own vitamin C. Somewhere along the road of survival of the fittest we apparently lost that life-sustaining ability.

18. Among primates, the hymen is only found in humans, Madagascar lemurs, and other *prosimians* (lemurs and tarsiers).

19. We are the only creature that blushes over relatively minor events, and we may be the only one that laughs at jokes. Chimps will laugh if tickled.

20. According to Pulitzer prize–winning author Jared Diamond in *Why Is Sex Fun?* human sexuality is different from all of the 30 million animal species. "By the standards of the world's 4300 other species of mammals, and even by the standards of our closest relatives, the great apes, we are the ones who are bizarre." He points to long-term partnerships, co-parenting, private sex, concealed ovulation, extended female receptivity, sex for fun, and female menopause.

21. According to Charles Kingsley Levy in *Evolutionary Wars,* no other animal even approaches the repertoire of sounds and skills that humans use to communicate.

22. There are different bone structures: Chimps' lumbar spine is shorter. Humans have a different kind of hip joint. Chimps do not have an arch in either foot.

23. Humans have a protruding nose.

24. Monkeys don't sweat.

25. Among primates, only humans have the capacity for blue eyes and curly hair.

26. Penguins, sea mammals, and humans seem to be the only creatures who can consciously hold their breath.

27. Monkeys and apes, despite any amount of training, will never be able to read a novel, understand a joke, drive a truck, fly a plane, sing the national anthem, or recite the Lord's Prayer. And note that the old idea that an infinite number of monkeys with an infinite amount of time and typewriters would type out a Shakespeare play was recently dispelled in Plymouth, England, when a group of monkeys were given computer keyboards for a month. Instead of typing words, they covered the keyboards with excrement. The ones that actually became interested in typing typed several pages of the letter "s."[11]

There are many major differences between man and monkey, and the gaps cannot be explained by minor internal adjustments, rare mutations, or survival of the fittest. Where's the tail? Why did we lose the fur (a disadvantage)? Why does our skin more resemble a dolphin's than a monkey's? Why can't we grasp fruit with our feet? Why is our brain more interested in literature than in dodging banana peels from the upper branches?

The only way naturalism can be false, is if reality is in fact a richer place than naturalism allows…In short, if we're going to show that naturalism is false, we need to locate observable features of the world that demonstrate design.

—William Dembski, *Intelligent Design: The Bridge Between Science & Theology*

I could prove God statistically. Take the human body alone—the chance that all the functions of the individual would just happen is a statistical monstrosity.

—George Gallup, 1984

24

Purposeful
Design

For some people the lingering question has been and may always be, are we the result of accidental changes (mutations) coupled with survival of the fittest, causing our complex systems to merely look like they might be purposefully designed; or are we truly purposefully designed and then modified by mutations and survival patterns over millions of years; or are we purposefully designed and modified additionally only by relatively recent, minor environmental changes? If design is not the primary cause, one needs to explain how multiple, intertwining chemical reactions came to be needed to accomplish every task within the body, such as clotting, immunity, hormonal regulation, and digestion, to mention only a few. Listed here are just some points that I believe stand out. Some are drawn from previous chapters; some are new.

Examples of Purposeful Design

1. *Blueprint size and capability:* The human egg is only one tenth of a millimeter (.004 inches) across, barely visible to the eye. The sperm is a hundred times smaller, and yet these two entities know how to find each other, combine, and set off a series of events that will determine nearly everything in a person's development—including external features, the biorhythms, symmetry, all cellular

interactions, hormone use and disposal, protein synthesis and breakdown, means to fight disease, personality styles (and possibly IQ), propensity toward certain diseases, and life expectancy.

2. *Smell and taste:* These senses are heightened whenever you are hungry. Food is not as appetizing when you are full. You feel like resting after a meal so that maximum blood can be diverted from muscles to the gastrointestinal tract. Babies sleep best after nursing.

3. *Temperature control:* Whenever you are chilled, every cell in your skin "fires up," and surface blood vessels constrict to maintain inner warmth. Temperature receptors tell you it's cold outside—tell you to get a coat or find shelter—and roughly how cold it is, and then they tell you if you are warm enough.

4. *Opposite sexes:* Having two sexes seems wasteful, yet most evolutionary theories favor the development of systems that are least wasteful. Is the presence of two sexes designed to ensure genetic variation? Or for pleasure? Could there ever have been an intermediate species with incompatible genitalia? Incompatible eggs and sperm?

5. *Early neurological development:* During the early period of fetal brain development the body adds more than 250,000 nerve cells per minute. Every neuron knows where to go, how to get there, and where to connect. A newborn has close to a trillion nerve cells, each with as many as 10,000 specific connections.

6. *Appetite and body responses:* The concentration of a hormone called *ghrelin* rises in the bloodstream before meals to enhance appetite, and levels of *cholecystokinin* rise after meals to suppress appetite. About 250 genes, working with 40 neurochemicals, regulate metabolism and appetite.

7. *Vision:* Eyelids blink to protect our eyes. Eyeballs roll up at night to protect them from injury when not being used. Tears bring

oxygen to the cornea, carry chemicals that kill bacteria and proteins to coat the eyes, wash the eyes, and move debris toward a lower drain, or lacrimal duct. Fifty milliseconds before we blink involuntarily, the visual section of the brain shuts down, retaining the image in anticipation of the blink, and we never see a blank visual screen. This happens hundreds of times a day. Not so with a voluntary blink, which is much slower. When we sneeze, our eyes automatically close, presumably to avoid contact with the expelled droplets. Not so with a cough, however. The reason may be related to speed—how fast the expelled droplets hit the air.

8. *Purposeful symmetry:* The presence of two ears helps to establish the distance and location of sounds. Two eyes give depth perception. Two nostrils help to locate smells. Two hands help grasp, and two legs are needed for locomotion and balance.

9. *Speech:* Is the fact that the sounds we speak are in the same frequency as the sounds we hear merely a matter of coincidence? What we have to say and how we say it can be quite elaborate and complex, much more so than any other animal. This is one of the ways we interact at very personal times. Would it make sense to have had our speech organs anatomically located elsewhere, perhaps at the back of the head? Did speech come as a whole package—including a tongue, cheeks, lips, a throat, vocal cords, changes in brain structure, and lungs? Some scientists think that the ability to speak arrived millions of years before humans began to converse. Why would that be?

10. *Automatic functions:* Most of us function on "automatic pilot" for breathing, absorption of oxygen, elimination of carbon dioxide, removal of metabolic products from the bloodstream, passage of waste products within the gastrointestinal tract, and regulation of heart rate and blood pressure to accommodate our level of activity.

11. *Constant vigilance:* The brain is our command center, and it is aided by five senses that are constantly looking for signs of danger.

12. *Fertilization:* The head of the sperm contains enzymes to break through the wall of the egg and set off a chemical reaction that leads to fertilization. How does the sperm DNA even know how to link up with the egg's DNA?

13. *Saliva:* It increases with the anticipation of a meal, moisturizes the food to aid in swallowing, helps digest certain nutrients, and kills germs. There is evidence suggesting that men and women have slightly different saliva and that it may act as an attractant; hence, perhaps, it adds to the pleasure of kissing. The *mucin* in saliva protects the mouth from injury; its antibodies are in the body's first line of defense; and its calcium and phosphorus help protect the enamel on our teeth. About one quart of saliva is secreted during the day, and nearly none at night. The reason we have "slimy teeth" in the mornings is bacterial overgrowth, which disappears with brushing and the resumption of salivation.

14. *Facial expressions:* According to Daniel McNeill in *The Face,* the human face is unique. Ours is flat—unique in a snarling animal world. The smooth face greatly expands possibilities for language, and it makes signals clearer, subtler, and more varied. The vanished muzzle may be the most puzzling evolutionary fact of all. A projecting mouth is essential for almost all animals. This is how they seize and carry their food.

15. *Nursing:* The size, shape, and weight of a newborn fits very well into the bent arm of its mother and leaves the mouth exactly opposite the nipple. Nursing sends a signal to the brain to release hormones to produce more milk—nursing begets nursing. The fact that babies don't get their first teeth until the age of seven months or so suggests design to lessen injury to the nipple. All babies can distinguish their mother's milk by smell, and they come

with a natural sucking reflex. Mother's milk has all of the nutrients and antibodies a baby needs, and lactation itself acts as a natural contraceptive, preventing competition for the mother's reserves. Immunological cells from the mother's intestinal tract (cells with memory of previous disease exposures) will migrate to the breast during lactation and begin secreting their memory-laden antibodies (*immunoglobulin A*) into the milk so the baby's body will develop its own defenses. Breast-fed babies have fewer hospital admissions, ear infections, respiratory infections, diarrhea, allergies, and rashes—and they score higher on IQ tests, especially if breast-fed for more than six months.

16. *Seals:* The mouth, vagina, urethra, and anus are sealed by mucus when not in use and yet can open and close in controlled ways as needs arise.

17. *Cellular complexity:* There are 10 to 75 trillion cells in the human body—200 different kinds of cells that know exactly what to do, when to do it, and how often, from the tiniest red blood cell at one-25,000th of an inch across to nerve cells that can stretch a few feet in length. Each cell is a universe of its own, filled with power generators, biochemical plant managers, messengers, and assembly lines.

18. *The mouth:* This orifice is uniquely suited to be a tasting chamber. It is here where bite-sized food is received, analyzed (tasted), temporarily retained, macerated and pulverized, hydrated, chemically cleaved, partially digested by enzymes, treated with antibodies, and reanalyzed before being allowed to pass.

19. *The teeth:* Permanent teeth are designed to push milk teeth out. The position and shape of our teeth seems to be deliberate. Incisors bite off chunks of food, and molars pulverize the food. The upper and lower teeth usually match in alignment and function. Could

intermediate species have had them reversed? Also, enamel is one of the hardest biological substances known.

20. *Smell:* Our nose flares when we sniff, to get a better sample of air. Olfactory cells within the nose tell us if food is tainted. The nose's two sides work together to locate the source of the scent. We derive some sexual desire through special tissues in the nose.

21. *The tongue:* This muscle can stretch forward to taste something with a lick, readily sense if a foreign body or bone is present in a bite and then easily ferret it out, scrape away lingering bits of food from the crevices between teeth, help form words and sounds, sense the temperature of food, shift food from cutting teeth to pulverizing teeth, help digest food by secreting an enzyme called *lingual lipase,* and initiate the swallowing process. The tongue will help you swallow saliva all day long without your conscious attention.

22. *Natural pain killers:* Endorphins and enkephalins are nature's internally produced pain killers. Their concentrations increase with stress, injuries, exercise, and laughter. During delivery, women's bodies will have very high levels of enkephalins.

23. *Hormones:* The pituitary gland, thyroid gland, adrenals, testes, and ovaries produce hormones that carry specific messages to target cells telling them what to do, how to do it, when, and how fast. There are more than 40 hormones known, and more are expected to be discovered.

24. *Memory:* We seem to have built-in mechanisms to cope with or to blot out memories of massive injuries. We can discard relatively useless material quickly, yet retain very important material for decades. We can arrange memories by dates. (Recall your high school friends and then arrange them by height, weight, age, or IQ.) We can remember how to ride a bike, cut a piece of meat, pass a test, calculate numbers on the basis of formulas, or plan

meals based on prior knowledge. Built-in circuits allow us to recognize people we haven't seen in decades.

25. *Tears:* Tears may help eliminate "sad"' proteins or hormones. (Go have a good cry and feel better.) Tears from crying have a different concentration of proteins than do natural tears for washing the eye or tears of happiness. And note that tears are manufactured at the upper, outer corner of the eye and drained at the lower, inner corner.

26. *Ovulation:* Females do not ovulate until they are old enough and are physically able to bear a child. Women will skip periods during times of famine, high stress, and war, presumably due to a built-in mechanism to limit childbirth when the child has less likelihood of surviving. On average, women will cease ovulating at age 52, presumably because they can no longer care for a newborn.

27. *Growth patterns:* Growth hormone controls growth during our formative years. The right hand mirrors the left; the right eye matches the left. Growth hormone also knows when to start up and when to turn off.

28. *Backup systems:* The pituitary gland releases ACTH in times of stress so that we will have more cortisol to cope better. The heart has backup pacemakers. The body can speed up the heart and breathing rate if there's a crisis. The bone marrow will make more red blood cells if there's been a blood loss or a drop in oxygen concentration. During water shortages the brain will initiate fluid conservation steps.

29. *Puberty:* The fact that females cannot bear children until they are old enough or if they are too old suggests design. Between the ages of 11 and 13, girls develop breasts, start periods, and grow pubic hair. In their mid-teens, boys start growing pubic and facial hair, and their voices change. Both sexes go from little interest in the opposite sex to intense interest; both are probably emitting pheromones. In the twentieth century, girls began their periods

earlier than those in the nineteenth century, presumably due to better nutrition. Girls in less developed countries start their periods later than girls in Western societies. Is this a designed mechanism responding to better environments?

30. *Breathing:* The air we inhale is sucked in by a bellows system and expelled by an elastic recoil system.

31. *The filtration system:* Air enters through the nose, where it is filtered by nasal hairs, cleansed by antibodies and killer cells, tested by smell sensors, humidified by mucus, and warmed by the sinus corridors. All of the captured debris (pollen, dirt, bacteria, viruses, fungi, smog particles) is collected and disposed of.

32. *Internal sensors:* We know when we are hungry, when we're full, and if we are thirsty. The bladder and rectum send signals when it's time. Our eyes tell us if the light is too bright; our ears tell us if the noise is too loud; and our body tells us if we are tired.

33. *The windpipe:* The cartilage rings in the trachea are strong enough to keep the windpipe open, yet soft and flexible enough to allow our necks to bend.

34. *Buffers:* The discs between the vertebrae in our back are soft enough not to damage bone, but sturdy enough to withstand constant day-to-day trauma. Cartilage lining the knees protects the bones from constant banging together. Acids and bases are adjusted on a minute-to-minute basis in the bloodstream to keep the body's pH within strict limits.

35. *Pain sensors:* Pain fibers warn us if we touch something that is too sharp, too cold, or too hot, or if we've overused our muscles or joints, stood too long on our feet, eaten something that was too spicy, too hot, or too cold, or if there's been an injury.

36. *Digestion:* On average we each spend three-and-a-half years of our life eating more than 25 tons of food, all of which is pulverized, hydrated, analyzed, sanitized, sorted, processed, organized, absorbed, modified, and distributed.

37. *Detoxification:* We are all exposed to scores of poisons and toxins, and yet our liver, kidneys, and bones know how to convert them to nontoxic compounds.

38. *Self-monitoring systems:* The brain monitors our hydration and nutrition on a minute-to-minute basis. Special sensors monitor our temperature and initiate measures to release or conserve heat. Balance is monitored by the cerebellum, the inner ears, and the musculoskeletal system. The kidneys watch our blood pressure.

39. *Vomiting:* The sudden expulsion of stomach contents is a coordinated function—initiated by special sentinels and involving the muscles of the stomach, esophagus, and mouth—to rid the body of something, such as tainted food, that might be dangerous. It may also be a community protective mechanism. When one person vomits, nearly everyone around either vomits or feels like it. Presumably, this is an alerting process to tell others they may have eaten something dangerous and they too need to get rid of it.

40. *Delivery systems:* Our hearts pump five to six quarts of blood per minute. This cycle is repeating itself during every second of a person's life. With each heartbeat, blood is propelled into a complex set of pipelines of decreasing diameter to deliver oxygen, water, nutrients, vitamins, hormones, and antibodies to every part of the body.

41. *Elimination systems:* The movement of feces through the large colon requires the coordination of several groups of muscles. Once a certain pressure is exceeded in the rectum, the need to defecate can be felt; the muscular opening relaxes, and another set of muscles expels the waste. Urine from both kidneys collects in the bladder, and once a certain pressure is exceeded, the need to urinate is felt. These exits are located in logical places.

42. *Recycling systems:* The body has a built-in mechanism to remove old or damaged red blood cells, converting them to bile salts to

aid digestion and then reabsorbing them. Saliva is swallowed, altered in the stomach, absorbed, and remade.

43.   *Compensatory mechanisms:* At a time of sudden, significant blood loss, plasma will diffuse into blood vessels to expand them, and adrenaline will constrict superficial blood vessels and make the heart work harder. The body will reroute the blood flow away from an injury. During a large meal, blood will be shifted to the stomach to aid in digestion. During exercise, blood will be shifted to the in-use muscle groups. As we age, our ears and noses become larger to better capture sounds and scents, and our gait widens to counter an aging balance mechanism.

44.   *Cellular loading and unloading docks:* Semiporous capillaries act like loading docks, allowing millions of different-shaped, different-charged, and different-sized particles to pass through. Cells can selectively absorb whichever nutrients they need and take a pass on those they don't.

45.   *Immunity:* Our immune system is structured to protect us from most infections. Millions of white cells patrol our circulation, while other white cells carry memories of previous infections and can readily manufacture specific antibodies.

46.   *The proteins:* Except for the red blood cells, every human cell has a nucleus that acts as a local command center. The nucleus sends out RNA messengers to make proteins at little factories called ribosomes. Experts in proteomics (a type of biotechnology concerned with proteins used at the gene level) estimate that the human body has as many as five million different types of protein. There may be only 5000 to 10,000 basic structures, but variations on each one account for the subtypes. Every conceivable shape can be found, many contorted and twisted like a pretzel but a thousand times more complex.

47.   *The enzymes:* Each cell also uses hundreds of different enzymes that can work at speeds of up to one ten-thousandth of a second, never

get in each other's way, and self-destruct after acting. Unneeded metabolites, hormones, and wastes in the cell are placed in bubbles and transported through microscopic highways called microtubules to the location of the lysosomes—extremely powerful enzymes—for dismantling.

48. *Clotting:* A mix of platelets, clotting factors, and chemicals from the blood will quickly patch an injury and begin the healing process according to a pre-prescribed plan.

49. *Skin protection:* People who live in the sunniest climates have the most melanin, presumably to protect their skins; and those in colder climates, where humans presumably migrated, have less.

50. *Opposing muscle groups:* The body has very clearly delineated opposing groups of muscles specifically suited to help initiate and undo every motion. Our joints are constructed to handle these motions and withstand the repeated trauma.

51. *Design integrity:* During growth, the body knows how to match the right side with the left, the bottom half with the top half, and the back with the front. Aging aside, every person's unique makeup is maintained even if 90 percent of their cells have been replaced several times. A freckle remains the same freckle, a dimple the same dimple. The new liver looks like the old liver. Ears and eyes mirror each other.

52. *Growth:* The growth plates located on the ends of long bones know how fast to grow, how long, wide, and thick to be, how to connect to other bones, and how much total calcium will be needed. They also know, or are told, when to shut off growth.

53. *Internal coordination:* The skull is a good example of millions of worker cells following a plan. What begins as a speck of cartilage grows into a bony casing with the right spaces for eyes, ears, nose, and throat.

54. *Self-defense:* Our senses keep guard 24/7. Our hair and skin protect us from ultraviolet damage. The skull protects the brain, the vertebrae protect the spinal cord, and the ribs protect the heart. Microbe-killing peptides are found in our sweat, probably to keep pores from getting infected. Instead of wearing photo IDs, all our cells carry unique MHCs on their surface that say "I'm self." Others are attacked.

55. *The hands:* The hands of a human embryo are paddlelike at first, but become separate fingers when specialized cells cut them apart. Twenty-seven bones in each hand work together superbly. We can find our way in the dark by feel, and the blind can read with their fingers.

56. *The hymen:* This membrane is possessed almost exclusively by humans. It is tough enough to protect the birth canal from injury or infection, yet weak enough to be penetrated by a penis. It is also constructed in a way that allows the loss of menstrual blood.

57. *Familiarity:* We can recognize a familiar face from among hundreds, maybe thousands, of people, even if there have been decades since the last contact.

58. *Menopause:* Are women designed not to have babies when they age or are physically less fit, or is it the reverse—that babies shouldn't be born to women who might not live until their children have grown up? Most women go through menopause around 52 years of age, and they all go through menopause in much the same way. It is clearly programmed. A similar pattern is found in men. As they approach 50, many have lower testosterone levels, lower sperm counts, and less interest in having sex.

59. *"Destruct mechanisms":* Adrenaline is released into the circulation in response to a crisis, but it remains active for only 10 to 30 minutes. Then it is quickly eliminated because it is too dangerous to keep around. Digestive enzymes from the pancreas are

quickly destroyed after they've done their work, or else they would start digesting the intestinal lining.

60. *Involuntary functions:* Too numerous to count. These include the kidneys clearing the bloodstream of wastes, the liver cleaning the blood of toxins and releasing stored sugars for energy, the collection of urine in the bladder, the transformation of food to chyme to stool in the GI tract, the heart's response to activity, hormone balance, and breathing.

61. *Regeneration and repair:* Broken bones can grow back together, a liver can replace a severed lobe, skin can heal itself, and lost blood is readily replaced by new blood. Wounds are sealed off, and an army of cellular workers reconstruct the same architecture. Mentally, we heal as well. Anger will often dissipate in hours. Depression can significantly resolve in weeks to months, grief in months to years.

62. *Special fat:* Human babies have a unique fat called brown fat to help them retain heat (stay warm). It is located across the shoulder blades, around the neck, and surrounding the kidneys. Brown fat cells are loaded with mitochondria (tiny powerhouses), which cause these fat pads to act like internal electric blankets.

63. *Antigravity mechanisms:* We all have systems in our body to counter gravity's pull. The heart pumps blood in such a way that the just-pumped cells push the previously pumped cells along. Having the heart and lungs located in the top third of the body makes pumping blood to the brain easier and takes advantage of gravity's pull for the lower parts. To aid blood's return to the heart, veins have one-way valves. Some of these benefits are lost under weightlessness, causing astronauts in space to have puffy faces and stuffy noses.

64. *Crying:* Could crying be a purposeful design to get attention? How else would a parent know a child is hungry or thirsty? How else would you know a baby is hurting? How would you know if someone is sad?

65. *The voice:* Our vocal cords provide sound, while our lungs supply
     airflow. The length and thickness of the cords provide pitch, but
     there are the resonating chambers in the throat and nasal cavities
     that make words more understandable. Muscles in the tongue,
     palate, and lips provide articulation. Our complex conversation
     skills are unique in nature.

66. *The heart:* Built to keep on going, repair itself on the run, nour-
     ish itself, take a daily pounding, and constantly adjust to
     moment-by-moment needs. The complexity and coordinated
     functions of this single organ could fill a large book.

67. *Bipedalism and an upright stature:* These characteristics allow us
     to see farther across the "savanna" and free up our hands for tool
     use, carrying food, and communication.

68. *Intercourse:* Face-to-face intercourse is relatively rare in the animal
     world, found only among whales, dolphins, dugongs, manatees,
     beavers, sea otters, centipedes, some crustaceans, a New Zealand
     songbird, and some primates like orangutans and bonobos.

     One might ask, how did human males and females evolve to
     be so perfectly compatible? Pelvic thrusting during intercourse
     stimulates both individuals and deposits the sperm in the deep-
     est possible spot. Vaginal *rugae* (folds) stimulate the penis. Every
     male aspect of intercourse—from the initial excitement set off by
     visual cues and pheromones, to a good mechanical fit, to stimu-
     lation, to the placement of sperm—matches up well with the
     female's equivalent interest, her means of being stimulated, the
     delivery of the egg, and her mechanisms to help the sperm on their
     voyage. Dopamine, a chemical responsible for feelings of reward
     and pleasure, is released into the bloodstream in males and females
     after sex, just as it is released after ingesting a good meal or certain
     illicit drugs.

69. *Independence:* Although it seems as if all of our cells are depend-
     ent on the functions of and interactions with other specialized cells,

many of them are capable of living isolated and reproducing in a petri dish. Skin cells can grow alone or connect up with others to form layers of cells resembling skin. Nerve cells will grow long tentacles to reach and attach to each other. Heart cells will beat on their own, and if several are clumped together, they will pump in unison.

70. *Biological canaries:* Cells in the testes are the quickest to self-destruct when exposed to pesticides, toxins, and radiation, presumably to prevent the passage of mutations to future generations (preventing evolution?). Morning sickness may be a defense against eating something especially harmful during an embryo's earliest formative days.

71. *A bacteria-controlling environment:* The air we breathe has millions of bacteria floating about in it, but it is screened by the nasal passages. The food we eat is loaded with bacteria, but they are killed by saliva and stomach acid. Our skin has a blanket of billions of bacteria, yet they rarely penetrate its surface. We have more than 500 different kinds of bacteria in our gut, which are controlled and sometimes used for nutrition, and they are not attacked by our immune system. Our intestinal cells also secrete a coating of *sialic acid,* which is protective. If, however, a bacterium were to penetrate the bowel wall, the body's defenses would attack it immediately. Since stool is loaded with quadrillions of bacteria, could defecation also be a form of crowd control?

72. *Self-identity:* The brain constantly works to keep reality in focus, always telling you the layout of your surroundings—such as where the windows, floor, furniture, and doors are located—and what you are doing. It automatically lets you know where your hands, feet, arms, legs, front, and back are in relation to everything else in the environment. At night, it keeps track of your positions in bed and makes sure that you do not lie in one position too long

(lessening the danger of bedsores). It will cause you to move or roll over, or even wake if there's a need.

73. *Internal "highs"*: Exercise increases endorphins—another name for internal morphine. This is the "runner's high" that athletes speak of. Endorphins lessen the pain of many athletic endeavors and probably encourage people to exercise. They aid in relaxation and generally make a person feel good. They may be critical to our day-to-day coping skills.

74. *Contagion:* Vomiting may be a feature to warn others in a group about contaminated foods. Could contagious yawning say it's time for everyone to take a rest? Women in dormitories will have their periods at the same time. Perhaps this is a throwback to the times when the hunters were home for short periods—all of the women had to be ready to conceive at the same time. And what about contagious fear? Is that a herd-protective mechanism?

75. *Warning signs:* Is a tension headache designed to tell you that you've had too much stress? Is muscle fatigue a warning to slow down? Are frequent bowel movements or too much gas a warning to change your diet? Is fatigue meant to encourage rest? Eye pain tells us that the light's too bright, ear ringing that the sound is too loud, and a burning sensation in the nose and throat that fumes may be noxious.

76. *Special engineering:* Our bones are thickest where we bear the most weight; they are studded with protrusions so muscles can attach and provide leverage; they are grooved for nerves and blood vessels to travel within and hollow to serve as sheltered nurseries for immature blood cells.

77. *The larynx:* All creatures are born with a non-descended larynx so they can nurse and breathe at the same time. The human larynx, however, descends at three to six months, while animals' larynxes don't. Presumably, this is because we need a lower larynx

to speak. If this were not the case, our voice might emanate from our nose.

78. *Hibernation:* Kidney cells go into a form of hibernation during times of severe infection and "re-awake" when the patient is stabilized. Heart cells along the margin of a heart attack and brain cells bordering a stroke will do the same.

79. *Crisis management:* We all have the emergency fight-or-flight response. During times of famine, the body slows metabolism to conserve calories. During water shortages, the kidneys will concentrate urine. During times of infection, white cells by the millions are dispatched. To save your life, your brain may divert blood to the more vital organs. To save your child's life, your body may give you extra strength.

80. *Lovable babies:* Are babies cute and cuddly by mutation, by survival of the fittest—or by design? Soft, small, needy, cute, defenseless creatures seem to bring out the nurturing, protective nature in most of us. These little human creatures also lack odor in their stools and have a pleasant breath. Evidence suggests that a newborn's hair is naturally scented with an opiate that promotes a relaxed, easygoing feeling in its parents. All babies are born with the ability to smile within three months (some can do it on their first day), and the ability to smile is present even if they are deaf or blind.

81. *Our birthday:* The day of our birth is the most dangerous day of our life—perhaps the most complicated—yet for the vast majority of us it occurs quite safely.

To the question why we do not find rich
fossiliferous deposits belonging to these assumed
earliest periods I can give no satisfactory answers.

—Charles Darwin, *On the Origin of Species*

There cannot be design without a designer.

—William Paley, *Natural Theology*

Darwin
Dissected

Throughout history, very few scientific theories have stood the test of time. With each new generation of scientists come the "correct" answers, yet, repeatedly, many of these well-conceived ideas are disproved; what was widely accepted as fact often turns out to be wrong. Sometimes, very wrong. Knowing whom to believe or what information is reliable has continued to be a challenge. It may remain so for a long time to come.

The ancient Greek philosophers felt that knowledge should come from thought and that embarking on experimental science was beneath their dignity. This premise, and those kinds of presumed "facts" persisted for centuries. The view that Earth was definitely flat and no one dare approach the dangerous edge was common until ships went way beyond the "edge" and returned home. If one bases the future on the past, it's very likely that much of what all of us presently believe will also be proven to be wrong.

Some examples of beliefs from the past include the following:

> Is there anyone anywhere such an idiot as to believe
> that there are people who stand with their feet opposite
> to ours, their legs in the air and their heads hanging
> down? Can there possibly be any place on earth where

everything is upside down, where trees grow downwards and rain and snow fall upwards? These mad ideas are the result of the crazy notion that the world is round.

—Firmianus Lactantius (fourth century A.D.), tutor to Crispus, son of Constantine the Great

The doctrine that the earth is not the center of the universe, that it is not immovable, but moves with a daily rotation, is absurd and both philosophically and theologically false.

—Findings of the Congregation of the Inquisition against Galileo, circa 1634

Pasteur's anti-rabies treatment is useless, dangerous and devoid of any scientific character. Pasteur is not curing rabies, he is actually communicating it. His laboratory should be closed.

—Professor Peter of the French Academy, circa 1872

To imagine that pain can ever be abolished in surgery is a daydream that is absurd to try to realize. Pain and the knife are two words that every patient must forever live with. And we who are doctors must recognize the fact.

—Ascribed to both Professor Alfred of the Paris Faculty of Medicine and the famed surgeon Alfred Velpeau, 1839

We can close the books on infectious diseases.

—U.S. Surgeon General William Stewart, 1979

In North America the black bear was seen by Hearne
swimming for hours with widely open mouth, thus
catching, like a whale, insects in the water. Even in so
extreme a case as this, if the supply of insects were
constant, and if better adapted competitors did not
already exist in the country, I can see no difficulty in a
race of bears being rendered by natural selection, more
and more aquatic in their structure and habits, with
larger and larger mouths, till a creature was produced
as monstrous as a whale.

—Charles Darwin, *On the Origin of Species,*
first edition

The ship of evidence that carries Darwin's theories is full of
gaping holes, and yet a huge following will not allow it to sink. Their
belief is as strong as that of those who oppose evolution, who are
often mocked as "religious"—yet, like a religion, the "science" of
evolution is actually based on a belief system. Karl Marx once called
Darwin's *On the Origin of Species* an epoch and asked permission
to dedicate his book *Das Kapital* to him. Darwin declined, presumably due to his pious wife. He said that he never meant to write
atheistically; it seems as if Darwin misinterpreted his own works.

Would Darwin's Theories Be Published Today?

The theory of evolution is like a connect-the-dots game. Some
dots are clearly connected, such as wolves to dogs, but the vast
majority, such as reptiles to mammals, cannot be connected without millions of intermediary dots (species). Darwin's theories do
not come close to explaining the enormous complexity even within
a simple cell (let alone the entire body), the whole-package phenomenon (WPP), and irreducible complexity. The fact that a series of

useless steps is needed to accomplish a tiny task forcefully argues against evolution. The fact that all bodily functions require the convergence of many useless steps and useless systems (when each is viewed in isolation) excludes evolution as an option. The presumed multiple mutations leading up to mankind would have had to be organized, purposeful, targeted, simultaneous, frequent, safe, and too numerous to count. The original blueprint would have had to contain all of the subsequent blueprints, such as how to make the next steps out of the many on the way to manufacturing insulin, hemoglobin, adrenalin, or growth hormone. It would also have had to include how to use these chemicals, how to control their concentrations (feedback loops), how to replace them, how to keep them from interacting with each other, how to concentrate them in areas or at times of need, how to use them within each cell, and how to dispose of them.

> If one bases the future on the past, it's very likely that much of what all of us presently believe will also be proven wrong.

Darwin knew little of genetics, hardly anything about human physiology, and nothing of conception. He could not tell the difference between a kidney cell and a liver cell, nor did he know they existed. His writings included inflammatory, sexist, and bigoted comments. He rarely gave credit to any scientific source. No such scientific article would be accepted for publication nowadays.

Darwin subscribed to Lamarck's theory of *pangenesis*, which essentially states that a lizard with its tail cut off could have offspring without tails (if that were a benefit to the species), or that a pregnant mother with a recent tan might give birth to a baby with a tan. (And tans may protect skin.) Many external forces affect individuals, such as toxins, ultraviolet light, climate, radiation, and prolonged inactivity, but they rarely affect offspring. Although

Lamarck has long since been dismissed, his main proponent remains a major force. Evolutionists tend to play down Darwin's support for Lamarck's ideas, yet Darwin wrote in a letter to Thomas Huxley, "I think some such view [as pangenesis] will have to be adopted, when I call to mind such facts as the inherited effects of use and disuse, etc." [12]

Very few educators seem to have taken an unbiased, in-depth look at the data. By observing farmers breed animals to get a better version, Darwin deduced that man could eventually breed one species into another. Simply stated, by making horses smaller and smaller, one might eventually get a dog or a cat. If Darwin's writings were scrutinized by today's standards, he probably would not be published. No one has ever shown that one species can change into another. Yet Darwin wrote that bears, who prefer to keep their heads above water, could evolve into whales that can dive many fathoms beneath the water's surface, sustain themselves permanently out at sea, withstand incredible hypothermia, migrate thousands of miles each year, and successfully give birth underwater. Not to mention such factors as growing blubber, shrinking four extremities, shedding all hair, growing fins, and developing a subsonic communication system.

The Fossil Record and Darwin

The mere finding of a million-year-old primate fossil does not prove that this species went on to become human. More than likely, it went on to become another monkey. Dolphins have not changed in five million years; why would humans change? The present-day whale, which is the largest animal in the world, has no clear-cut fossil predecessors. These monstrous 60-ton mammals seem to have merely appeared. One would think that a huge, fossilized pre-whale skull or vertebra might be found somewhere.

Flies found in amber that is estimated to be 225 million years old are the same as today's flies. The giraffe, with its incredibly long neck, has not changed in two million years, and it has no shorter-neck predecessors among the fossils. Rodents also appeared suddenly in the fossil record. Fish arrived without preceding fish-like fossils. Insects showed up without any precedents. Thousands of new species, discovered at the Burgess Shale in Canada and at a counterpart in China, exploded on the scene during the Cambrian period (sometimes called the biological big bang) 540 million years ago. No predecessor fossils have ever been found for 99 percent of some quite large and weird-looking animals. The *opabinia* had five eyes; there were worms with thorny noses to snag prey; and we've even found evidence of crawling creatures with eyes on the ends of stalks. There are no new phyla since the Cambrian period.

Most species, according to the fossil record, evolved very little, if at all, before becoming extinct; the life expectancy of a species of animal might have extended a hundred thousand generations or a few million years, yet each generation continued to look much like, if not identical to, the previous generations. Take the beetle. It has not changed in two million years. Or the bowfin fish, which has not changed in 100 million years. The lungfish has not changed in 350 million years.

Herbert Nilsson of Lund University, Sweden, stated, "It is not even possible to make a caricature of evolution [Darwin's gradualism] out of paleobiological facts. The fossil material is now so complete that the lack of transitional series cannot be explained by the scarcity of material. The deficiencies are real, they will never be filled." Or consider the words of paleontologist Steven Stanley: "The known fossil record is not, and never has been in accord with gradualism." Or those of paleontologist David Raup: "Different species usually appear and disappear from the fossil record without showing the transitions that Darwin postulated." Or those of biologist and curator of the American Museum of Natural History, Ernst Mayr: "With curious frequency it is even stated today that Darwin's method was largely one of speculation and deduction." Or those of Francis Hitching in *The Neck of the Giraffe*, who states that most scientists now discount the idea of the lungfish having evolved into an amphibian, based on its head structure and lack of true legs.

More Questions for Darwin's Theories

Are we designed to change, or is there a genetic inertia? No one knows, but Hitching writes, "On the face of it, the prime function of the genetic system would seem to be to resist change." Stasis and extinction are the patterns seen in fossils. Freaks of nature are shunned, such as a zebra born without stripes. Animals will often kill different-looking or different-acting offspring even if they might grow up to be stronger or faster (but how would they know?).

Once in every ten million cell divisions, a cell makes a copying mistake. The chance of the mistake passing into the next generation is one in two. The odds are six to one that it will disappear by the tenth generation and fifty to one that it will be gone by the hundredth generation.

According to F.B. Livingston, it would take approximately 20,000 generations, or 400,000 years, for an advantageous gene to spread among the hominid populations of the Pleistocene Era. If we are descendants of the famous Lucy, the australopithecine skull found in Ethiopia in 1974 and thought to be three million years old, then there would have been time for only *seven* advantageous genes to have changed. That's barely enough of a change to tell a difference, let alone make a monkey into a person.

Some scientists think that one beneficial mutation happens per 20,000 mutations. Or reverse this: 19,999 out of 20,000 mutations are useless, dangerous, or quickly diluted out. To calculate the statistical chance of man's DNA codes having so come about—correctly and by mere chance—multiply 6,000,000,000 by a number just short of infinity. Nesse and Williams estimate the likelihood of any gene being altered as one in a million per generation—and most often these changes are either lethal or lead to freaks. How could so many efficient and effective changes have taken place so quickly?

Law or Conjecture?

If survival of the fittest is an evolutionary law, why do men and women seem to prefer attractive partners over healthier ones? Health and good looks do not necessarily go together. Why do many of us go out of our way to help the disabled and the elderly? That's contrary to survival of the fittest.

Why did we lose most of our body hair, when it should have been protective for us? Fur protects animals from scratches, cuts, scrapes, insect bites, and stings; it also keeps them warm and dry. Why did we shift to two legs, when running on all fours is known to be faster? Darwinians assume that upright posture aids distant seeing, yet many four-legged animals can stand on two legs to see farther or reach for fruit. Why are our brains still enlarging, when intellectually we're way beyond the

> By observing farmers breed animals to get a better version, Darwin deduced that man could eventually breed one species into another. Simply stated, by making horses smaller and smaller, one might eventually get a dog or cat.

needs of survival of the fittest? Why are we so dependent upon our parents for so long a period, when survival of the fittest should have forced earlier emancipation?

What Are the Chances?

According to Richard Milton, who wrote *Shattering the Myths of Darwinism*, the chances of forming protein and self-replicating DNA randomly are as likely as "winning the state lottery by finding the winning ticket in the street, and then continuing to win the lottery every week for a thousand years by finding the winning ticket in the street each time" (in other terms, one chance in 10^{65}).

The human body develops from an ovum the size of a dot, yet this speck of biological material contains vast encyclopedias of information—huge dictionaries defining every molecule and convoluted recipes to make every chemical moiety, or component. Conception sets in motion domino-like changes in this speck so that it becomes a human being—a multitrillion cell organism with 200 different kinds of cells that make five million different proteins. In this organism, sometimes a billion or more neurons will work on the same task and accomplish it in less than one-hundredth of a second. Just the fact that billions of newly formed neurons know where to set up shop, how to interact with thousands of neighboring neurons in a meaningful way, and yet be flexible enough to learn and change throughout a person's life is beyond calculation. It's beyond understanding.

Try to imagine an animal that lacks a way to find food, a means to ingest it, or a mechanism to eliminate wastes. These processes are critical for sustaining life, yet many of us view them as being relatively simple, like filling one's gas tank at a service station, burning the fuel, and leaving a few exhaust fumes. It would have taken millions, if not billions, of fortuitous genetic mutations to create teeth, saliva, a tongue, a liver, a pancreas, a gallbladder, and a complex gastrointestinal conveyor belt that includes acid to digest the food, bases to neutralize the acid, antibodies to kill worrisome bacteria, antitoxins to neutralize toxins, and hundreds of different enzymes that steadily break food down. Everything has to be done in tandem or parallel and in very special ways—or none of it can work. Each step is dependent on previous steps; each step complements the others before it.

The ability to talk had to have anticipated conversation. Our new species would have had to have the correct anatomy for communication and a frontal cortex to process language. Without ears we wouldn't know what another human being is saying. Without mental filtering devices we would be driven crazy by every sound around us. How did we end up with a naked face, which enhances possibilities for language, when a muzzle is best suited for seizing food?

And no one knows why or how we could have changed from cold-blooded creatures into warm-blooded ones. Every aspect of metabolism would have been affected. Were there ever any animals that were half warm-blooded and half cold-blooded? This change would have required a massive genetic makeover.

And why did the tail just drop off?

What the Facts Demand

Did we evolve; were we created as we are; or were we created subject to natural laws, like survival of the fittest, that have helped shape our past and will help shape our present and future? Or, is there another, not-yet-conceived theory that can explain our complexity, even our existence? The answers to these questions and many more are not truly found among archaeological and pale-ontological digs. Evolution, much like a religion, requires a lot of faith. There are no conclusive facts that reliably support Darwin's theories—yet there are millions of facts that challenge them. Maybe. billions. Some people may always have difficulty accepting that there is a Designer—a very personal choice for all of us—but an alternative explanation for the exquisite design and complexity of the human body has yet to be found.

I am not a theologian, nor do I pretend to be. I'm merely a collector and analyzer of biological and medical facts. The data, as I see it, points directly to an Intelligent Designer, much like a car speaks for an automaker, a soufflé for a chef, and a play for a playwright. Alternative explanations may yet be found or proposed, but the theory of evolution cannot satisfy what the facts demand. The idea that humans evolved from unicellular organisms belongs to an overflowing crate of flat worlds, gods living on mountaintops, and superstitions.

I love fools' experiments.
I am always making them.
—Charles Darwin

Notes

1. Illustration taken from *The World's Best Anatomical Charts* (Skokie, IL: The Anatomical Chart Company, 1993), p. 3. Used by permission.

2. Illustration taken from Frank H. Netter, *Atlas of Human Anatomy*, 2nd ed. (Teterboro, NJ: Icon Learning Systems, LLC, 1989), plate 153. Copyright 1989 Icon Learning Systems, LLC, a subsidiary of MediMedia USA Inc. Reprinted with permission from ICON Learning Systems, LLC, illustrated by Frank H. Netter, MD. All rights reserved.

3. Illustration taken from *World's Best*, p. 16. Used by permission.

4. Illustration taken from Netter, *Atlas*, plate 77. Copyright 1989 Icon Learning Systems, LLC, a subsidiary of MediMedia USA Inc. Reprinted with permission from ICON Learning Systems, LLC, illustrated by Frank H. Netter, MD. All rights reserved.

5. Illustration taken from Netter, *Atlas*, plate 87. Copyright 1989 Icon Learning Systems, LLC, a subsidiary of MediMedia USA Inc. Reprinted with permission from ICON Learning Systems, LLC, illustrated by Frank H. Netter, MD. All rights reserved.

6. Illustration taken from Netter, *Atlas*, plate 511. Copyright 1989 Icon Learning Systems, LLC, a subsidiary of MediMedia USA Inc. Reprinted with permission from ICON Learning Systems, LLC, illustrated by Frank H. Netter, MD. All rights reserved.

7. Illustration taken from *World's Best*, p. 5. Used by permission.

8. Illustration taken from *World's Best*, p. 11. Used by permission.

9. Illustration taken from *World's Best*, p. 1. Used by permission.

10. Illustration taken from Netter, *Atlas*, plate 21. Copyright 1989 Icon Learning Systems, LLC, a subsidiary of MediMedia USA Inc. Reprinted with permission from ICON Learning Systems, LLC, illustrated by Frank H. Netter, MD. All rights reserved.

11. David Adam, "Give six monkeys a computer, and what do you get? Certainly not the Bard," *The Guardian* (Manchester, UK), May 9, 2003. Available on-line at <http://www.guardian.co.uk/uk_news/story/0,3604,952227,00.html>.

12. Charles Darwin, *Life and Letters*, vol. 3, p. 44.

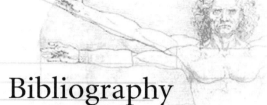

Bibliography

Ackerman, Diane. *A Natural History of the Senses.* Random House, Inc., 1990.

———. *A Natural History of Love.* Vintage Books, 1995.

Agosta, William. *Bombardier Beetle and Fever Trees: A Close-up Look at Chemical Warfare and Signals in Animals and Plants.* Addison-Wesley Publishing Company, 1995.

Aidley, David J. *The Physiology of Excitable Cells.* 4th ed. Cambridge University Press, 1998.

Andrews, Nancy C. "Disorders of Iron Metabolism." *The New England Journal of Medicine.* 1999 (341:1986-1995).

Ankerberg, John, and John Weldon. *Darwin's Leap of Faith: Exposing the False Religion of Evolution.* Harvest House Publishers, 1998.

Arking, Robert. *Biology of Aging.* 2nd ed. Sinauer Associates, Inc., 1998.

Ashcroft, Frances. *Life at the Extremes: The Science of Survival.* University of California Press, 2000.

Augros, Robert, and George Stancu. *The New Biology: Discovering the Wisdom in Nature.* New Science Library, 1988.

Baker, Robin. *Sperm Wars.* HarperCollins Publishers, Ltd., 1996.

Banchereau, Jacques. "The Long Arm of the Immune System." *Scientific American,* November 2002, pp. 52-59.

Barash, David P., and Judith Eve Lipton. *Making Sense of Sex: How Genes and Gender Influence Our Relationships.* Island Press/Shearwater Books, 1997.

Behe, Michael J. *Darwin's Black Box: The Biochemical Challenge to Evolution.* Simon and Schuster, 1996.

Birkhead, Tim. *Promiscuity: An Evolutionary History of Sperm Competition.* Harvard University Press, 2000.

Bodanis, David. *The Secret Family: Twenty-four Hours Inside the Mysterious World of Our Minds and Bodies.* Simon and Schuster, 1997.

Bogin, Barry. *Patterns of Human Growth.* Cambridge University Press, 1997.

Bower, Bruce. "Faces of Perception." *Science News,* July 7, 2001, pp. 10-12.

Boylan, Jeanne. *Portraits of Guilt.* Simon and Schuster, Inc., 2000.

Cadbury, Deborah. *Altering Eden: The Feminization of Nature.* St. Martin's Press, 1997.

Calais-Germain, Blandine. *Anatomy of Movement*. Eastland Press, 1991.

Carina, Dennis, and Richard Gallagher. *The Human Genome*. Nature Publishing Group, 2001.

Cerf, Christopher, and Victor Navasky. *The Experts Speak: The Definitive Compendium of Authoritative Misinformation*. Random House, Inc., 1998.

Children's Hospital Boston. *The Children's Hospital Guide to Your Child's Health and Development*. Perseus Publishing, 2001.

Coleman, William. *Biology in the Nineteenth Century: Problems of Form, Function and Transformation*. Press Syndicate of the University of Cambridge, 1971.

Cross, Patricia C., and K. Lynne Mercer. *Cell and Tissue Ultrastructure: A Functional Perspective*. W.H. Freeman and Company, 1993.

Cvancara, Alan M. *Sleuthing Fossils: The Art of Investigating Past Life*. John Wiley and Sons, Inc., 1990.

Czerner, Thomas B. *What Makes You Tick: The Brain in Plain English*. John Wiley and Sons, Inc., 2001.

Darwin, Charles. *On the Origin of Species: A Facsimile of the First Edition*. Harvard University Press, 1964. (Reprint ed. London: John Murray, Albemarle Street 1859.)

———. *The Descent of Man, and Selection in Relation to Sex*. Princeton University Press, 1981. (Reprint ed. London: J. Murray, 1871.)

———. *The Expression of the Emotion in Man and Animals: Definitive Edition*. Oxford University Press, 1999. (Reprint ed. London: John Murray, 1872.)

Davies, Paul. *The Cosmic Blueprint: New Discoveries in Nature's Creative Ability to Order the Universe*. Simon and Schuster, Inc., 1988.

Dawkins, Richard. *The Blind Watchmaker*. W.W. Norton and Company, 1986.

———. *The Selfish Gene*. Oxford University Press, 1976.

de Becker, Gavin. *The Gift of Fear: Survival Signals that Protect Us from Violence*. Little, Brown and Company, 1997.

Dembski, William A. *Intelligent Design: The Bridge Between Science & Theology*. InterVarsity Press, 1998.

———, ed. *Mere Creation: Science, Faith, and Intelligent Design*. InterVarsity Press, 1998.

———. *No Free Lunch*. Rowman & Littlefield Publishers, 2002.

Dennett, Daniel C. *Consciousness Explained*. Little, Brown and Company, 1991.

Diamond, Jared. *Why Is Sex Fun? The Evolution of Human Sexuality*. Basic Books, 1997.

Dolhinow, Phyllis, and Agustin Fuentes. *The Nonhuman Primates*. Mayfield Publishing Company, 1994.

Downer, John. *Weird Nature: An Astonishing Exploration of Nature's Strangest Behavior*. Firefly Books, Inc. 2002.

Eccles, John C. *Evolution of the Brain: Creation of the Self*. Routledge, 1989.

Eldredge, Niles. *The Triumph of Evolution and Failure of Creationism*. W.H. Freeman and Company, 2000.

Ellis, Richard. *Aquagenesis: The Origin and Evolution of Life in the Sea.* Penguin Putnam, Inc., 2001.

Etcoff, Nancy. *Survival of the Prettiest: The Science of Beauty.* Doubleday, 1999.

Ewald, Paul W. *Evolution of Infectious Disease.* Oxford University Press, 1994.

Ganong, William F. *Review of Medical Physiology.* 19th ed. Simon and Schuster, 1999.

Gazzaniga, Michael S., Richard B. Irvy, and George B. Mangun. *Cognitive Neuroscience: The Biology of the Mind.* W. W. Norton and Company, 1981.

Gee, Henry. *Beyond the Fossil Record to a New History of Life.* The Free Press, 1999.

Glynn, Patrick. *God, the Evidence: The Reconciliation of Faith and Reason in a Postsecular World.* Prima Publishing Forum, 1999.

Gould, E., and C. Gross. "Neurogenesis in the neocortex of adult primates." *Science,* October 1999, pp. 584-552.

Gould, Stephen Jay. *Hen's Teeth and Horse's Toes: Further Reflections in Natural History.* W.W. Norton and Company, 1983.

———. *The Mismeasure of Man.* W.W. Norton and Company, 1981.

———. *The Panda's Thumb: More Reflections in Natural History.* W.W. Norton and Company, 1982.

———. *Rocks of Ages: Science and Religion in the Fullness of Life.* The Ballantine Publishing Group, 1999.

Gross, Michael. *Life on the Edge: Amazing Creatures Thriving in Extreme Environments.* Perseus Publishing, 1998.

Hall, Susan. *Basic Biomechanics.* Mosby Year Book, 1999.

Hamer, Dean, and Peter Copeland. *Living With Our Genes.* Random House, 1998.

Harris, Henry. *The Birth of the Cell.* Yale University Press, 1999.

Hawley, R. Scott, and Catherine A. Mori. *The Human Genome: A User's Guide.* Harcourt Brace and Company, 1999.

Hellman, Hal. *Great Feuds in Science: Ten of the Liveliest Disputes Ever.* John Wiley and Sons, Inc. 1998.

Hitching, Francis. *The Neck of the Giraffe: Where Darwin Went Wrong.* Ticknor and Fields, 1982.

Hughes, Howard C. *Sensory Exotica: A World Beyond Human Experience.* The MIT Press, 1999.

Johnson, Phillip E. *Defeating Darwinism by Opening Minds.* InterVarsity Press, 1997.

Johnston, Victor S. *Why We Feel: The Science of Human Emotions.* Perseus Books, 1999.

Jones, Steve. *Darwin's Ghost: The Origin of Species Updated.* Random House, 2000.

Kardong, Kenneth V. *Vertebrates: Comparative Anatomy, Function, and Evolution.* 2nd ed. McGraw-Hill, 1998.

Kay, Lily E. *Who Wrote the Book of Life? A History of the Genetic Code.* Stanford University Press, 2000.

Kliegman, Behrman. *Nelson Essentials of Pediatrics.* 3rd ed. W.B. Saunders, 1998.

Kropotkin, P. *Mutual Aid: A Factor of Evolution*. Trans. William Heinemann. Alfred A. Knopf, 1902.

Lesk, Arthur. *Introduction to Protein Architecture*. Oxford University Press, 2001.

Levy, Charles Kingsley. *Evolutionary Wars: A Three-Billion-Year Arms Race*. W.H. Freeman and Company, 1999.

Lewin, Roger. *Principles of Human Evolution: A Core Textbook*. Blackwell Science, Inc., 1998.

Litvak, Stuart, and A. Wayne Senzee. *Toward a New Brain: Evolution and the Human Mind*. Prentice-Hall, Inc. 1986.

Loewenstein, Werner R. *The Touchstone of Life: Molecular Information, Cell Communication and the Foundations of Life*. Oxford University Press, 1999.

Lubenow, Marvin L. *Bones of Contention: A Creationist Assessment of Human Fossils*. Baker Books, 1992.

Lutz, Tom. *Crying: The Natural and Cultural History of Tears*. W.W. Norton and Company, Inc., 1999.

Malacinski, George M., and David Friefelder. *Essentials of Molecular Biology*, 3rd ed. Jones and Bartlett Publishers, 1998.

Margulis, Lynn. *Symbiotic Planet: A New Look at Evolution*. Basic Books, 1998.

———, and Dorion Sagan. *Origins of Sex: Three Billion Years of Genetic Recombination*. Yale University Press, 1986.

McGowan, Kathleen. "The Biology of...Appetite." *Discover*, September 2002.

McLain, Bill. *What Makes Flamingos Pink?* HarperCollins Publishers, 2001.

McNeill, Daniel. *The Face: A Natural History*. Little, Brown and Company, 1998.

Mead, James, G., and Joy P. Gold. *Whales and Dolphins in Question: The Smithsonian Answer Book*. Smithsonian Institute, 2002.

Miller, Kenneth R. *Finding Darwin's God: A Scientist's Search for Common Ground Between God and Evolution*. HarperCollins Publishers, 1999.

Milton, Richard. *Shattering the Myths of Darwinism*. Park Street Press, 1997.

Moody, Raymond A., Jr., *Life After Life*. Bantam, 1976.

Moore, John A. *From Genesis to Genetics: The Case of Evolution and Creationism*. University of California Press, 2002.

Moore, Keith L., and T.V.N. Persaud. *The Developing Human: Clinically Oriented Embryology*. W.B. Saunders, 1998.

Moreland, J.P., ed. *The Creation Hypothesis: Scientific Evidence for an Intelligent Designer*. InterVarsity Press, 1994.

Morgan, Elaine. *The Scars of Evolution: What Our Bodies Tell Us About Human Origins*. Oxford University Press, 1990.

Moser, Penny. "Eye of the Beast." *Discover*, December, 1999, pp. 92-101.

Murchie, Guy. *The Seven Mysteries of Life*. Houghton Mifflin Company, 1978.

Nesse, Randolph M., and George C. Williams. *Why We Get Sick: The New Science of Darwinian Medicine*. Random House, Inc., 1994.

Paley, William. *Paley's Natural Theology.* Richardson, Lord, Holbrook, and Crocker & Brewster. 1831.

Palmer, John D. *The Living Clock: The Orchestrator of Biological Rhythms.* Oxford University Press, 2002.

Panjabi, Manohar M., and Augustus White. *Biomechanics in the Musculoskeletal System.* Churchill Livingstone, 2001.

Parker, Steve. *The Practical Paleontologist.* Simon and Schuster, 1990.

Peckenpaugh, Nancy J., and Charlotte M. Poleman. *Nutrition Essentials and Diet Therapy.* 8th ed. W.B. Saunders Company, 1999.

Potts, Malcolm, and Roger Short. *Ever Since Adam and Eve: The Evolution of Human Sexuality.* Cambridge University Press, 1999.

Provine, Robert R. *Laughter: A Scientific Investigation.* Penguin Group, 2000.

Reader's Digest. *1000 Wonders of Nature.* The Reader's Digest Association Limited, 2002.

Rensberger, Boyce. *Life Itself: Exploring the Realm of the Living Cell.* Oxford University Press, 1996.

Restak, Richard. *The Secret Life of the Brain.* Joseph Henry Press, 2001.

———. *Mysteries of the Mind.* National Geographic, 2000.

Rich, Patricia Vickers, Thomas Hewitt Rich, Mildred Adams Fenton, and Carroll Lane Fenton. *The Fossil Book: A Record of Prehistoric Life.* Dover Publications, Inc., 1996.

Ridley, Mark, ed. *The Darwin Reader.* W.W. Norton & Company, 1987.

Rose, Kenneth Jon. *The Body in Time.* John Wiley and Sons, Inc., 1988.

Sabom, Michael B. *Recollections of Death: A Medical Investigation.* Harper and Row, 1982.

Saign, Geoffrey C. *The Great Apes.* Grolier Publishing, 1998.

Saladin, Kenneth S. *Anatomy and Physiology: The Unity of Form and Function.* McGraw-Hill, 1998.

Scheibel, Arnold B., and J. William Schopf. *The Origin and Evolution of Intelligence.* Jones and Bartlett Publishers, 1997.

Schroeder, Gerald L. *The Science of God.* The Free Press, 1997.

———. *The Hidden Face of God: How Science Reveals the Ultimate Truth.* The Free Press, 2001.

Schwartz, Jeffrey H. *Sudden Origins: Fossils, Genes and the Emergence of Species.* John Wiley and Sons, Inc., 1999.

Scott, Andrew. *The Creation of Life: Past, Future, Alien.* Basil Blackwell, Ltd., 1986.

Sherr, Lynn. *Tall Blondes.* Andrew McMeel Publishing, 1997.

Spetner, Lee. *Not By Chance!: Shattering the Modern Theory of Evolution.* The Judaica Press, 1998.

Springer, Sally P., and Georg Deutsch. *Left Brain, Right Brain.* Rev. ed. W.H. Freeman and Company, 1985.

Steele, Edward J., Robin A. Lindley, and Robert V. Blanden. *Lamarck's Signature: How Retrogenes Are Changing Darwin's Natural Selection Paradigm.* Perseus Books, 1998.

Stewart, Ian. *Life's Other Secret: The New Mathematics of the Living World.* John Wiley and Sons, Inc., 1998.

Strogatz, Steven. *SYNC: The Emerging Science of Spontaneous Order.* Theia, 2003.

Sykes, Bryan. *The Seven Daughters of Eve: The Science that Reveals Our Genetic Ancestry.* W.W. Norton and Company, Inc., 2001.

Tattersall, Ian, and Jeffrey H. Schwartz. *Extinct Humans.* Westview Press, 2001.

Treffert, Darold A. *Extraordinary People: Understanding "Idiot Savants."* Harper and Row, 1989.

Turek, V., J. Marek, and J. Benes. *Fossils of the World: A Comprehensive, Practical Guide to Collecting and Studying Fossils.* Arch Cape Press, 1988.

Van De Graaff, Kent M., and R. Ward Rhees. *Human Anatomy and Physiology.* 2nd ed. McGraw-Hill, 1997.

Vogel, Steven. *Prime Mover: A Natural History of Muscle.* W.W. Norton and Company, Inc., 2001.

Wakefield, Tom. *Liaisons of Life: From Hornworts to Hippos, How the Unassuming Microbe Has Driven Evolution.* Perseus Publishing, 2000.

Walker, Evan Harris. *The Physics of Consciousness: The Quantum Mind and the Meaning of Life.* Perseus Publishing, Inc., 2000.

Watson, Lyall. *Jacobson's Organ and the Remarkable Nature of Smell.* W. W. Norton and Company, 2000.

Wells, Jonathan. *Icons of Evolution: Science of Myth?* Regnery Publishing, Inc., 2000.

Widmaier, Eric P. *Why Geese Don't Get Obese (And We Do): How Evolution Strategies Affect Our Everyday Lives.* W. H. Freeman and Company, 1999.

Williams, Charles J.B. *Principles of Medicine: General Pathology and Therapeutics.* Lea and Blanchard, 1848.

Williams, Guy. *The Age of Miracles: Medicine and Surgery in the Nineteenth Century.* Constable and Company, Ltd., 1981.

Winston, Mark L. *Nature Wars: People Versus Pests.* Harvard University Press, 1997.

Wright, Robert. *The Moral Animal: Why We Are We The Way We Are.* Random House, Inc., 1994.

Youngson, Robert. *Scientific Blunders: A Brief History of How Wrong Scientists Can Be.* Carroll & Graf Publishers, Inc., 1998.

Zimmer, Carl. *Parasite Rex: Inside the Bizarre World of Nature's Most Dangerous Creatures.* The Free Press, 2000.

Zuidema, George D. *The Johns Hopkins Atlas of Human Functional Anatomy.* 4th ed. The Johns Hopkins University Press, 1997.